Circular Economy: Business, Technology, and Policy

(Part 2)

Edited by

Vijaya Kittu Manda
Perspectives on Business Management, Economics & Information Technology (PBMEIT)
Visakhapatnam, Andhra Pradesh
India

Theodore Tarnanidis
International Hellenic University
Thermi, Thessaloniki
Greece

&

Vivek Gupta
Indian Institute of Management Lucknow (IIM)
Lucknow, Tamil Nadu
India

Circular Economy: Business, Technology, and Policy ***(Part 2)***

Editors: Vijaya Kittu Manda, Theodore Tarnanidis and Vivek Gupta

ISBN (Online): 979-8-89881-663-6

ISBN (Print): 979-8-89881-664-3

ISBN (Paperback): 979-8-89881-665-0

Published by Bentham Science Publishers Pte. Ltd. Singapore,

in collaboration with Eureka Conferences, USA.

First published in 2026.

need for a court order if at any point you breach any terms of this License Agreement. In no event will any delay or failure by Bentham Science Publishers in enforcing your compliance with this License Agreement constitute a waiver of any of its rights.

3. You acknowledge that you have read this License Agreement, and agree to be bound by its terms and conditions. To the extent that any other terms and conditions presented on any website of Bentham Science Publishers conflict with, or are inconsistent with, the terms and conditions set out in this License Agreement, you acknowledge that the terms and conditions set out in this License Agreement shall prevail.

Bentham Science Publishers Pte. Ltd.
No. 9 Raffles Place
Office No. 26-01
Singapore 048619
Singapore
Email: subscriptions@benthamscience.net

BENTHAM SCIENCE

CONTENTS

FOREWORD

This volume arrives at a critical juncture when humanity must reconcile economic imperatives with ecological boundaries. While Part 1 lays the foundational concepts of the circular economy, Part 2 confronts the real-world complexities of implementation - where policy meets practice and innovation meets infrastructure.

The chapters in this section address the often-overlooked dimensions of circular transition: the legal frameworks that enable or constrain circular practices, government policies that incentivize sustainable behavior, and community-led initiatives that demonstrate circularity works at the grassroots level. From eco-design principles that extend product lifecycles to digital tools that track material flows, these contributions offer concrete pathways for organizations seeking to operationalize circularity.

What distinguishes this section is its emphasis on the human and financial dimensions of the circular economy. Chapter 8 examines the critical need to reinvent employee skills for circular economies, recognizing that workforce transformation is as essential as technological innovation. Chapter 10 addresses the financing gap that often stalls circular projects, offering insights into investment strategies, green bonds, and blended finance models that can unlock capital for circular initiatives.

The inclusion of sector-specific case studies, such as the footwear industry's efforts to reduce carbon footprints, demonstrates that circularity is achievable across diverse contexts. Similarly, the focus on community-based waste management initiatives, including lessons from India's Haritha Karma Sena, highlights how decentralized, participatory approaches can drive sustainable transformation where top-down models often fail.

Business leaders will find actionable strategies for transforming operations and supply chains. Policymakers will encounter regulatory approaches that balance ecological protection with economic growth. Academics and students will appreciate the rigorous research underpinning each chapter, while practitioners will value the real-world applications and empirical evidence presented.

This section reinforces that the circular economy is not a distant ideal but an achievable reality. The transition requires collective action across sectors and stakeholders - and it begins with the insights and inspiration found within these pages. I invite you to approach this volume not only as a collection of research but as a catalyst for transformation in your sphere of influence.

Vijaya Rama Raju
Andhra University Waltair
Visakhapatnam, Andhra Pradesh
India

PREFACE

The concept of a Circular Economy (CE) is rapidly reshaping how businesses, policymakers, and technologists approach sustainability and economic growth. Businesses have to move out of traditional linear models of "take, make, and dispose". The circular economy emphasizes resource efficiency, waste reduction, and regenerative systems. This book, Circular Economy: Business, Technology, and Policy, provides a comprehensive exploration of CE principles, implementation strategies, and their impact across industries.

This collection of research and case studies brings together leading experts from diverse fields, offering insights into consumer engagement, reverse logistics, manufacturing transformations, sustainable finance, AI-driven solutions, and regulatory frameworks. The chapters bridge theoretical discussions with practical applications. The book as a whole highlights how organizations can transition toward circularity without compromising economic viability or technological innovation.

Each chapter delves into crucial aspects of circularity - from the role of digital tools and artificial intelligence to government policies and grassroots waste management initiatives. Special attention is given to emerging business models, financing strategies, and the role of eco-design in prolonging product life cycles.

As we face the pressing challenges of climate change, resource scarcity, and economic resilience, this book serves as a valuable resource for academics, policymakers, and industry leaders committed to a sustainable future.

Vijaya Kittu Manda
Perspectives on Business Management, Economics
& Information Technology (PBMEIT)
Visakhapatnam, Andhra Pradesh
India

Theodore Tarnanidis
International Hellenic University
Thermi, Thessaloniki
Greece

&

Vivek Gupta
Indian Institute of Management Lucknow (IIM)
Lucknow, Tamil Nadu
India

List of Contributors

Ajoy Kanti Das	Department of Mathematics, Tripura University, Agartala, Tripura, India
Abhijit Bhattachrya	Department of Education (ITEP), NIT West Tripura, Jirania, Tripura, India
Anjan Mukherjee	Department of Chemistry, Bir Bikram Memorial College, Agartala, Tripura, India
Amanda Adelina Harun	Faculty of Law, Universitas Negeri Gorontalo, Gorontalo, Indonesia
Ankit Tiwari	Department of Electrical Engineering, Madhav Institute of Technology & Science, Gwalior, Madhya Pradesh, India
Akash Kumar Shukla	Department of Electrical Engineering, Madhav Institute of Technology & Science, Gwalior, Madhya Pradesh, India
Ali Tufail	School of Digital Science, Universiti Brunei Darussalam, Bandar Seri Begawan, Brunei Darussalam
Abdallah Namoun	AI Centre, Faculty of Computer and Information Systems, Islamic University of Madinah, Madinah, Saudi Arabia
Carlos Granados	Estudiante de Doctorado en Matemáticas, Magister en Ciencias Matemáticas, Universidad de Antioquia, Medellín, Colombia
Dinesh Nilkant	CMS Business School, JAIN (Deemed-to-be University), Bengaluru, Karnataka, India
Deepak Rathod	Department of Electrical and Electronics Engineering, Shri Vaishnav Institute of Technology and Science, Shri Vaishnav Vidyapeeth Vishwavidyalaya, Indore, Madhya Pradesh, India
Hemanth Kumar S.	CMS Business School, JAIN (Deemed-to-be University), Bengaluru, Karnataka, India
Hemavathi G.P.	R N S Institute of Technology, Bangalore, Karnataka, India
Krishna Koppa	CMS Business School, JAIN (Deemed-to-be University), Bengaluru, Karnataka, India
Karolina Wilamowska	Business Attorney and Mediator, Poland
Krishnashree Achuthan	Center for Cybersecurity Systems and Networks, Amrita Vishwa Vidyapeetham, Amritapuri, Kerala, India
Kartikey Singh	School of Business and Management, Christ University, Banglore, Karnataka, India
Liyanage Chandratilak De Silva	School of Digital Science, Universiti Brunei Darussalam, Bandar Seri Begawan, Brunei Darussalam
Mona Mahecha	Faculty of Law, Manipal University, Jaipur, Rajasthan, India
Mohammed Majeed	Department of Marketing, Tamale Technical University, Tamale, Ghana
Nandini Gupta	Department of Environmental Science, Bir Bikram Memorial College, Agartala, Tripura, India
Oksana Polyakova	Department of Regional Geology and Mineral Resources, Kazan Federal University, Kazan, Russian Federation

Prabha Kiran	Westminster Business School, Westminster International University in Tashkent, Tashkent, Uzbekistan
Padma Rao Sahib	Faculty of Economics and Business, University of Groningen, Groningen, The Netherlands
P. Bhanumathi	M S Ramaiah Institute of Management, Bangalore, Karnataka, India
Rakhal Das	Department of Mathematics, The ICFAI University Tripura, Mohanpur, Tripura, India
Renju Chandran	School of Contemporary Knowledge Systems, Chinmaya Vishwa Vidyapeeth (Deemed to be University), Ernakulam, Kerala, India
Rosyzie Anna Awg Haji Mohd Apong	School of Digital Science, Universiti Brunei Darussalam, Bandar Seri Begawan, Brunei Darussalam
Suman Patra	Department of Mathematics, Tripura University, Agartala, Tripura, India
Suman Das	Department of Mathematics, Tripura University, Agartala, Tripura, India
Sanya Yadav	School of Law, Bennett University, Greater Noida, Uttar Pradesh, India
Sarath Chandran M.C.	Amrita School of Arts, Humanities and Commerce, Amrita Vishwa Vidyapeetham, Amritapuri, Kerala, India
Swati Beniwal	Faculty of Law, Manipal University, Jaipur, Rajasthan, India
Sushila Choudhary	Faculty of Law, Manipal University, Jaipur, Rajasthan, India
Surabhi Sangal	School of Business and Management, Christ University, Banglore, Karnataka, India
Tej Singh	Centre of AI, Madhav Institute of Technology & Science, Gwalior, Madhya Pradesh, India
Wasswa Shafik	School of Digital Science, Universiti Brunei Darussalam, Bandar Seri Begawan, Brunei Darussalam Dig Connectivity Research Laboratory (DCRLab), Kampala, Uganda

CHAPTER 1

Eco-Design Principles for Product Life Cycle Management: Insights from Multi-Criterion Decision-Making

Ajoy Kanti Das[1,*], **Nandini Gupta**[2], **Suman Patra**[1], **Carlos Granados**[3], **Rakhal Das**[4], **Suman Das**[1], **Abhijit Bhattachrya**[5] and **Anjan Mukherjee**[6]

[1] *Department of Mathematics, Tripura University, Agartala, Tripura, India*

[2] *Department of Environmental Science, Bir Bikram Memorial College, Agartala, Tripura, India*

[3] *Estudiante de Doctorado en Matemáticas, Magister en Ciencias Matemáticas, Universidad de Antioquia, Medellín, Colombia*

[4] *Department of Mathematics, The ICFAI University Tripura, Mohanpur, Tripura, India*

[5] *Department of Education (ITEP), NIT West Tripura, Jirania, Tripura, India*

[6] *Department of Chemistry, Bir Bikram Memorial College, Agartala, Tripura, India*

Abstract: This chapter explores the integration of eco-design principles within Product Life Cycle Management (PLCM) systems through the lens of Multi-Criteria Decision-Making (MCDM). It emphasizes innovative strategies aimed at significantly reducing resource consumption and waste generation throughout the Product Life Cycle (PLC). The chapter examines key eco-design methodologies such as Design for Environment (DFE), Cradle-to-Cradle (C2C), and modular design, offering insights into how these approaches can be effectively incorporated into product development processes. Special attention is given to the role of MCDM in eco-design, highlighting how MCDM frameworks support the evaluation of multiple, often conflicting, environmental, economic, and social criteria. Tools like eco-design checklists, Life Cycle Assessment (LCA) software, and other analytical instruments are discussed in the context of aiding companies in making informed, sustainable decisions. The chapter also addresses how eco-design principles align with corporate strategies, enhancing sustainability efforts while meeting the growing consumer demand for environmentally responsible products. Furthermore, it explores how eco-design helps navigate complex regulatory frameworks, ensuring compliance while promoting environmental stewardship. Through case studies and real-world examples, the chapter showcases successful eco-design implementations, demonstrating tangible benefits such as cost savings, improved brand reputation, and increased market share. The integration of eco-design with PLCM systems, supported by MCDM tools, is positioned as a pivotal

* **Corresponding author Ajoy Kanti Das:** Department of Mathematics, Tripura University, Agartala, Tripura, India; E-mail: ajoykantidas@gmail.com

Theodore Tarnanidis, Vijaya Kittu Manda, Vivek Gupta (Eds.)

step toward fostering a circular economy, where products are designed with sustainability in mind, optimizing resource efficiency and minimizing environmental impact. This chapter offers valuable insights for practitioners, researchers, and policymakers striving to advance eco-design practices and promote sustainable product development.

Keywords: Design for environment, Eco-design, Life cycle assessment, Modular design, Product life cycle management, Sustainability, Waste reduction.

INTRODUCTION

As concerns about the environment gain greater significance in global discussions, eco-design has emerged as a crucial approach for advancing sustainability in product development. Eco-design encompasses the incorporation of environmental factors into the design process, with the goal of reducing negative ecological effects throughout a product's entire life cycle. This methodology is closely aligned with the principles of the circular economy, which prioritize the creation of products that can be reused, repaired, and recycled, ultimately minimizing waste and lowering resource consumption (Arruda *et al.*, 2021).

The shift from a traditional linear model characterized by a “take-make-dispose” approach to a circular economy framework requires a profound re-evaluation of how products are conceived, designed, and developed. This transformation emphasizes the importance of resource efficiency, sustainability, and the creation of a closed-loop system where materials are continually cycled back into use rather than discarded. By embracing eco-design, companies not only contribute to environmental protection but also unlock new opportunities for innovation, cost savings, and competitive advantage in the marketplace. The integration of eco-design practices can lead to enhanced product performance and a more sustainable future, reflecting the growing demand from consumers for environmentally responsible choices.

The implementation of PLCM has become crucial for organizations aiming to effectively integrate eco-design into their operations. PLCM is a comprehensive and systematic methodology that oversees all stages of a product’s life cycle, starting from the initial conception and design, progressing through production and use, and culminating in end-of-life disposal. By embracing PLCM, organizations can ensure that sustainability principles are woven into every phase of the product's journey, allowing them to address environmental impacts in a comprehensive and cohesive manner (Bocken *et al.*, 2014; Giwa *et al.*, 2022). This holistic approach not only enhances resource efficiency and minimizes waste but also empowers companies to stay competitive in an increasingly eco-aware market. As consumers become more discerning about the environmental implications of their purchases, businesses that prioritize sustainability through PLCM can differentiate themselves and build stronger brand loyalty. Furthermore, PLCM facilitates collaboration among various stakeholders, fostering innovation and the development of greener technologies. Ultimately, by embedding eco-design principles within the framework of PLCM, organizations can contribute positively to environmental stewardship while reaping the benefits of improved operational efficiency and market positioning.

A key aspect of eco-design is its alignment with DfE initiatives, which prioritize environmental considerations during the design phase. DfE encourages designers to select materials that are less harmful to the environment, utilize energy-efficient production processes, and develop products that are easier to recycle or repurpose (Lee *et al.*, 2023). This methodology extends beyond product design to include supply chain management, emphasizing the need for collaboration with suppliers to ensure sustainable practices are maintained throughout the supply chain. Additionally, effective eco-design practices can help organizations anticipate and comply with stringent environmental regulations, thus reducing legal and financial risks. Furthermore, the C2C design philosophy serves as a powerful illustration of how eco-design can promote sustainability by advocating for a regenerative approach to product development. The C2C framework encourages the creation of products that positively impact environmental health rather than deplete it. It emphasizes the development of closed-loop systems in which waste is minimized, and materials are perpetually reused (Zuo & Zhao, 2014; Kong *et al.*, 2021). This regenerative strategy not only supports ecological balance but also fosters brand loyalty and consumer trust. As environmentally conscious consumers increasingly gravitate towards products that reflect their values, businesses that adopt C2C principles stand to benefit significantly in terms of market positioning. Moreover, research focusing on the regeneration and reusability of innovative low-cost adsorbents demonstrates effective methods for treating wastewater. These advancements contribute to broader objectives such as resource recovery and pollution reduction (El Messaoudi *et al.*, 2024). By integrating these eco-design principles, companies can enhance their environmental stewardship while simultaneously appealing to a growing demographic of sustainability-minded consumers. This alignment not only cultivates a positive brand image but also positions companies as leaders in the shift towards a more sustainable future.

Despite advancements in eco-design practices, significant challenges remain in their widespread implementation. Organizations often face obstacles such as high initial costs, lack of technical expertise, and resistance to change within organizational cultures (Popoff & Millet, 2017; Kong *et al.*, 2022). High upfront costs can deter businesses from investing in eco-design, particularly small and medium enterprises that may have limited resources. Moreover, the integration of sustainability into existing processes may require retraining employees and restructuring workflows, leading to resistance from stakeholders accustomed to traditional practices. However, companies that successfully embrace eco-design and PLCM are likely to reap long-term benefits, including improved brand reputation, increased customer loyalty, and reduced operational costs (Wang *et al.*, 2022; Yu *et al.*, 2022). Recent advances in life cycle-oriented low-carbon product design, based on constraint satisfaction problems, demonstrate that organizations can effectively balance sustainability goals with operational efficiency (Kong *et al.*, 2023).

Eco-design focuses on creating environmentally friendly products throughout their life cycle. To support this, MCDM under uncertainty is essential. Various fuzzy, soft set, and neutrosophic models have been developed to enhance MCDM in such complex environments (Das, 2016; Das, 2018; Das & Granados, 2021). The concept of intuitionistic fuzzy rough relations was introduced to deal with vague and partial information (Das, 2016). Later, a weighted fuzzy soft multiset model was proposed to improve MCDM where multiple options and preferences exist (Das, 2018). This approach enables better prioritization in sustainable product development.

In group MCDM, advanced fuzzy soft models like weighted average ratings, fuzzy parameterized intuitionistic fuzzy soft multisets, and hesitant fuzzy structures have been developed to allow multiple experts to express their views even when they are uncertain (Das & Granados, 2021; Das & Granados, 2022a; Das & Granados, 2022b; Das & Granados, 2023a). These models provide a strong foundation for assessing conflicting eco-design criteria. Operations on fuzzy soft sets and new theoretical extensions have been applied in different MCDM contexts to compare and rank alternatives more efficiently (Das *et al.*, 2022; Das & Granados, 2023b). Such models are especially useful in selecting eco-friendly materials, energy-efficient designs, and recyclable components in PLCM.

Recent applications of these models include water quality evaluation and pollution rating using weighted hesitant fuzzy soft sets and fuzzy MCDM approaches (Das *et al.*, 2023; Das *et al.*, 2025a; Das *et al.*, 2025b). These works demonstrate how uncertainty-based models can support environmental assessments aligned with eco-design objectives. The development of neutrosophic structures and soft multisets also contributed to MCDM under higher levels of uncertainty (Das *et al.*, 2025c; Das *et al.*, 2025d). These frameworks have been applied in areas such as adaptive inventory management and expert-based group MCDM (Das *et al.*, 2025d; Das *et al.*, 2025e). In addition, new decision tools using neutrosophic distributions, soft multisets, and hesitant bipolar fuzzy sets have been proposed to enhance sustainability assessments and product evaluations (Granados *et al.*, 2022; Granados *et al.*, 2023; Das *et al.*, 2025f).

Earlier foundational work on fuzzy soft multisets and their relations also laid the theoretical groundwork for applying these models to sustainability-oriented problems (Mukherjee & Das, 2015a; Mukherjee & Das, 2015b; Mukherjee & Das, 2015c; Mukherjee & Das, 2016a; Mukherjee & Das, 2016b; Mukherjee & Das, 2022; Mukherjee & Das, 2023). These include applications in investment planning, product evaluation, and complex system modeling.

Recent studies have shown their applicability in water pollution analysis and river quality monitoring (Das *et al.*, 2024a; Das *et al.*, 2024b), aligning well with eco-design principles. Lastly, models integrating AI, IoT, and MCDM in flood detection and environmental monitoring show the expanding scope of MCDM tools in sustainability applications (Das *et al.*, 2025g). These studies collectively highlight how fuzzy logic, soft set theories, and neutrosophic models provide valuable tools for supporting eco-design decisions, particularly when environmental, social, and economic criteria must be balanced.

In light of these challenges and opportunities, this chapter explores the transformative potential of eco-design within the framework of PLCM. It highlights best practices, case studies, and strategic implications for organizations aiming to enhance sustainability in their product offerings. By analyzing the intersections between eco-design, PLCM, and corporate sustainability strategies, this research aims to contribute valuable insights into pathways toward a more sustainable future. Ultimately, the integration of eco-design principles into PLCM can serve as a catalyst for innovation and sustainable growth, positioning organizations to meet the challenges of the 21st century while contributing positively to the environment.

TOOLS AND METHODOLOGIES FOR ECO-DESIGN: INSIGHTS FROM MCDM

To address the growing environmental challenges, eco-design has become a crucial strategy in product development, embedding sustainability throughout the PLCM. This section examines the definition, importance, methodologies, and tools essential for effectively implementing eco-design, with a particular emphasis on how MCDM can enhance eco-design practices.

Definition and Importance

Eco-design, often synonymous with sustainable design, integrates environmental considerations into every phase of the product development process. It emphasizes reducing negative environmental impacts at all stages of a product's life cycle from raw material extraction to manufacturing, use, and eventual disposal.

The significance of eco-design lies in its ability to create products that not only meet consumer needs but also minimize environmental harm. By prioritizing sustainability, eco-design fosters the efficient use of resources, encourages waste reduction, and promotes circular economy principles, where materials are reused, and waste is minimized. This approach supports a more sustainable future while meeting the increasing demand for environmentally friendly products.

The adoption of eco-design principles also provides businesses with a competitive advantage. As consumers become more environmentally conscious, companies that implement eco-design can differentiate themselves in the marketplace by demonstrating a commitment to sustainability. Moreover, eco-design can improve a company's reputation, leading to increased customer loyalty and market share.

Methodologies

Eco-design methodologies provide structured frameworks to incorporate sustainability into product development, ensuring that environmental factors are considered at each stage. By integrating these methodologies, designers can create products that are both functional and eco-friendly. The application of MCDM supports the evaluation of multiple, often conflicting, sustainability criteria during the design process.

Step 1: Design for Environment (DFE)

- **Concept:** DFE encourages designers to prioritize environmental impacts from the earliest stages of product development. This includes selecting sustainable materials, designing for energy efficiency, and ensuring ease of disassembly for recycling.
- **Benefits:** By incorporating environmental considerations early on, companies can minimize waste, reduce production costs, and increase product appeal to environmentally conscious consumers. MCDM tools help prioritize these environmental criteria when selecting materials and design features.

Step 2: Cradle-to-Cradle (C2C) Design

- **Concept:** The C2C methodology advocates for designing products with the aim of creating closed-loop systems, where materials can be fully reclaimed and reused without degradation of quality.
- **Benefits:** C2C design contributes to a circular economy by eliminating waste and enabling continuous material flow, supported by MCDM models that weigh the feasibility and environmental benefits of material recovery and reuse.

Step 3: Modular Design

- **Concept:** Modular design focuses on creating products made of interchangeable parts, allowing for easy upgrades, repairs, and replacements, which can extend product life and reduce waste.
- **Benefits:** Modular products adapt to changing consumer needs and technological advancements, offering enhanced sustainability and long-term economic value. MCDM can aid in evaluating the trade-offs between modularity and other design factors, such as cost, performance, and recyclability.

TOOLS

A variety of tools and resources are available to help designers integrate eco-design principles into their products, improving MCDM and supporting sustainable product development. These tools are particularly effective when paired with MCDM approaches, which assist in balancing environmental, economic, and social criteria in the design process.

Eco-Design Checklists and Guidelines

- **Overview:** Eco-design checklists and guidelines provide structured frameworks to help designers evaluate sustainability considerations at each stage of product development. These resources typically include criteria for material selection, energy efficiency, recyclability, and waste reduction.
- **Use:** Designers can use these checklists as a basis for evaluating their designs against established sustainability benchmarks. By integrating MCDM tools, they can further assess the trade-offs between different design alternatives and select the most sustainable options based on a comprehensive analysis of environmental impacts.

Software Tools

- **SimaPro:** SimaPro is a widely used LCA software that allows designers to model the environmental impacts of their products. It provides access to a comprehensive database of environmental data and enables the application of MCDM techniques to evaluate multiple sustainability criteria.

- **GaBi:** Similar to SimaPro, GaBi offers tools for LCA and eco-design, supporting users in analyzing the life cycle impacts of products and optimizing designs for sustainability. MCDM can be employed in GaBi to prioritize criteria such as carbon footprint, energy usage, and material efficiency.
- **Other Tools:** Additional software tools such as OpenLCA and Umberto offer LCA capabilities and facilitate eco-design analysis. These tools, when combined with MCDM methods, allow for the evaluation of various environmental, economic, and social impacts, ensuring a balanced and informed MCDM process.

By leveraging these tools and methodologies, companies can effectively integrate eco-design into their product development processes, optimizing sustainability outcomes while also addressing consumer demands and regulatory requirements. The use of MCDM enhances the MCDM process, providing a systematic approach to evaluating trade-offs and selecting the most sustainable design options.

EXAMPLE OF MCDM IN ECO-DESIGN

To illustrate how MCDM supports eco-design decisions, consider the case of selecting a material for manufacturing a laptop casing. The company must evaluate three conflicting criteria:

- *Cost (C1) - Lower is better*
- *Recyclability (C2) - Higher is better*
- *Durability (C3) - Higher is better*

Step 1: Identify Alternatives

Let the company consider three materials:

- *A1: Recycled Plastic*
- *A2: Aluminum*
- *A3: Magnesium Alloy*

Step 2: Construct Decision Matrix

Table **1** shows how different materials (Recycled Plastic, Aluminum, and Magnesium Alloy) are compared based on three criteria: cost, recyclability, and durability. This helps in choosing the best material for an eco-friendly laptop casing using the MCDM method.

Table 1. Decision matrix for material selection using MCDM in eco-design.

Criteria →	Cost (INR/kg) ↓	Recyclability (%) ↑	Durability (Score) ↑
*A*1	100	80	6
*A*2	180	95	9
*A*3	150	85	8

Step 3: Normalize Values

Since some criteria are cost-minimizing and others are benefit-maximizing, normalization is applied.

Step 4: Apply Weights

Assume the weights assigned based on expert judgment:

- **Cost:** 0.4
- **Recyclability:** 0.3
- **Durability:** 0.3

Use a simple method like the Weighted Sum Model to compute scores:

$A1 = (0.4\times1) + (0.3\times0.67) + (0.3\times0.5) = 0.4 + 0.201 + 0.15 = 0.751$
$A2 = (0.4\times0.33) + (0.3\times1) + (0.3\times1) = 0.132 + 0.3 + 0.3 = 0.732$
$A3 = (0.4\times0.5) + (0.3\times0.75) + (0.3\times0.89) = 0.2 + 0.225 + 0.267 = 0.692$

Step 5: Decision

The best material, based on the weighted criteria, is A1 (Recycled Plastic), offering the best trade-off between low cost and moderate recyclability and durability.

This example clarifies how MCDM can be practically applied in real-world eco-design problems, where stakeholders must evaluate alternatives with conflicting sustainability criteria.

INTEGRATION OF ECO-DESIGN INTO PLCM

Integrating eco-design principles into PLCM is essential for organizations aiming to enhance sustainability while achieving their business objectives. This approach involves aligning eco-design strategies with broader corporate goals, ensuring that sustainability becomes a central component of product development rather than an afterthought. By incorporating eco-design into every phase of the PLCM, from design to disposal, companies can minimize environmental impacts and drive long-term value through innovative, sustainable practices.

Aligning Eco-Design with Business Goals

Effectively integrating eco-design into PLCM requires aligning sustainability initiatives with the company's core business objectives. This alignment not only supports environmental goals but also enhances overall performance by creating value through sustainable design solutions that resonate with both consumers and stakeholders.

Cost Savings and Efficiency

Eco-design principles can significantly improve resource efficiency, leading to cost savings. Optimizing material use, reducing waste, and minimizing energy consumption during production can lower operational costs. Companies like Interface, a modular carpet manufacturer, have demonstrated that adopting eco-design strategies focused on sustainability can result in substantial savings and improved profitability. By applying MCDM methods, businesses can identify the most cost-effective design options that balance environmental impacts with resource use, improving both economic and environmental performance.

Market Differentiation

Eco-design can also serve as a powerful differentiator in competitive markets. By prioritizing sustainable practices, businesses can enhance their brand image and build loyalty among eco-conscious consumers. For example, Patagonia has successfully used its commitment to environmental responsibility as a key marketing tool, cultivating a strong connection with customers who value sustainability. This market differentiation can lead to increased consumer trust and long-term brand loyalty. Through MCDM techniques, companies can assess various eco-design alternatives and identify the most impactful ways to align product development with consumer demand for sustainability.

Role of Leadership in Promoting Eco-Design Initiatives

Strong leadership is vital for embedding eco-design into PLCM. Senior executives must champion sustainability initiatives and foster a company-wide culture that values environmental responsibility. Research shows that when leaders prioritize sustainability, this commitment influences MCDM throughout the organization, encouraging employees to consider the environmental impacts of their actions.

Training and Development

Leaders should invest in training programs that equip employees at all levels with the knowledge and skills needed to implement eco-design principles. For example, Unilever offers training on sustainable practices, enabling employees to actively contribute to eco-design initiatives. By integrating eco-design training into organizational development, companies ensure that sustainability considerations are embedded throughout the PLCM, from concept to end-of-life.

Examples of Companies Successfully Integrating Eco-Design

Numerous companies across industries are demonstrating how integrating eco-design principles into PLCM can drive sustainability, enhance brand reputation, and improve operational efficiency. These examples show how businesses can effectively incorporate eco-design into their strategic planning and product development processes.

- **Unilever:** Unilever's Sustainable Living Plan illustrates how the company integrates eco-design principles to minimize environmental impact while promoting the health and well-being of consumers. By applying eco-design throughout its product development cycle, Unilever has created products that use less water and generate less waste. This integration of sustainability with business growth objectives not only reduces the company's ecological footprint but also aligns its product portfolio with consumer demands for more responsible products. Using MCDM approaches, Unilever can evaluate the trade-offs between different eco-design options, ensuring that sustainability goals are met without compromising product performance.
- **Patagonia:** Patagonia is known for its dedication to environmental activism and has successfully integrated eco-design principles into its PLCM. The company prioritizes the use of recycled materials and designs products that are durable and repairable, which enhances their sustainability by extending their life cycle. Patagonia's "Worn Wear" program further promotes responsible consumption by encouraging customers to repair and reuse their garments. By embedding eco-design in its business strategy, Patagonia demonstrates how companies can align environmental stewardship with innovation, creating products that inspire consumers to adopt more sustainable practices.
- **IKEA:** IKEA's commitment to becoming a circular business by 2030 highlights its integration of eco-design into its PLCM. The company focuses on using renewable and recycled materials, designing products that can be easily disassembled for recycling, and ensuring that its products promote sustainable living. Through MCDM tools, IKEA can assess the environmental impacts of different design alternatives, optimizing its product development to meet

sustainability targets while satisfying consumer needs for affordable, eco-friendly products.

Integrating eco-design into PLCM is not only a sustainable practice but also a strategic business decision. By aligning eco-design with business goals, investing in leadership commitment, and drawing inspiration from successful examples, organizations can enhance their sustainability efforts while also realizing economic benefits. MCDM provides a systematic framework for evaluating the environmental, economic, and social impacts of different design options, ensuring that companies can make informed decisions that support both sustainability and business performance. By embedding eco-design into PLCM, businesses can create more sustainable products, reduce their environmental impact, and strengthen their position in the market.

REGULATORY FRAMEWORKS AND ECO-DESIGN

Regulations and standards play a crucial role in shaping eco-design practices, promoting sustainability across various industries. These frameworks provide mandatory requirements for product sustainability and can drive innovation by encouraging companies to integrate environmental considerations into their design processes.

Extended Producer Responsibility

Extended Producer Responsibility (EPR) policies transfer the obligation of managing products at the end of their life cycle from consumers and governments to manufacturers. Under these policies, producers are mandated to design their products in ways that facilitate easier recycling, reuse, and environmentally sound waste management. This paradigm shift not only encourages manufacturers to consider the entire life cycle of their products from the outset but also fosters innovation in sustainable product design.

By holding producers accountable for the environmental impacts of their products after they reach the end of their useful life, EPR policies incentivize companies to adopt eco-design principles. This includes using materials that are recyclable or biodegradable, reducing waste generation, and enhancing the overall sustainability of their products. As a result, manufacturers are motivated to integrate environmentally friendly practices into their design and production processes, ultimately contributing to a more circular economy and reducing the burden of waste on society and the environment. EPR thus plays a critical role in promoting sustainability and ensuring that environmental considerations are embedded in product development from the very beginning.

Global Standards

Countries and regions worldwide have implemented their own regulations aimed at promoting eco-design. For instance, Japan has established the Law for the Promotion of Measures to Cope with Global Warming, which actively encourages eco-design through a comprehensive framework of guidelines and standards. This legislation focuses on reducing greenhouse gas emissions associated with various products, emphasizing the importance of sustainable practices in product design and development.

These standards often outline specific requirements for manufacturers to follow, encouraging them to adopt eco-friendly materials, improve energy efficiency, and enhance the recyclability of their products. By setting clear expectations, these regulations help drive innovation and foster a culture of sustainability within industries.

In addition to Japan, other countries and regions have also introduced similar eco-design regulations, reflecting a global commitment to addressing environmental challenges. By aligning product design with sustainability objectives, these standards not only benefit the environment but also provide businesses with opportunities to differentiate themselves in the market and meet the growing consumer demand for environmentally responsible products. Ultimately, global standards play a crucial role in facilitating the transition toward a more sustainable future.

Driving Innovation

Regulatory frameworks frequently act as catalysts for innovation by motivating companies to create new technologies and materials that align with sustainability goals. For example, compliance with the Ecodesign Directive has spurred significant advancements in the development of energy-efficient appliances and sustainable packaging solutions.

These regulations challenge manufacturers to rethink their design processes, prompting them to integrate eco-friendly practices that minimize environmental impact. As businesses strive to meet stringent sustainability criteria, they often invest in research and development, leading to innovative solutions that not only fulfill regulatory requirements but also enhance product performance and consumer appeal.

Moreover, the push for compliance encourages collaboration between various stakeholders, including suppliers, manufacturers, and research institutions, fostering an ecosystem of innovation. This collaborative effort often results in the emergence of breakthrough technologies and sustainable materials that contribute to a circular economy. By driving innovation through regulatory frameworks, businesses can not only meet compliance standards but also position themselves as leaders in sustainability, ultimately benefiting both the environment and their bottom line.

Market Differentiation

Adhering to environmental regulations can offer companies a competitive edge, especially as consumer preferences shift toward sustainable products. As awareness of environmental issues grows, consumers are increasingly inclined to choose products that reflect eco-friendly practices.

By integrating eco-design principles into their offerings, companies can significantly enhance their brand reputation, positioning themselves as responsible and forward-thinking. This commitment to sustainability not only resonates with eco-conscious consumers but also fosters loyalty among customers who value environmentally friendly practices.

Furthermore, companies that prioritize eco-design can differentiate themselves in a crowded marketplace. They can leverage their commitment to sustainability as a Unique Selling Proposition (USP), appealing to consumers looking for brands that align with their values. This differentiation can lead to increased market share and profitability, as more consumers are willing to pay a premium for products that are both sustainable and responsibly made.

In essence, embracing eco-design not only fulfills regulatory obligations but also serves as a strategic approach for companies to enhance their market position, attract a dedicated customer base, and contribute positively to environmental sustainability.

Challenges in Complying with Eco-Design Regulations

Navigating the intricate landscape of eco-design regulations poses significant challenges for companies. The diversity of standards and regulations across various regions can complicate compliance, particularly for multinational corporations that operate in multiple jurisdictions. This complexity can lead to confusion and inconsistencies in adherence to eco-design principles.

- **Cost Implications:** The transition to eco-design practices in line with regulatory requirements often necessitates substantial investments in several key areas. Companies may need to allocate significant resources for research and development, employee training, and the adoption of new technologies that support sustainable practices. For smaller enterprises, these financial commitments can be particularly daunting, as they may lack the resources and infrastructure to meet compliance demands effectively. The high costs associated with implementing eco-design can deter these companies from pursuing sustainability initiatives, potentially limiting their market competitiveness.

- **Limited Access to Information:** Organizations frequently encounter difficulties in accessing up-to-date information regarding evolving eco-design regulations and best practices. This knowledge gap can significantly hinder their ability to implement effective eco-design strategies. Without comprehensive insights into regulatory changes and emerging standards, companies may struggle to align their practices with compliance expectations. The lack of access to pertinent information can lead to unintentional violations of regulations, resulting in potential legal ramifications and reputational damage.

In conclusion, while eco-design regulations play a crucial role in promoting sustainability, the associated challenges such as compliance complexity, cost implications, and limited information access can create significant barriers for companies. Addressing these challenges will require concerted efforts from industry stakeholders, regulators, and organizations to foster a more supportive environment for the adoption of eco-design practices.

Potential Solutions

- **Enhanced Training and Resources:** To address the challenges companies face in implementing eco-design practices and ensuring regulatory compliance, enhanced training and resource availability are essential. Providing businesses, particularly small and medium-sized enterprises, with targeted training sessions, workshops, and practical resources can greatly facilitate their understanding of eco-design principles. Organizations like the European Commission offer valuable guidance and tools that assist companies in navigating complex regulations and incorporating sustainable practices into their operations.
- **Collaborative Approaches:** Fostering collaboration among various stakeholders including governments, businesses, industry associations, and research institutions can promote knowledge sharing and the establishment of best practices in eco-design. By creating platforms for dialogue and partnership, stakeholders can work together to develop innovative solutions that address common challenges, enhance compliance, and drive the adoption of sustainable design practices across sectors.
- **Streamlining Regulations:** Efforts to harmonize eco-design regulations across different regions can significantly reduce compliance complexity for companies operating in multiple markets. By establishing a unified set of guidelines and

standards, businesses can more easily align their practices with regulatory requirements, minimizing confusion and fostering a smoother implementation process. Streamlined regulations can encourage more companies to adopt eco-design principles, ultimately contributing to a more sustainable economy.

In summary, regulatory frameworks play a crucial role in shaping eco-design practices by establishing clear guidelines and standards that promote sustainability. While these regulations drive innovation and create opportunities for market differentiation, challenges such as regulatory complexity and cost implications must be addressed. By enhancing training resources, promoting collaborative approaches, and streamlining regulations, stakeholders can facilitate the successful integration of eco-design principles, leading to a more sustainable and innovative future.

REAL-WORLD APPLICATIONS AND THEIR ENVIRONMENTAL IMPACTS IN PLCM

Eco-design principles have been widely adopted across various industries, resulting in substantial environmental benefits and innovative solutions that enhance the sustainability of PLCs. By integrating eco-design with MCDM, companies are able to evaluate the long-term environmental, economic, and social impacts of their products, ensuring that sustainability is embedded throughout the entire life cycle. Below are key examples of companies applying eco-design principles in PLCM, showcasing the integration of sustainability at various stages from production to disposal.

Consumer Electronics: Apple Inc.

Apple has made significant strides in incorporating eco-design into its PLCM. By focusing on reducing material usage and enhancing recyclability, Apple has integrated sustainability into the design, production, and disposal phases. For example, Apple uses recycled aluminum in the casings of its MacBooks, which reduces the demand for virgin materials and lowers environmental impacts. Moreover, the company has committed to powering all its production facilities with 100% renewable energy, significantly reducing its carbon footprint.

Through MCDM, Apple can assess and optimize the environmental impact of its PLC, evaluating the trade-offs between material selection, energy use, and recyclability at each stage. This holistic approach to eco-design has not only helped Apple reduce its environmental footprint but has also driven consumer demand for more sustainable products, enhancing brand loyalty.

Automotive Industry: Ford Motor Company

Ford has integrated eco-design principles into its automotive PLC, focusing on sustainability from the design phase through to end-of-life disposal. By using recycled plastics and renewable materials in vehicle interiors, Ford has reduced waste and resource consumption in manufacturing. The company's "Ford Smart Mobility" initiative further extends the application of eco-design by promoting sustainable transportation systems, which include exploring electric vehicles and smart infrastructure to reduce environmental impacts.

Ford's use of MCDM enables them to assess the sustainability of different materials and technologies throughout the vehicle's life cycle. By evaluating the environmental impact of various design choices such as material sourcing, energy consumption during manufacturing, and the vehicle's end-of-life recyclability Ford can optimize its PLC to achieve sustainability goals while maintaining product performance and consumer appeal.

Packaging Industry: Unilever

Unilever has implemented eco-design principles in its packaging strategy to minimize environmental impact throughout the PLC. The company focuses on reducing plastic usage and promoting recyclable, reusable, or compostable materials in its packaging. By 2025, Unilever aims to ensure that all its plastic packaging is capable of being recycled, reused, or composted, significantly reducing plastic waste in the environment.

Unilever's adoption of MCDM tools allows for the evaluation of various packaging materials across multiple sustainability criteria, including resource efficiency, recyclability, and environmental impact. This MCDM approach enables the company to make informed choices about the materials used in packaging, ensuring that environmental considerations are prioritized without compromising product safety and functionality.

Environmental Impacts of Eco-Design in PLCM

The integration of eco-design principles in PLCM has led to significant environmental improvements, which can be evaluated through MCDM approaches that consider factors such as waste reduction, resource efficiency, and sustainability perception. Below are the key environmental impacts of eco-design.

- **Waste Reductio**n: Eco-design has been shown to significantly reduce waste by promoting recyclability and extending PLCs. Products designed with a focus on end-of-life recyclability ensure that materials can be reused or recycled, leading to a reduction in landfill contributions. By applying MCDM models, companies can assess the trade-offs between product durability, recyclability, and waste reduction, optimizing the PLC to minimize environmental harm.

- **Resource Efficiency:** Eco-design enhances resource efficiency by minimizing material usage and promoting sustainable sourcing of raw materials. Companies that adopt eco-design principles report reductions in raw material consumption, which correlates to lower environmental impacts from resource extraction. By integrating MCDM, businesses can evaluate the life cycle impacts of different materials and production methods, identifying opportunities to reduce resource consumption while maintaining product quality and performance.
- **Sustainability Perception:** The growing adoption of eco-designed products has positively influenced consumer perceptions of sustainability. Studies show that consumers are increasingly inclined to favor brands that prioritize environmental responsibility in their PLCs. As a result, businesses that implement eco-design principles experience longer product life spans, higher customer satisfaction, and enhanced brand loyalty. MCDM tools can help companies assess how sustainability influences consumer decisions at each stage of the PLC, from design to disposal, fostering long-term customer relationships and strengthening market positioning.

The integration of eco-design principles into PLCM provides significant environmental benefits and fosters innovation across industries. By using MCDM models, companies can evaluate and optimize the sustainability of their products at each stage of the life cycle. This approach allows businesses to make informed decisions about material selection, resource efficiency, waste reduction, and product durability, ensuring that sustainability is achieved without compromising product quality or market competitiveness. Through these strategies, companies can not only minimize their environmental footprint but also meet the growing demand for eco-friendly products, thereby enhancing brand value and consumer loyalty in an increasingly sustainability-conscious marketplace.

CIRCULAR ECONOMY INTEGRATION THROUGH ECO-DESIGN

Eco-design plays a crucial role in advancing the principles of the circular economy by creating products with lifecycle thinking in mind, aiming for minimal environmental impact, optimized resource use, and facilitating reuse, recycling, and repurposing. As global focus shifts from linear consumption models to circularity, eco-design strategies allow companies to rethink how products are manufactured, used, and discarded, extending their lifespan and reducing waste.

Design for Durability and Longevity

One of the fundamental principles of eco-design is creating products that last. Designing for durability means selecting materials and production techniques that withstand wear, reducing the need for frequent replacements. Durable products not only benefit consumers but also reduce waste by limiting the frequency of discarded goods. In the fashion industry, for example, companies like Patagonia have embraced durable materials and repair services that enable customers to extend the life of their purchases. This approach reduces textile waste and reinforces customer loyalty.

Strategies for Durability:

- Use high-quality, resilient materials.
- Minimize components that may wear quickly or become obsolete.
- Design modular components that are replaceable or upgradeable.

Design for Repairability and Upgradability

Products that are easy to repair or upgrade are less likely to be discarded prematurely. By designing components that can be easily accessed, disassembled, and replaced, manufacturers empower consumers to fix products instead of discarding them. This strategy is commonly seen in electronics, where companies like Fairphone have designed smartphones with replaceable batteries, screens, and other components, allowing consumers to extend the life of the device.

Strategies for Repairability and Upgradability:

- Use standardized parts and screws for easy disassembly.
- Design products with clear repair instructions and accessible repair kits.
- Incorporate software or hardware upgradability to keep products relevant over time.

Design for Recyclability

Eco-design principles encourage the use of recyclable materials and components, facilitating the circular economy's goal of repurposing materials instead of extracting new resources. By choosing materials that can be recycled at the end of a product's life, companies ensure that the product’s value is retained in the economy. For instance, companies like Apple and Dell are increasingly using aluminum, glass, and other recyclable materials in their devices and designing components to be easily separated during recycling.

Strategies for Recyclability:

- Opt for single-material or easily separable multi-material components.
- Avoid materials that are difficult to recycle, like mixed plastics or materials with complex coatings.
- Use identifiable markers or codes on parts to guide recycling facilities in material separation.

Design for Reusability and Remanufacturing

Products designed for reuse or remanufacturing can undergo multiple life cycles, thereby extending their value. Remanufacturing involves restoring used products to like-new condition, often with updated components, which conserves resources while reducing waste. Companies like Caterpillar and Xerox have successfully implemented remanufacturing programs, refurbishing machinery and office equipment for continued use. This approach reduces material use, lowers production costs, and supports a circular supply chain.

Strategies for Reusability and Remanufacturing:

- Design products with modular components that are easy to replace and refurbish.
- Implement take-back programs where consumers can return used products for remanufacturing.
- Use durable materials that withstand multiple remanufacturing cycles without degradation.

Design for Biodegradability and Compostability

In cases where recycling or reuse is not feasible, eco-design can focus on materials that are biodegradable or compostable, ensuring minimal environmental impact at the end of life. This is particularly important for single-use products and packaging, where biodegradable materials can help reduce landfill waste and pollution. For example, companies like Lush have developed compostable product packaging, such as shampoo bars wrapped in biodegradable paper.

Strategies for Biodegradability and Compostability:

- Use plant-based or natural materials that decompose harmlessly in the environment.
- Avoid chemical treatments or coatings that prevent materials from breaking down.
- Educate consumers on how to properly dispose of compostable items.

Minimizing Environmental Impact with Lifecycle Assessments (LCA)

Lifecycle Assessments (LCAs) enable designers to understand and minimize the environmental impact of products across all stages from material extraction to production, distribution, usage, and disposal. LCA can help identify areas for improvement and optimize material choices, manufacturing processes, and logistics to reduce emissions and resource consumption. Companies can implement LCA results into their eco-design process to ensure a product's environmental impact remains low throughout its lifecycle.

Strategies for Lifecycle Optimization:

- Use LCA tools to evaluate energy, water, and material use across the product's life stages.
- Identify and reduce hotspots with high environmental impact, such as transportation emissions or resource-intensive materials.
- Implement circular economy principles in high-impact areas highlighted by the LCA.

By integrating eco-design into circular economy models, companies can maximize product life, retain material value, and reduce waste. Adopting these strategies not only leads to environmental benefits but also offers companies economic advantages, as resource efficiency and product longevity lower production costs and create brand value through sustainability. Eco-design is thus a powerful catalyst for achieving circularity, promoting a future where products are designed with their end-of-life in mind, closing the loop on resource use and advancing sustainability goals across industries.

ECONOMIC AND MARKET ANALYSIS OF ECO-DESIGN ADOPTION

The economic implications of eco-design adoption are becoming increasingly significant as companies and stakeholders recognize the potential for long-term profitability, enhanced brand reputation, and alignment with market trends toward sustainability. Analyzing the cost-benefit dynamics, Return on Investment (ROI), and evolving consumer preferences highlights the tangible advantages of eco-design, providing insights that are essential for business stakeholders aiming to make informed decisions.

Cost-Benefit Analysis of Eco-Design Adoption

Eco-design adoption often requires an initial investment in sustainable materials, innovative technologies, and redesigning product lifecycles. However, these upfront costs can be balanced or even outweighed by the long-term benefits that eco-design offers, especially as regulatory and consumer pressures increase.

- **Reduced Material Costs:** Eco-design can lead to more efficient use of materials, reducing waste and associated costs. By designing products with modular or recyclable components, companies can cut down on raw material costs over time. For example, modular furniture makers, such as SteeLCAse, use interchangeable parts, reducing waste and allowing customers to repair or upgrade parts instead of replacing entire units.
- **Waste Reduction and Cost Savings:** By minimizing waste generation, companies can also reduce disposal costs, align with zero-waste goals, and potentially capitalize on circular revenue streams. Philips, for example, shifted to a circular business model for lighting systems, offering "lighting as a service," where they retain ownership of lighting materials and repurpose components, thus reducing costs and waste disposal expenses.
- **Lower Energy Expenditures:** Eco-design can include energy-efficient production processes, leading to significant savings. Products designed to consume less energy during manufacturing or operation benefit both the company and the end-user. Many consumer electronics companies, such as HP and Apple, have integrated energy efficiency into product design, lowering production costs and enhancing consumer appeal.

Return on Investment (ROI) of Eco-Designed Products

The ROI of eco-designed products can vary depending on industry, product complexity, and the level of sustainable investment. However, numerous case studies reveal that eco-design investments often generate high returns due to increased consumer demand, brand differentiation, and regulatory advantages.

- **Enhanced Sales through Brand Differentiation:** Companies that adopt eco-design practices often experience increased consumer loyalty and higher sales. For example, Patagonia's focus on environmentally friendly products and sustainable supply chains has solidified its position in the outdoor apparel market. Consumers perceive Patagonia as a leader in sustainability, leading to strong sales growth and an expanded customer base willing to pay a premium for its eco-conscious products.
- **Reduced Operational Costs:** Eco-design often leads to reduced operational costs due to savings in energy, materials, and waste management. In manufacturing, sustainable design can decrease resource use, improving overall production efficiency. For instance, Unilever reports significant savings by adopting sustainable production processes across its product lines, yielding long-term financial returns that offset initial investments.

- **Access to Green Financing and Incentives:** Many governments offer grants, tax incentives, or low-interest loans for businesses that prioritize sustainability. By integrating eco-design, companies may access green financing options or benefit from regulatory incentives, ultimately enhancing ROI. This is especially true in industries like construction, where certifications (*e.g.*, LEED) linked to eco-design can yield tax breaks and lower financing costs.

Long-Term Economic Benefits of Eco-Design

The long-term economic benefits of eco-design are multifaceted, enhancing financial performance while positioning companies for sustained growth in a green economy.

- **Risk Mitigation and Regulatory Compliance:** As governments worldwide impose stricter environmental regulations, companies that adopt eco-design practices can avoid future compliance costs and potential penalties. By proactively implementing eco-design, businesses position themselves as leaders in sustainability and reduce their exposure to regulatory risks. For instance, companies that have embraced eco-design find it easier to comply with regulations like the European Union's Green Deal, which mandates eco-friendly product criteria for import and export.
- **Value Retention through Product Longevity:** Eco-designed products are often more durable, reparable, and reusable, creating extended PLCs. This longevity reduces the need for frequent replacements, decreasing long-term manufacturing costs while increasing product value for consumers. Brands like Fairphone focus on modular smartphones, allowing customers to replace or upgrade parts easily, thereby retaining product value over time and fostering consumer loyalty.
- **Improved Brand Value and Investor Interest:** Eco-design adoption positively impacts brand value, attracting environmentally conscious consumers and investors alike. Many investment firms and funds are increasingly focused on Environmental, Social, and Governance (ESG) factors. A commitment to eco-design enhances a company's ESG profile, drawing interest from investors seeking sustainable, ethical investment opportunities. According to Morgan Stanley, over 85% of investors are now interested in sustainable investing, emphasizing the economic advantage of integrating eco-design.

Market Trends and Consumer Behaviors

As eco-design continues to gain traction, consumer preferences and market demands for sustainable products shape the competitive landscape. Eco-conscious consumers increasingly prefer brands with sustainable practices, and many are willing to pay a premium for eco-designed products.

- **Growing Demand for Sustainable Products:** Research shows that younger generations, especially Millennials and Gen Z, prefer sustainable products and are more likely to choose brands with eco-friendly practices. Nielsen reports that 73% of global consumers are willing to change their consumption habits to reduce environmental impact, illustrating a growing market for eco-designed products.
- **Premium Pricing Opportunities:** Consumers perceive eco-friendly brands as high quality and are often willing to pay more for products that align with their values. For example, Tesla's electric vehicles attract premium prices not only for their innovation but also for their environmental benefits, as consumers value emissions-free transportation.
- **Shifts in Corporate Procurement:** Corporations are adopting green procurement policies, prioritizing eco-designed products in their supply chains. Large companies, such as Walmart, require suppliers to meet sustainability criteria, creating new markets and revenue opportunities for companies offering eco-designed products.

Competitive Advantage and Economic Impact of Eco-Design

Eco-design creates a distinct competitive advantage, enabling companies to differentiate in crowded markets. It also fosters loyalty among eco-conscious consumers and attracts employees interested in working for purpose-driven organizations.

- **Increased Market Share:** Eco-design can attract new customers and capture market share from competitors. Companies that prioritize sustainability can tap into growing eco-conscious markets, as seen with brands like Seventh Generation in the household cleaning industry, which has captured a substantial share by emphasizing eco-friendly ingredients and packaging.
- **Employment and Talent Attraction:** Organizations with strong sustainability values are attractive to employees who prioritize environmental and social responsibility. This leads to higher employee retention and recruitment advantages, which translates to long-term cost savings.
- **Lifecycle Profitability through Product as a Service:** By adopting these models, companies generate recurring revenue from products designed for durability and reuse. This model enhances lifecycle profitability and reduces waste. For example, Philips offers lighting as a service to commercial buildings, retaining ownership of materials and repurposing components for future use, resulting in reduced material costs and consistent revenue streams.

Eco-design adoption offers substantial economic benefits by aligning companies with market trends, consumer preferences, and regulatory frameworks that prioritize sustainability. The integration of eco-design allows businesses to reduce costs, improve ROI, capture new market share, and enhance brand reputation. As the global market increasingly values sustainable practices, companies that embrace eco-design are not only supporting environmental goals but also securing long-term economic viability.

IMPACT MEASUREMENT AND PERFORMANCE INDICATORS FOR ECO-DESIGN

Measuring the impact of eco-design initiatives is essential for businesses to understand the effectiveness of their sustainability efforts, identify areas for improvement, and communicate achievements to stakeholders. Tracking specific Key Performance Indicators (KPIs) enables companies to quantify the positive environmental, economic, and social impacts of their eco-design practices. Below are some of the most relevant KPIs for evaluating eco-design success, along with strategies for data collection and analysis.

Carbon Footprint Reduction

A significant goal of eco-design is to minimize greenhouse gas emissions across the product lifecycle, from raw material extraction to disposal. Tracking carbon footprint reduction offers insight into the environmental benefits of eco-design and highlights improvements in manufacturing, transportation, and product disposal.

- **KPIs for Carbon Footprint:**
    - **Total Emissions (CO_2)**: Measure the overall carbon emissions in CO_2 equivalent for the entire lifecycle of a product or within a specific process.
    - **Carbon Intensity:** Measure emissions relative to production output (*e.g.*, kg CO_2 per unit produced).
    - **Reduction in Emissions Year-over-Year:** Track the percentage reduction in carbon emissions over time as eco-design practices are implemented.
- **Measurement Strategies:**
- Use Lifecycle Assessment (LCA) tools to quantify emissions across each phase of the product lifecycle.
- Apply carbon accounting software to track emissions data, ensuring consistency and accuracy.
- Utilize supplier data to understand emissions in the supply chain, which is critical for products with complex sourcing.

Energy Efficiency

Eco-design often aims to reduce energy consumption in product manufacturing and operation. By tracking energy efficiency, companies can assess their progress in lowering energy use, leading to cost savings and reduced environmental impact.

- **KPIs for Energy Efficiency:**
  - **Energy Use per Unit Produced:** Measure the energy consumed per product unit to identify energy efficiency improvements over time.
  - **Energy Efficiency Ratio:** Calculate the ratio of output (*e.g.*, product units or revenue) to energy consumed.
  - **Renewable Energy Percentage:** Track the percentage of energy derived from renewable sources *versus* non-renewable sources.
    - **Measurement Strategies:**
  - Implement real-time energy monitoring systems in facilities to track consumption accurately.
  - Conduct energy audits to identify high-energy-consuming processes and evaluate the impact of eco-design modifications.
  - Collaborate with suppliers to collect energy data for outsourced production stages, as energy use can vary significantly within supply chains.

Resource Efficiency and Material Use

Reducing resource use through efficient material selection and product design is a core objective of eco-design. Monitoring resource efficiency helps companies understand their impact on raw material consumption and waste generation, ensuring responsible and sustainable resource management.

- **KPIs for Resource Efficiency:**
  - **Material Intensity:** Measure the total weight or volume of materials used per unit of output, tracking reductions in raw material consumption.
  - **Percentage of Recycled or Sustainable Materials:** Track the percentage of total materials that come from recycled or renewable sources.
  - **Waste Generation per Unit:** Measure the amount of waste generated per product or during production, including scrap, rework, and packaging waste.
    - **Measurement Strategies:**
  - Conduct regular materials audits to assess the quantity and types of materials used, focusing on opportunities to reduce or replace non-sustainable materials.
  - Set up tracking systems within manufacturing processes to monitor waste

generation at different stages.

- Use advanced software to track resource use across the supply chain, particularly for products with high raw material dependencies.

Product Lifecycle and Durability

Eco-design emphasizes creating products with extended lifecycles and durability, which reduces the frequency of replacement and the environmental impact of production. Measuring product longevity and post-use options (such as recyclability or biodegradability) helps quantify sustainability achievements.

- **KPIs for Product Lifecycle:**
  - **Product Longevity:** Track the average lifespan of a product to assess improvements in durability.
  - **Repairability and Upgradability Index:** Measure the ease with which a product can be repaired or upgraded, which supports lifecycle extension.
  - **Percentage of Recyclable Components:** Track the proportion of product components that are recyclable or biodegradable, reducing end-of-life environmental impact.
    - **Measurement Strategies:**
  - Conduct durability testing to establish baseline lifespan data and track improvements over time.
  - Use data from repair facilities or customer feedback to evaluate product repairability and upgradability.
  - Work with recycling partners or use recyclability certifications to assess the end-of-life impact of materials and components.

Water Usage and Wastewater Management

Water consumption and wastewater generation are critical factors in assessing the environmental impact of eco-design, especially for industries with high water use, such as manufacturing and textiles. Monitoring water-related KPIs enables companies to minimize their water footprint and ensure responsible water management.

- **KPIs for Water Usage:**
  - **Water Use per Unit Produce**d: Measure water consumption in production processes relative to output.
  - **Wastewater Reduction:** Track reductions in wastewater volume and pollutants as a result of eco-design improvements.
  - **Water Recycling Rate:** Measure the percentage of water recycled within processes, reducing dependence on fresh water sources.

- **Measurement Strategies:**
  - Install water meters to track usage at specific stages in the production process.
  - Use wastewater treatment systems with monitoring capabilities to measure pollutants and track wastewater output.
  - Partner with external stakeholders to assess water impacts within the supply chain, particularly for water-intensive materials like cotton or leather.

Social and Economic Performance

Beyond environmental impacts, eco-design initiatives often produce social and economic benefits, such as cost savings, job creation, and customer satisfaction. Tracking these indicators can provide a holistic view of eco-design impact, helping companies to align with broader sustainability goals.

- **KPIs for Social and Economic Impact:**
  - **Customer Satisfaction and Product Return Rates:** Track customer satisfaction related to eco-designed products and monitor return rates as a proxy for product quality and durability.
  - **Eco-Design ROI:** Measure the return on investment for eco-design initiatives by analyzing cost savings, new revenue from eco-designed products, and overall profitability.
  - **Employee Engagement in Eco-Design Initiatives:** Track participation in eco-design programs and training sessions, which often correlates with a stronger organizational commitment to sustainability.
- **Measurement Strategies:**
  - Gather feedback from customers on product satisfaction, focusing on eco-design aspects such as durability and eco-friendly features.
  - Conduct financial analyses to calculate cost savings from material efficiency, energy reductions, and other eco-design-related savings.
  - Survey employees or monitor participation in eco-design programs to gauge organizational engagement with sustainability goals.

Tracking the success of eco-design initiatives using specific KPIs provides businesses with a clear picture of their sustainability progress. By focusing on carbon footprint, energy efficiency, resource usage, product lifecycle, water management, and social impact, companies can align eco-design practices with their financial and environmental objectives. Regularly monitoring these KPIs allows businesses to make data-driven improvements, communicate impact to stakeholders, and further integrate eco-design principles across their operations.

COLLABORATIONS AND PARTNERSHIPS FOR SUSTAINABLE INNOVATION IN ECO-DESIGN

Sustainable innovation in eco-design often requires the integration of knowledge, resources, and capabilities that extend beyond a single organization. Collaborations with external stakeholders such as Non-Governmental Organizations (NGOs), governments, research institutions, and industry partners can significantly accelerate the development and implementation of eco-design practices. By combining efforts, businesses can leverage diverse expertise, access funding, and influence policy changes that facilitate the adoption of sustainable technologies and products. Below, we explore how these collaborations can drive innovation in eco-design.

Partnerships with Non-Governmental Organizations (NGOs)

NGOs play a crucial role in driving sustainability by advocating for environmental protection, supporting community-based environmental projects, and pushing for corporate accountability. Partnering with NGOs provides businesses with insights into best practices, emerging sustainability trends, and social issues related to environmental impacts.

- **Benefits of Collaborating with NGOs**:
  - **Access to Expertise:** NGOs often have deep expertise in environmental issues, such as biodiversity, pollution, and climate change. This expertise can guide businesses in designing products that minimize negative environmental impacts.
  - **Community Engagement:** NGOs can facilitate outreach and collaboration with local communities, helping businesses integrate social considerations into eco-design, such as supporting circular economy initiatives or providing fair labor conditions in supply chains.
  - **Influence on Consumer Behavior:** NGOs can help businesses better understand consumer preferences for sustainable products, which can inform eco-design decisions. They also provide credibility and legitimacy, which can increase customer trust in the company's sustainability claims.
- **Examples**:
  - **Patagonia and Fair Trade:** Patagonia, an outdoor apparel company, partners with NGOs to ensure that its supply chain meets social and environmental standards. Through collaborations with Fair Trade USA, the company has improved labor conditions and promotes sustainable material sourcing.
  - **Unilever's Sustainable Living Plan:** Unilever collaborates with various NGOs such as the World Wildlife Fund to tackle environmental issues,

promote sustainability in its supply chain, and improve the recyclability of its products.

Collaborations with Government Entities

Governments can play a pivotal role in shaping eco-design innovation through regulatory frameworks, funding programs, and public-private partnerships. Collaborative efforts with governments can help businesses stay compliant with sustainability regulations while gaining access to incentives and funding for green initiatives.

- **Government Support for Eco-Design**:
  - **Policy and Regulatory Influence:** Governments can create incentives for eco-design by introducing policies such as EPR, eco-labeling, and sustainability regulations. Companies can collaborate with government agencies to ensure compliance with these regulations while helping shape future policies.
  - **Public Funding for Research and Development:** Governments often provide funding and grants for Research and Development (R&D) in sustainable technologies. Partnerships with governmental bodies can enable businesses to access financial support for developing eco-designed products and technologies.
  - **Market Access and Incentives:** Governments can facilitate market access for eco-designed products through public procurement policies or tax incentives for businesses that adopt sustainable practices.
- **Examples**:
  - **The European Union's Circular Economy Action Plan:** The EU has been at the forefront of supporting eco-design through regulatory measures and funding opportunities. Programs such as Horizon 2020 have provided financial support to businesses working on circular economy innovations, encouraging them to adopt eco-design principles in product development.
  - **The US Green Building Council (USGBC):** USGBC's partnership with various local, state, and federal agencies has contributed to the rise of green building standards such as LEED, which promotes eco-design in construction and architecture.

Collaboration with Research Institutions

Research institutions are hubs of innovation, driving advancements in sustainable materials, manufacturing technologies, and eco-design methodologies. Collaborating with academic and research organizations enables businesses to access cutting-edge research, enhance product design with scientific insights, and accelerate the commercialization of new technologies.

- **Benefits of Collaborating with Research Institutions**:
  - **Access to Advanced Technologies:** Universities and research centers often work on the development of new, sustainable materials and manufacturing processes. Collaborating with these institutions allows businesses to integrate these innovations into their products early in the development phase.
  - **Joint R&D:** Businesses can partner with research institutions to fund joint R&D initiatives focused on eco-design, exploring areas such as biodegradable materials, energy-efficient production techniques, or smart, resource-saving technologies.
  - **Knowledge Transfer and Innovation:** Research collaborations facilitate the transfer of knowledge between academic researchers and industry practitioners, fostering the development of novel solutions and accelerating the commercialization of sustainable technologies.
- **Examples**:
  - **Ford and the University of Michigan:** Ford Motor Company collaborates with the University of Michigan on sustainable transportation research, including eco-design of automotive components such as lightweight, recyclable materials and energy-efficient technologies.
  - **Philips and Fraunhofer Institute:** Philips, a global leader in lighting and healthcare, works with the Fraunhofer Institute to develop energy-efficient and sustainable LED lighting solutions, as well as new materials for circular economy applications.

Cross-Industry Collaborations

Eco-design innovation thrives when businesses across different sectors come together to share knowledge, resources, and best practices. Cross-industry collaborations allow for the exchange of innovative ideas and solutions that can be adapted to various product categories, leading to breakthroughs in sustainability.

- **Benefits of Cross-Industry Collaborations**:
  - **Shared Resources and Expertise:** Companies from diverse industries such as electronics, automotive, and fashion can collaborate to share insights on material sourcing, energy efficiency, and recycling practices, which can be applied across different sectors.
  - **Standardization of Practices:** By working together, industries can develop common sustainability standards that streamline eco-design efforts, making it easier for businesses to adopt sustainable practices and for consumers to identify eco-friendly products.
  - **Innovative Supply Chains:** Collaborative efforts between industries can lead to more resilient and sustainable supply chains by sharing materials, components, and recycling networks.

- **Examples**:
    - **The Ellen MacArthur Foundation's Circular Economy Network:** This network brings together businesses from various industries to promote circular economy practices. Through collaborations with brands like IKEA, Google, and Unilever, the foundation has helped companies integrate eco-design into their product development processes.
    - **BMW and the Ellen MacArthur Foundation:** BMW partnered with the Ellen MacArthur Foundation to explore opportunities for designing products with longer lifecycles and using renewable and recyclable materials, supporting the transition toward a circular economy.

Leveraging Industry Consortia and Sustainable Standards

Collaborations through industry consortia or through developing and adopting sustainability standards can accelerate the adoption of eco-design. Consortia bring together stakeholders from across sectors to align on common goals, share knowledge, and create industry-wide benchmarks for eco-design practices.

- **Benefits of Industry Consortia**:
    - **Collective Problem Solving:** Consortia provide a platform for businesses to work together to solve complex sustainability challenges that no single company can address alone.
    - **Scaling Sustainable Practices:** Industry-wide collaborations can help scale eco-design practices across sectors, creating a broader impact on sustainability.
    - **Sustainability Standards Development:** Through collaboration, industry consortia can establish sustainability standards that shape the future of eco-design, such as certifications, eco-labels, and material guidelines.
- **Examples**:
    - **Global e-Sustainability Initiative:** It is an industry consortium dedicated to promoting sustainability in the information and communication technology sector. It focuses on eco-design initiatives that reduce the environmental footprint of digital products.
    - **Cradle to Cradle Products Innovation Institute:** The Cradle to Cradle certification is a globally recognized standard for eco-designed products. Companies that join the institute's network gain access to resources and tools to improve the sustainability of their product designs.

Collaboration is key to fostering innovation in eco-design and achieving sustainable outcomes across industries. Partnerships with NGOs, governments, research institutions, and across industries allow companies to access expertise, resources, and funding, facilitating the development and implementation of eco-designed products. By working together, these partnerships can accelerate the transition toward a circular economy, promote the adoption of sustainable practices, and drive long-term innovation for environmental sustainability.

CHALLENGES AND BARRIERS TO ECO-DESIGN ADOPTION

While eco-design offers significant environmental, social, and economic benefits, its widespread adoption by companies faces several challenges. These barriers can arise from various factors, including financial constraints, technical limitations, and consumer misconceptions. Understanding these obstacles is crucial for businesses as they navigate the complexities of integrating eco-design into their product development processes. Below are the primary challenges and barriers that companies encounter when adopting eco-design principles.

Cost Constraints and Economic Pressures

One of the most significant barriers to the adoption of eco-design is the perceived high initial cost. Designing products with minimal environmental impact often requires investing in new materials, technologies, and processes, which can lead to higher upfront costs. These expenses can be particularly challenging for small and medium-sized enterprises that may already operate under tight financial margins.

- **High R&D Costs:** The development of new sustainable materials, energy-efficient manufacturing processes, and innovative recycling systems can require substantial investment in R&D. Companies may hesitate to allocate funds for these initiatives without a clear, short-term return on investment.
- **Initial Capital Investment:** Eco-design often necessitates the purchase of new machinery, technology, or materials that are more expensive than traditional alternatives. This can lead to reluctance from businesses that are not willing to commit significant resources without assurance of profitability.
- **Longer Payback Periods:** While eco-design can lead to long-term cost savings through resource efficiency and waste reduction, the payback period can be lengthy. Many companies, particularly those under financial pressure, may not have the financial flexibility to invest in such long-term solutions.
- **Example:** In the electronics industry, companies like Apple have faced criticism for the high cost of their recycling programs and the use of recycled materials in their products. Although these practices contribute to sustainability, the associated costs can lead to higher prices for consumers, which companies may be reluctant to pass on.

Supply Chain Limitations and Resource Availability

Eco-design often requires sourcing sustainable raw materials, utilizing renewable energy in production processes, and collaborating with suppliers who adhere to sustainability standards. These factors introduce complexities and limitations in the supply chain that can hinder the adoption of eco-design.

- **Sourcing Sustainable Materials:** While demand for sustainable materials is increasing, these resources can be limited or more expensive than conventional alternatives. Additionally, the availability of materials like recycled plastics, biodegradable polymers, and responsibly sourced metals is often restricted by geographic, logistical, and production constraints.
- **Supplier Capability and Compliance:** Not all suppliers are equipped to meet the environmental standards required for eco-designed products. Businesses may struggle to find suppliers who can provide materials with a low environmental footprint or who follow ethical and sustainable practices in their operations.
- **Complex Supply Chains:** Many products rely on global supply chains, and ensuring sustainability at every stage from raw material extraction to product assembly can be a daunting task. Companies may face difficulties in monitoring their supply chain for environmental impact or enforcing compliance with sustainability standards.
- **Example:** The fashion industry is often criticized for its lack of sustainable practices across global supply chains. Companies that attempt to use eco-friendly materials may face challenges in sourcing them at scale, leading to inconsistencies in product offerings.

Technological and Knowledge Gaps

While the potential for eco-design is vast, the integration of new technologies and practices into existing business models can be challenging. Companies may lack the technical expertise required to design products with minimal environmental impact, or they may face difficulties integrating sustainable practices into established production systems.

- **Lack of Knowledge and Skills:** Many companies may not possess the in-house expertise needed to implement eco-design principles effectively. This includes knowledge of sustainable materials, energy-efficient production techniques, and waste management strategies.
- **Technological Limitations:** In some cases, the required technologies to support eco-design may not be readily available, or they may not yet be commercially viable. The transition to new technologies may involve significant technical and operational hurdles, such as retooling production lines or retraining staff.

- **Integration with Existing Systems:** Eco-design requires a systemic approach that integrates sustainable practices across the entire product lifecycle. This can be difficult to achieve, particularly for companies with complex production systems or existing infrastructure that is not designed for sustainability.
- **Example:** In the automotive industry, manufacturers face challenges in integrating electric vehicle technologies into their existing production lines, which were originally designed for traditional combustion engine vehicles. This requires substantial investment in new machinery, staff training, and reconfiguration of supply chains.

Consumer Misconceptions and Market Demand

Consumer understanding and demand for eco-designed products can significantly influence a company's decision to adopt sustainable practices. However, misconceptions and reluctance from consumers can pose obstacles to the widespread adoption of eco-design.

- **Lack of Consumer Awareness:** Many consumers are not fully aware of the environmental benefits of eco-designed products or the long-term value they provide. As a result, they may not be willing to pay a premium for sustainable products or may prioritize price over environmental impact.
- **Greenwashing Concerns:** Companies may face skepticism about the authenticity of their eco-design claims. The phenomenon of "greenwashing," where companies falsely market products as environmentally friendly, has led to consumer distrust. As a result, businesses that genuinely adopt eco-design principles may face challenges in differentiating their products in the market.
- **Perceived Quality Trade-Off:** Some consumers may associate eco-designed products with lower quality or performance due to their environmentally friendly nature. This misconception can deter them from purchasing eco-friendly alternatives, particularly in industries where performance and durability are prioritized, such as electronics or automotive.
- **Example:** In the food industry, there has been resistance to organic and sustainably produced foods in certain markets. While consumer interest in eco-design is growing, many shoppers still perceive these products as too expensive or inferior in quality, which can limit demand.

Regulatory and Policy Challenges

While governments are increasingly introducing regulations to encourage sustainability, the regulatory environment around eco-design can be complex and inconsistent. Companies may struggle to navigate these regulations or find that existing standards do not align with their eco-design goals.

- **Lack of Standardization:** There is no universally accepted standard for eco-design, and regulations vary widely by region and sector. This can make it difficult for companies to adopt consistent practices across their operations and products. The absence of clear guidelines may also cause confusion or lead to inconsistencies in how eco-design is applied.
- **Changing and Uncertain Regulations:** Regulatory landscapes can change rapidly, with governments periodically introducing new sustainability mandates, carbon taxes, or recycling requirements. Companies may struggle to keep up with these changes, particularly if they are not sufficiently equipped to track evolving standards.
- **Example:** The electronics industry faces challenges with EPR regulations, which mandate manufacturers to take responsibility for the recycling and disposal of their products. Companies often find it challenging to keep up with varying regional requirements for recycling programs, which can affect their ability to comply and design for sustainability.

While the adoption of eco-design offers significant environmental and economic benefits, companies face a range of challenges in its integration. From cost constraints and supply chain limitations to consumer misconceptions and regulatory complexity, businesses must overcome multiple barriers to implement sustainable product design practices effectively. To address these challenges, companies need strategic planning, investment in innovation and education, and collaboration with stakeholders across the value chain. By understanding and tackling these barriers, companies can take meaningful steps toward adopting eco-design and driving sustainability in their product offerings.

FUTURE TRENDS IN ECO-DESIGN AND SUSTAINABLE MANUFACTURING

As the global focus on sustainability intensifies, eco-design and sustainable manufacturing are evolving rapidly. Companies are increasingly adopting innovative approaches to minimize environmental impact, reduce waste, and promote resource efficiency. The future of eco-design is shaped by advancements in technology, changing consumer expectations, and a growing commitment to circular economy principles. Below are several key trends that are likely to define the future of eco-design and sustainable manufacturing.

Biodegradable and Compostable Products

Biodegradable and compostable materials are becoming an essential part of eco-design, addressing the global challenge of plastic pollution. These materials break down naturally over time, reducing their environmental impact when discarded.

The growing concern over single-use plastics and their impact on ecosystems has spurred innovations in biodegradable alternatives.

- **Trend Overview:** New biodegradable materials, such as bioplastics made from plant-based resources, are being developed to replace traditional plastics in packaging, products, and components. Additionally, compostable materials are being designed for use in industries like food packaging, textiles, and medical products.
- **Impact:** This trend could drastically reduce the amount of plastic waste entering landfills and oceans, contributing to a cleaner environment. Additionally, biodegradable products could help meet tightening regulations on plastic usage and disposal, offering companies an opportunity to comply with evolving environmental policies.

Eco-Packaging Innovations

The packaging industry is undergoing a major transformation as companies and consumers alike demand more sustainable alternatives. Packaging often constitutes a significant portion of a product's overall environmental impact, and minimizing its ecological footprint has become a key focus for eco-design.

- **Trend Overview:** Innovations in eco-packaging are shifting away from plastic-based materials towards sustainable options, such as recyclable, reusable, or biodegradable packaging. Companies are also exploring minimalist packaging designs that reduce material waste, as well as refillable packaging systems that extend the lifecycle of the packaging.
- **Examples:** Companies like Unilever and Nestlé are increasingly moving towards biodegradable and recyclable packaging for their products. Lush, a cosmetics brand, has led the charge with packaging-free products, focusing on eliminating waste altogether. Meanwhile, Loop is pioneering a circular economy model with reusable packaging for everyday consumer goods, which is collected, cleaned, and refilled for reuse.
- **Impact:** The transition to eco-friendly packaging not only reduces environmental impact but also meets consumer demand for more sustainable and transparent practices. This could lead to widespread changes across industries, from food and beverage to consumer goods and electronics.

Zero-Waste Manufacturing

Zero-waste manufacturing refers to the practice of designing and operating production processes that aim to eliminate waste by reducing, reusing, and recycling materials. The focus is on creating closed-loop systems where resources are continuously reused, minimizing the need for raw materials and reducing the environmental impact of waste disposal.

- **Trend Overview:** Companies are beginning to embrace zero-waste practices, such as designing production lines that minimize waste generation, using recycled materials in manufacturing, and optimizing production to reduce resource consumption. This includes embracing the principles of circular manufacturing, where products and materials are reused or refurbished rather than discarded.
- **Examples:Patagonia**, a leader in sustainable outdoor apparel, has pioneered a zero-waste approach in its production processes by using recycled materials and creating a closed-loop system for its clothing line. Interface, a global carpet tile manufacturer, has implemented sustainable manufacturing techniques that incorporate recycled materials, renewable energy, and waste-free production processes.
- **Impact:** The zero-waste manufacturing trend is driving greater resource efficiency, lowering the carbon footprint of production processes, and reducing the overall environmental impact of manufacturing. It also offers cost-saving potential for businesses by reducing the need for raw materials and improving operational efficiency.

Smart Eco-Design with AI and IoT

Emerging technologies like Artificial Intelligence (AI) and the Internet of Things (IoT) are beginning to play a critical role in eco-design and sustainable manufacturing. These technologies enable real-time monitoring of production processes, optimization of resource usage, and more effective management of supply chains, leading to more efficient and sustainable outcomes.

- **Trend Overview:** AI and IoT can be integrated into eco-design to create smarter products and manufacturing processes. AI algorithms can optimize product design to reduce material waste, while IoT sensors can monitor energy and resource consumption in manufacturing facilities, helping to minimize inefficiencies. Additionally, AI-powered systems can predict and optimize the lifecycle of products, ensuring that they are designed for reuse or recycling.
- **Examples:** Companies like **Tesla** are using AI to optimize energy usage in manufacturing, while **Siemens** uses IoT to monitor and improve the efficiency of production lines. In consumer products, AI-driven design tools are allowing companies to reduce the amount of material needed for production by predicting and designing for the most efficient product shapes and sizes.

- **Impact:** The integration of AI and IoT can lead to more sustainable products and manufacturing processes by improving resource efficiency and reducing waste. This trend also opens new possibilities for products that can self-monitor and adjust their performance to extend their lifespan, further supporting the principles of circular economy and eco-design.

Upcycled and Regenerative Products

The trend towards upcycled and regenerative products is gaining momentum as companies recognize the value in repurposing waste materials. Upcycling involves transforming waste products into higher-value items, while regenerative design goes beyond sustainability to restore ecosystems or create products that contribute positively to the environment.

- **Trend Overview:** More companies are exploring how waste materials, such as discarded textiles, plastics, and industrial by-products, can be upcycled into new products. Regenerative design goes even further, focusing on creating products that actively restore the environment, such as through carbon sequestration, soil regeneration, or habitat restoration.
- **Impact:** Upcycled and regenerative products contribute to the reduction of waste, encourage resource recovery, and promote a restorative approach to product design. This trend will likely expand as both consumers and businesses recognize the potential for waste to become a valuable resource, offering opportunities for innovation and new business models in various industries.

Carbon-Neutral and Net-Zero Products

As the urgency to address climate change grows, there is a strong focus on carbon neutrality and net-zero products in eco-design. Companies are aiming to create products with minimal or zero carbon footprints by adopting sustainable production methods and offsetting emissions through carbon credits or other initiatives.

- **Trend Overview:** The concept of carbon-neutral and net-zero products focuses on reducing emissions across the entire product lifecycle, from raw material extraction to end-of-life disposal. This includes designing products with energy-efficient production processes, sourcing renewable energy, and using carbon offset strategies to neutralize the environmental impact.
- **Impact:** The carbon-neutral and net-zero trend is pushing companies to adopt more sustainable practices across their operations. This shift is not only essential for mitigating climate change but also opens up new opportunities for companies to demonstrate leadership in sustainability, enhancing their brand reputation and appealing to eco-conscious consumers.

The future of eco-design and sustainable manufacturing is poised to be defined by innovations that prioritize the environment while meeting the demands of consumers and industries. From biodegradable materials and zero-waste manufacturing to AI-driven eco-design and carbon-neutral products, these emerging trends promise to reshape how products are conceived, produced, and consumed. As businesses continue to embrace these practices, we can expect to see a more sustainable and circular economy emerge, where resource use is minimized, waste is reduced, and environmental impact is actively mitigated across industries.

CONCLUSION

The integration of eco-design principles into PLCM is increasingly critical for addressing the environmental challenges we face today. As consumer demand for sustainable products grows, businesses must adapt by embedding sustainability into their product development processes. This chapter has explored the role of eco-design in PLCM, with a focus on MCDM methods that help companies make informed choices regarding sustainability throughout a product's life cycle. The analysis of consumer perceptions shows a growing willingness to invest in sustainable products, highlighting the potential for businesses to differentiate themselves in a competitive market. By applying MCDM, companies can better understand the trade-offs between various sustainability criteria, such as resource efficiency, recyclability, and product longevity. This enables businesses to optimize product designs that meet both consumer expectations and environmental objectives, enhancing brand loyalty and market position. Effective marketing strategies, supported by clear communication of the eco-design features of products, further amplify consumer engagement. Transparency in how products align with sustainability goals such as energy efficiency, material sourcing, and recyclability can improve consumer confidence. By utilizing MCDM, companies can evaluate the effectiveness of different marketing approaches, ensuring that eco-design benefits are communicated in ways that resonate with target audiences and reinforce a company's commitment to sustainability. Regulatory frameworks, including the EU Ecodesign Directive and EPR policies, play a vital role in driving sustainability in PLCs. These regulations set mandatory requirements for design and end-of-life management, encouraging companies to innovate and integrate eco-design into their product offerings. However, the complexity of these regulations presents challenges, particularly for smaller businesses with fewer resources. MCDM techniques can help companies navigate these complexities by evaluating various compliance strategies and choosing the most efficient ways to integrate regulatory requirements into their design processes.

Looking forward, the future of eco-design in PLCM will likely be shaped by emerging trends such as digital design optimization tools, which allow for the simulation of different design scenarios to assess their environmental and economic impacts. Furthermore, the alignment of eco-design with circular economy principles will play a critical role in driving sustainable product development. MCDM will continue to be an essential tool in helping businesses navigate these emerging trends, enabling them to make data-driven decisions that optimize both sustainability and performance.

REFERENCES

Arruda, E.H., Melatto, R.A.P.B., Levy, W., Conti, D.M. (2021). Circular economy: A brief literature review (2015–2020). *Sustainable Operations and Computers, 2*, 79-86.
[http://dx.doi.org/10.1016/j.susoc.2021.05.001]

Bocken, N.M.P., Short, S.W., Rana, P., Evans, S. (2014). A literature and practice review to develop sustainable business model archetypes. *J. Clean. Prod., 65*, 42-56.
[http://dx.doi.org/10.1016/j.jclEPRo.2013.11.039]

Das, A.K. (2016). On partially included intuitionistic fuzzy rough relations. *Afrika Matematika, 27*, 993-1001.
[http://dx.doi.org/10.1007/s13370-016-0395-2]

Das, A.K. (2018). Weighted fuzzy soft multiset and decision-making. *Int. J. Mach. Learn. Cybern., 9*, 787-794.
[http://dx.doi.org/10.1007/s13042-016-0607-y]

Das, A.K., Granados, C. (2021). An advanced approach to fuzzy soft group decision-making using weighted average ratings. *SN Computer Science, 2*, 471.
[http://dx.doi.org/10.1007/s42979-021-00873-5]

Das, A.K., Granados, C. (2022). A new fuzzy parameterized intuitionistic fuzzy soft multiset theory and group decision-making. *Journal of Current Science and Technology, 12*(3), 547-567.
[http://dx.doi.org/10.14456/jcst.2022.42]

Das, A.K., Granados, C. (2022). FP-intuitionistic multi-fuzzy N-soft set and its induced FP-Hesitant N soft set in decision-making. *Decision Making: Applications in Management and Engineering, 5*(1), 67-89.
[http://dx.doi.org/10.31181/dmame181221045d]

Das, A.K., Granados, C. (2023). IFP-intuitionistic multi fuzzy N-soft set and its induced IFP-hesitant N-soft set in decision-making. *J. Ambient Intell. Humaniz. Comput., 14*, 10143-10152.
[http://dx.doi.org/10.1007/s12652-021-03677-w]

Das, A.K., Granados, C. (2023). Preference intuitionistic fuzzy rough relation and its theoretical approach. *J. Indian Math. Soc., 90*(3-4), 199-212.

Das, A.K., Granados, C., Bhattacharya, J. (2022). Some new operations on fuzzy soft sets and their applications in decision-making. *Songklanakarin J. Sci. Technol., 44*(2), 440-449.
[http://dx.doi.org/10.14456/sjst-psu.2022.61]

Das, A.K., Gupta, N., Granados, C. (2023). Weighted hesitant bipolar-valued fuzzy soft set in decision-making. *Songklanakarin J. Sci. Technol., 45*(6), 681-690. Available from: https://sjst.psu.ac.th/journal/45-6/10.pdf

Das, A.K., Gupta, N., Mahmood, T., Tripathy, B.C., Das, R., Das, S. (2025). An efficient water quality evaluation model using weighted hesitant fuzzy soft sets for water pollution rating.*Mechatronics: Concepts, Tools, Applications, and New Trends.* CRC Press.

Das, A.K., Gupta, N., Mahmood, T., Tripathy, B.C., Das, R., Das, S. (2025). An innovative fuzzy multi-

criteria decision-making model for analyzing anthropogenic influences on urban river water quality. *Iran Journal of Computer Science, 8*, 103-124.
[http://dx.doi.org/10.1007/s42044-024-00211-x]

Das, A.K., Das, R., Das, S., Debnath, B.K., Granados, C., Shil, B., Das, R. (2025). A comprehensive study of neutrosophic SuperHyper BCI-semigroups and their algebraic significance. *Transactions on Fuzzy Sets and Systems, 4*(2), 80-101.
[http://dx.doi.org/10.71602/tfss.2025.1198050]

Das, A.K., Mahmood, T., Das, R., Das, S. (2025). Optimizing Inventory Levels in Retail: Fuzzy Logic-Based Decision Support Systems for Adaptive Inventory Management.*Applications of Fuzzy Logic in Decision Making and Management Science. Information Systems Engineering and Management.* (Vol. Vol. 29). Cham: Springer.

Das, A.K., Das, R., Datta, R., Granados, C. (2025). An Innovative Approach to Group Decision-Making Based on Weighted Hypersoft Expert System.*Neutrosophic and Plithogenic Inventory Models for Applied Mathematics.* IGI Global Scientific Publishing.

Das, A.K., Patra, S., Granados, C. (2025). An innovative approach to hesitant bipolar fuzzy soft sets in multi-criteria group decision-making. Adv. in Comp. *Int., 5*, 4.
[http://dx.doi.org/10.1007/s43674-025-00082-0]

Das, A.K., Gupta, N., Mahmood, T., Tripathy, B.C., Das, R., Das, S. (2024). Assessing anthropogenic influences on the water quality of Gomati River using an innovative weighted fuzzy soft set-based water pollution rating system. *Discover Water, 4*, 73.
[http://dx.doi.org/10.1007/s43832-024-00136-3]

Das, A.K., Gupta, N., Granados, C., Das, R., Das, S. (2024). Neutrosophic Approach to Water Quality Assessment: A Case Study of Gomati River, the Largest River in Tripura, India. *Neutrosophic Systems with Applications, 22*, 1-12.
[http://dx.doi.org/10.61356/j.nswa.2024.22386]

Das, A.K., Gupta, N., Granados, C., Mahmood, T., Das, S. (2025). Integrating AI and ML with IoT for Real-Time Flood Detection and Monitoring: A Comprehensive Approach.*Advancements in AI and ML for Early Warning Systems in Natural Disaster Detection: Future Trends and Innovations.*

El Messaoudi, N., El Khomri, M., El Mouden, A. (2024). Regeneration and reusability of non-conventional low-cost adsorbents to remove dyes from wastewaters in multiple consecutive adsorption–desorption cycles: A review. *Biomass Convers. Biorefin., 14*, 11739-11756.
[http://dx.doi.org/10.1007/s13399-022-03604-9]

Giwa, T., Akbari, M., Kumar, A. (2022). Assessment of the greenhouse gas emission footprint of a biorefinery over its life cycle. *Energy Convers. Manage., 271*, 116327.
[http://dx.doi.org/10.1016/j.enconman.2022.116327]

Granados, C., Das, A.K., Das, B. (2022). *Some continuous neutrosophic distributions with neutrosophic parameters based on neutrosophic random variables.*

Granados, C., Das, A.K., Osu, B. (2023). *Weighted neutrosophic soft multiset and its application to decision making.*

Kong, L., Wang, L., Li, F., Tian, G., Li, J., Cai, Z., Zhou, J., Fu, Y. (2022). A life-cycle integrated model for product eco-design in the conceptual design phase. *J. Clean. Prod., 363*, 132516.
[http://dx.doi.org/10.1016/j.jclEPRo.2022.132516]

Kong, L., Wang, L., Li, F., Li, J., Wang, Y., Cai, Z., Zhou, J., Guo, J., Wang, G. (2023). Life cycle-oriented low-carbon product design based on the constraint satisfaction problem. *Energy Convers. Manage., 286*, 117069.
[http://dx.doi.org/10.1016/j.enconman.2023.117069]

Kong, L., Wang, L., Li, F., Lv, X., Li, J., Ma, Y., Chen, B., Guo, J. (2021). Multi-layer integration framework for low carbon design based on design features. *J. Manuf. Syst., 61*, 223-238.

[http://dx.doi.org/10.1016/j.jmsy.2021.09.008]

Lee, W.L., Chung, Y., Tan, S., Koh, M.H., Lu, F., Low, S.C. (2023). Enhancing the environmental sustainability of products through ecodesign: A systematic review. *J. Eng. Des., 34*(10), 814-843. [http://dx.doi.org/10.1080/09544828.2023.2261094]

Mukherjee, A., Das, A.K. (2015). Application of interval valued intuitionistic fuzzy soft set in investment decision making *2015 Fifth International Conference on Advances in Computing and Communications (ICACC),* Kochi, India201561-64.

Mukherjee, A., Das, A.K. (2015). Interval valued intuitionistic fuzzy soft multi set theoretic approach to decision making problems, 2015 International Conference on Computer, Communication and Control (IC4), Indore, India, 2015, pp. 1-5.

Mukherjee, A., Das, A.K. (2015). Relations on intuitionistic fuzzy soft multi-sets. *Information Science and Applications. Lecture Notes in Electrical Engineering.* (Vol. Vol. 339). Berlin, Heidelberg: Springer.

Mukherjee, A., Das, A.K. (2016). Application of fuzzy soft multi-sets in decision-making problems.

Mukherjee, A., Das, A.K. (2016). Topological structure formed by intuitionistic fuzzy rough relations. *J. Indian Math. Soc., 83*(1-2), 135-144.

Mukherjee, A., Das, A.K. (2022). Einstein operations on fuzzy soft multisets and decision making. *Boletim da Sociedade Paranaense de Matematica, 40*, 1-10. [http://dx.doi.org/10.5269/bspm.32546]

Mukherjee, A., Das, A.K. (2023). Essentials of fuzzy soft multisets: Theory and applications, Springer Nature Singapore Pte Ltd., 1-151. ISBN: 978-981-19-2759-1.

Popoff, A., Millet, D. (2017). Sustainable life cycle design using constraint satisfaction problems and quality function deployment. *Procedia CIRP, 61*, 75-80. [http://dx.doi.org/10.1016/j.procir.2016.11.147]

Wang, J., Li, R., Ding, G., Qin, S., Cai, Z. (2022). Product-service system engineering characteristics design for life cycle cost based on constraint satisfaction problem and Bayesian network. *Adv. Eng. Inform., 52*, 101573. [http://dx.doi.org/10.1016/j.aei.2022.101573]

Yu, F., Fu, J., Guo, J., Tan, R., Yang, B. (2022). An approach for radical innovative design based on cross-domain technology mining in patents. *Int. J. Prod. Res., 61*(21), 7502-7523. [http://dx.doi.org/10.1080/00207543.2022.2151659]

Zuo, J., Zhao, Z.Y. (2014). Green building research Current status and future agenda: A review. *Renew. Sustain. Energy Rev., 30*, 271-281. [http://dx.doi.org/10.1016/j.rser.2013.10.021]

CHAPTER 2

Digital Tools for Circularity Tracking and Monitoring

Dinesh Nilkant[1], **Hemanth Kumar S.**[1,*], **Krishna Koppa**[1] and **Prabha Kiran**[2]

[1] *CMS Business School, JAIN (Deemed-to-be University), Bengaluru, Karnataka, India*

[2] *Westminster Business School, Westminster International University in Tashkent, Tashkent, Uzbekistan*

Abstract: The shift from linear economic models to a sustainable circular economy is progressively propelled by the incorporation of digital technologies, including the Internet of Things (IoT), Artificial Intelligence (AI), blockchain, and digital twins. These technologies provide real-time monitoring, resource optimization, and secure data transmission, enhancing the efficiency and transparency of supply chains. This chapter examines the transformative impact of digital tools on boosting circularity in several industries, emphasizing critical applications such as predictive maintenance, ethical sourcing, product lifecycle management, and resource recovery. Additionally, the chapter addresses the social and ethical considerations of digital circularity, including data privacy, labor standards, and equitable access to technology for Small and Medium-sized Enterprises (SMEs) and emerging economies. Finally, the chapter outlines future prospects for scaling digital circularity, discussing the potential of AI-driven processes, 5G-enabled IoT, and blockchain advancements. Strategic recommendations for policymakers and businesses are provided, emphasizing the need for standardization, workforce development, data security, and public-private partnerships to foster a resilient global circular economy.

Keywords: 5G, Artificial Intelligence (AI), Blockchain, Circular economy, Circular supply chain, Data privacy, Digital innovation, Digital twins, Equitable access, Ethical sourcing, Internet of Things (IoT), Predictive maintenance, Supply chain transparency, Sustainable resource management.

INTRODUCTION TO CIRCULARITY IN THE DIGITAL AGE

Definition and Importance of Circular Economy

In recent years, the Circular Economy (CE) has garnered much attention as a crucial solution to the environmental issues associated with the conventional lin-

* **Corresponding author Hemanth Kumar S.:** CMS Business School, JAIN (Deemed-to-be University), Bengaluru, Karnataka, India; E-mail: dr.hemnthkumar@cms.ac.in

Theodore Tarnanidis, Vijaya Kittu Manda, Vivek Gupta (Eds.)

ear economic model, characterized by the "take, make, dispose" approach. The circular economy aims to reduce waste, enhance material reuse, and maximize resource efficiency by fostering the regeneration of products and materials throughout their existence (Geissdoerfer *et al.*, 2017) . This strategy allows enterprises and economies to diminish their dependence on limited resources while concurrently tackling critical environmental issues, including climate change and resource constraints.

The significance of shifting to a circular economy is highlighted by its capacity to markedly decrease global waste and carbon emissions. Research conducted by the Ellen MacArthur Foundation (Ellen MacArthur Foundation, 2023) demonstrates that the use of circular principles could potentially decrease global greenhouse gas emissions by 45% and diminish waste by 80%. The circular economy offers significant economic advantages, potentially generating up to $4.5 trillion in global economic benefits by 2030 through the creation of new employment opportunities in recycling, refurbishment, and renewable energy sectors (World Economic Forum, 2022).

Limitations of Linear Economies

While the linear economy has driven industrial growth and consumer prosperity, it has created significant inefficiencies and environmental degradation. The linear model depletes finite natural resources at unsustainable rates and generates excessive waste, which contributes to pollution and climate change. As highlighted in the Circle Economy report (Circle Economy, 2023), only 8.6% of the 100 billion tons of resources extracted annually are recycled or reused, leaving the vast majority as waste. This waste accumulates in landfills and contributes to environmental degradation and increased resource costs (Circle Economy, 2023).

The limitations of linear economic systems are evident in key industries:

- **Fashion:** The fashion industry accounts for up to 10% of global carbon emissions and generates significant waste, with about 85% of textiles ending up in landfills each year (Fashion for Good, 2023).
- **Electronics:** Electronic waste (e-waste) poses a growing challenge, as only 20% of e-waste is properly recycled. This results in the loss of valuable metals such as gold and copper, which could otherwise be recovered and reused (World Economic Forum, 2022).
- **Construction:** The construction industry is responsible for approximately 39% of global CO_2 emissions, driven by inefficient resource use and waste from building materials (International Energy Agency, 2022).

These examples demonstrate the urgent need to transition from linear to circular economic models that prioritize resource optimization and waste minimization.

Digital Transformation in Circular Practices

Digital technologies are essential for facilitating circular economy activities by offering tools for resource tracking, waste minimization, and lifecycle management. Technologies include the Internet of Things (IoT), Blockchain, Artificial Intelligence (AI), and Geospatial Technologies, which provide innovative methods for real-time monitoring and management of resource flows, hence improving efficiency and sustainability across many industries (Accenture, 2023).

1. **IoT and Sensor Networks:** IoT enables real-time monitoring of resources and energy use, allowing companies to optimize processes and reduce waste. For example, IoT sensors in logistics help reduce fuel consumption by optimizing delivery routes (McKinsey & Company, 2023).
2. **Blockchain Technology:** Blockchain offers secure, transparent tracking of materials through the supply chain, ensuring that products are ethically sourced and recycled. Industries such as fashion and electronics have adopted blockchain to improve traceability and support circular supply chains (World Economic Forum, 2022).
3. **AI and Machine Learning:** AI enhances resource efficiency by providing predictive analytics that help companies optimize production and minimize waste. In the recycling industry, AI-driven systems can accurately identify recyclable materials, improving sorting efficiency (Ellen MacArthur Foundation, 2023).
4. **Geospatial and Remote Sensing Technologies:** Geospatial technologies help monitor environmental factors such as land use, water availability, and ecosystem health, aiding in sustainable resource management (United Nations Environment Programme, 2022).

According to Accenture, the adoption of digital technologies could reduce material costs by up to 30% and lower energy consumption by up to 20% (Accenture, 2023). These advancements offer critical insights that empower businesses to adopt sustainable practices and adhere to global circular economy standards. As digital tools evolve, their integration into circular systems will become increasingly essential for achieving sustainability goals and reducing the environmental impact of industries.

CORE DIGITAL TECHNOLOGIES DRIVING CIRCULARITY TRACKING AND MONITORING

IoT and Sensor Networks for Real-Time Monitoring

The Internet of Things (IoT) plays a pivotal role in advancing circular economy practices by enabling real-time tracking and monitoring across a product's lifecycle. IoT consists of interconnected devices and sensors that gather data from various stages, from production to end-of-life, to optimize resource use and reduce waste (Bressanelli *et al.*, 2023).

In agriculture, for instance, IoT sensors track soil moisture and nutrient levels, enabling precise irrigation and crop management. This practice reduces water consumption by up to 30%, significantly contributing to sustainable agricultural practices (Food and Agriculture Organization, 2023). Similarly, the food industry utilizes IoT in cold chain logistics to monitor temperature and humidity in real time, preventing spoilage and reducing food waste by approximately 15% during transportation (World Economic Forum, 2022).

In the automotive sector, IoT sensors embedded in vehicle components support predictive maintenance by collecting data on usage and wear. Companies like Ford and Tesla rely on this data to perform maintenance based on actual usage patterns, thus extending the lifespan of parts and minimizing the need for replacements (European Automobile Manufacturers' Association, 2023). These applications of IoT not only improve operational efficiency but also align with the principles of the circular economy by promoting resource longevity and minimizing waste.

Blockchain for Transparent and Traceable Supply Chains

Blockchain technology provides an immutable and decentralized platform for tracking transactions and materials within supply chains, enhancing transparency and accountability. Blockchain has become integral to the circular economy by ensuring that products and materials are ethically sourced, recycled, and managed responsibly throughout their lifecycle (Saberi *et al.*, 2023).

A prominent example of blockchain's application is in the electronics industry, where companies such as IBM and MineHub have implemented blockchain platforms to trace critical minerals like cobalt and lithium. These minerals, essential for batteries and electronics, are tracked from extraction to manufacturing, ensuring ethical sourcing and reducing the risks associated with illegal or unsustainable mining practices (McKinsey & Company, 2023).

Similarly, in the fashion industry, platforms like Provenance and Everledger utilize blockchain to track the production lifecycle of garments. These technologies allow brands to verify the ethical sourcing of materials and labor practices, as well as environmental standards. Everledger, for instance, tracks diamonds, ensuring their ethical production and fostering greater consumer trust (Ellen MacArthur Foundation, 2023). The ability of blockchain to provide such traceability supports circular economy goals by promoting transparency and accountability across global supply chains.

AI and Machine Learning for Predictive Analytics

Artificial Intelligence (AI) and Machine Learning (ML) are essential for facilitating data-driven decision-making, which improves resource management and minimizes waste. These technologies examine extensive datasets to discern patterns and generate precise forecasts on future resource requirements, thus enhancing operational efficiency and facilitating circular practices. An important application of AI in industry is predictive maintenance, wherein AI systems identify anomalies and forecast equipment breakdowns prior to their occurrence, hence minimizing downtime and prolonging machinery lifespan (Siemens, 2023).

In the waste management sector, AI-driven robotic systems like those from AMP Robotics have revolutionized sorting processes by using machine learning algorithms to identify and separate recyclable materials with 90% accuracy. This technology has significantly improved recycling rates and reduced the amount of waste sent to landfills (AMP Robotics, 2023) . Additionally, in the food industry, IBM Food Trust employs AI to predict supply and demand, allowing production levels to align with market needs and reducing the risk of overproduction and waste (IBM, 2023). These AI-powered tools not only enhance efficiency but also help industries transition to more sustainable, circular models.

Geospatial Technology and Remote Sensing for Environmental Monitoring

Geospatial technologies, such as Geographic Information Systems (GIS) and remote sensing, offer critical instruments for assessing environmental conditions and overseeing resource management. These technologies provide critical data on land utilization, resource availability, and ecological effects, allowing enterprises to make educated decisions that adhere to circular economy principles (World Bank, 2022).

In agriculture, remote sensing is used to monitor crop health, soil quality, and water usage, helping farmers optimize resource allocation and minimize waste. The Food and Agriculture Organization (FAO) leverages satellite imagery to track land usage, helping prevent over-extraction and promoting sustainable farming practices (Food and Agriculture Organization, 2023).

In the mining industry, remote sensing technologies support circular practices by monitoring extraction activities and assessing environmental impacts, aiding companies in minimizing ecological damage and identifying areas for resource recovery and land restoration (United Nations Environment Programme, 2022).

Urban planning and smart city initiatives also benefit from geospatial technology. These tools monitor parameters such as air quality, pollution levels, and green space distribution, helping cities design eco-friendly infrastructures and foster sustainable urban development. The use of geospatial tools is crucial for advancing circular economy models in various sectors, enabling data-driven resource management and reducing environmental footprints (United Nations Environment Programme, 2022).

IMPLEMENTATION OF DIGITAL TOOLS ACROSS THE PRODUCT LIFECYCLE

Eco-Design and Production Stages

The eco-design and production stages are critical in integrating sustainability into the product lifecycle. Eco-design focuses on minimizing environmental impacts by optimizing material use, enhancing recyclability, and reducing emissions. Tools like Life Cycle Assessment (LCA) software and Computer-Aided Design (CAD) systems help companies assess environmental impacts early in the design phase, mitigating these impacts before products are manufactured (Bevilacqua *et al.*, 2022).

For example, LCA platforms enable companies to evaluate the carbon footprint, energy consumption, and recyclability of materials throughout a product's lifecycle. Automotive manufacturers use these tools to select lightweight, durable, and recyclable materials that reduce emissions and waste. General Motors employs LCA to evaluate vehicle components, aiming to lower emissions per mile and enhance the recyclability of parts (European Automobile Manufacturers' Association, 2023).

In the fashion industry, Levi Strauss & Co. utilizes LCA to track water and energy usage in denim production, leading to design choices that significantly reduce resource consumption. Similarly, 3D printing, or additive manufacturing, is used in sectors like aviation and automotive to create lightweight, eco-efficient parts that reduce both energy and raw material requirements. General Electric has harnessed 3D printing in aviation to cut down on waste during production, manufacturing complex designs with fewer resources while maintaining durability (Accenture, 2023).

By adopting digital tools for eco-design, industries can substantially improve their sustainability in the production process. These technologies offer critical insights that empower companies to optimize resource efficiency and minimize waste.

Optimizing Distribution and Logistics

Digital tools are crucial in the distribution and logistics phases of the product lifecycle, since they diminish emissions, enhance resource utilization, and optimize supply chains. Technologies like IoT, AI, and blockchain provide real-time tracking, route optimization, and effective inventory management, leading to reduced emissions and improved resource usage. UPS demonstrates the efficacy of AI in logistics with its On-Road Integrated Optimization and Navigation (ORION) system, which enhances delivery routes, conserving 10 million gallons of fuel and reducing carbon dioxide emissions by 100,000 metric tons each year (World Economic Forum, 2022). UPS employs GPS data and machine learning algorithms to dynamically optimize delivery routes, thereby reducing fuel usage and improving overall efficiency.

Blockchain further improves transparency in logistics by recording product journeys, a practice particularly useful in industries like pharmaceuticals that prioritize ethical sourcing. For example, Walmart employs blockchain to track supply chain transactions, reducing waste and preventing costly product recalls (McKinsey & Company, 2023). AI-driven predictive analytics also help companies anticipate demand, thereby reducing excess inventory and storage costs. This is especially valuable in retail and e-commerce, where AI tools forecast demand to prevent stockpiling and overproduction (IBM, 2023).

IoT sensors are critical in cold chain logistics for industries such as pharmaceuticals and food, where maintaining precise temperatures is essential. These sensors monitor environmental conditions in real-time, ensuring that perishable products remain viable, reducing food and medical waste, and protecting consumer health (Food and Agriculture Organization, 2023).

Usage, Maintenance, and Extending Product Lifecycle

Extending the product lifecycle is a cornerstone of the circular economy, enabled by digital tools such as predictive maintenance and the product-as-a-service (PaaS) model. Predictive maintenance utilizes IoT sensors embedded in products to monitor performance data in real-time, detecting signs of wear and tear before failures occur. This proactive approach reduces downtime, cuts repair costs, and prolongs product life, ultimately decreasing the environmental impact associated with premature replacements.

Caterpillar, for example, employs predictive maintenance in its heavy machinery, using IoT sensors to monitor equipment performance. This system minimizes breakdowns, extends equipment longevity, and reduces the demand for raw materials needed for replacement parts (Caterpillar, 2023). This approach not only generates operational savings but also supports circularity by encouraging durable and maintainable product designs.

The PaaS model shifts consumer behavior from ownership to usage, allowing companies to retain product ownership while providing it as a service. Philips Lighting has adopted this model for commercial lighting solutions, taking responsibility for maintenance and eventual recycling. This model incentivizes manufacturers to design products for durability and easy maintenance, promoting circular practices that prioritize longevity over disposability (Accenture, 2023).

Digital tools also aid in usage tracking and collecting data on consumer behavior and product performance. In the automotive sector, manufacturers use telematics to refine vehicle design, enhancing durability while minimizing the environmental impact (World Economic Forum, 2022).

End-of-Life Management and Reverse Logistics

End-of-life management and reverse logistics are essential components of the circular economy, facilitating the reuse, recycling, or responsible disposal of products and materials. Digital technologies such as blockchain, RFID tracking, and AI-driven sorting systems augment these processes by enhancing efficiency and transparency.

Reverse logistics involves moving used products from consumers back to manufacturers or recycling facilities. Dell, for example, uses blockchain to track returned electronics, ensuring responsible recycling and material recovery (McKinsey & Company, 2023). This system allows for precise tracking, enabling Dell to recover valuable materials, such as rare metals, and reintegrate them into new devices.

AI-driven sorting systems, like those developed by AMP Robotics, use machine learning algorithms to improve material recovery at recycling facilities. These systems can identify and sort recyclable materials with high accuracy, reducing landfill waste and increasing recycling rates by up to 30% (AMP Robotics, 2023). These digital tools are transformative in waste management, automating the sorting process and minimizing the need for manual labor.

Companies are creating closed-loop systems that facilitate the continual recycling of products and materials. Apple's "Daisy" robot disassembles iPhones to reclaim important components, exemplifying a closed-loop process that facilitates resource recovery and reduces environmental impact (Apple, 2023). Similarly, Patagonia's take-back program encourages customers to return used garments, which are then recycled into new products, exemplifying a circular approach to material use (Ellen MacArthur Foundation, 2023).

By improving reverse logistics and recycling processes, digital tools enable cost-effective and efficient end-of-life management, aligning with the broader goals of a circular economy.

ENGAGING CONSUMERS AND DRIVING BEHAVIOR CHANGE

Digital Platforms for Consumer Awareness

Digital platforms have become pivotal in engaging consumers with sustainable practices, making circular economy concepts more accessible and interactive. Through mobile apps, websites, and social media, companies can offer transparency about product lifecycles, educating consumers on topics such as sourcing, sustainability, and recycling options while inviting them to participate in environmentally responsible actions.

For example, IKEA's mobile app provides detailed information about product sustainability, from sourcing to recyclability. By encouraging users to engage in its take-back program, IKEA promotes consumer involvement in circular practices, allowing products to be recycled or refurbished rather than discarded. This strategy fosters a sustainable relationship with customers, raising environmental awareness and reinforcing commitment to circularity (IKEA, 2023).

Another innovative model is Unilever's use of QR codes on packaging, allowing consumers to scan the codes and learn about the product's origin, environmental impact, and proper disposal methods. This engagement not only raises awareness but also fosters trust by offering transparency regarding each product's journey from raw materials to end-of-life (Unilever, 2022). In the fashion sector, brands like Levi's and Patagonia provide similar digital tools to inform consumers about their sourcing, manufacturing, and waste-reduction efforts, promoting sustainability alongside the customer experience.

Digital platforms have transformed the consumer experience by providing educational tools and fostering engagement that empowers consumers to make informed and sustainable choices in alignment with circular economy principles.

Education on Sustainable Consumption

Digital tools play a crucial role in educating consumers about sustainable consumption. E-learning platforms, social media campaigns, and educational websites enable companies and organizations to communicate circular economy principles, urging consumers to rethink waste, reuse products, and support recycling initiatives.

Patagonia's digital platform, Patagonia Action Works, serves as a hub for sustainability-related resources, educating users about environmental issues, connecting them with activist groups, and inspiring them to adopt sustainable practices in their everyday lives. This platform amplifies Patagonia's commitment to environmental education, helping consumers understand the impact of their purchasing decisions on the planet (Ellen MacArthur Foundation, 2023).

Similarly, H&M's Conscious Collection incorporates a digital learning experience that allows consumers to explore sustainable fashion practices. By offering insights into sustainable fabrics, low-water textile production, and waste-reduction techniques, H&M encourages consumers to make more informed fashion choices, fostering a consumer base that values circular economy practices (H&M, 2023).

Nike also provides online educational modules detailing the environmental benefits of their recycled materials and energy-efficient production processes in sportswear. This outreach reinforces Nike's sustainability commitment while empowering consumers to consider the ecological impact of their purchases (Nike, 2023).

By integrating digital educational tools, these brands enhance consumer understanding and foster a culture of sustainability, motivating consumers to embrace and support circular economy practices.

Consumer Data and Feedback Loops

In a circular economy, understanding consumer behavior and preferences is crucial for designing products that align with sustainability goals. Digital tools enable companies to gather real-time data on product usage, satisfaction, and end-of-life practices, providing insights that inform product improvement and innovation. Establishing a continuous feedback loop with consumers helps companies optimize design, functionality, and material choices for better sustainability outcomes.

Nike's circular product line, Nike Grind, exemplifies this feedback-driven approach. By collecting data from consumers, Nike monitors product performance, evaluates customer satisfaction, and adjusts materials and designs based on insights from usage data. This iterative feedback loop enables Nike to make informed changes that support product longevity and recyclability, advancing their alignment with circular economy objectives (Nike, 2023).

In the food and beverage sector, Nestlé leverages consumer feedback to improve packaging sustainability. By collecting data on recycling habits and packaging preferences, Nestlé refines its designs to enhance recyclability and usability. This ongoing engagement allows the company to continuously adapt to consumer expectations and improve packaging sustainability (Nestlé, 2023).

Companies must responsibly manage consumer data in compliance with privacy requirements, including the General Data Protection Regulation (GDPR) in the European Union. These requirements necessitate transparency in data collection and obligate corporations to disclose their methods of gathering, storing, and utilizing consumer information.

By complying with these regulations, companies can maintain consumer trust and encourage participation in sustainability initiatives, as consumers feel confident their data is being used ethically.

Leveraging digital tools for consumer feedback and data collection supports continuous product improvement and innovation within circular economy practices. By prioritizing data privacy and transparency, companies can foster consumer trust and create a positive feedback loop that benefits both the environment and brand reputation.

CASE STUDIES OF DIGITAL TOOLS FACILITATING CIRCULAR PRACTICES

Blockchain in Fashion for Ethical Sourcing and Traceability

Blockchain technology has emerged as a crucial tool for promoting ethical sourcing and traceability in the fashion industry. With an estimated 10% of global carbon emissions attributed to the fashion sector, implementing sustainable practices has become essential (World Economic Forum, 2022). Blockchain's decentralized ledger provides transparency by recording each stage of the supply chain, from raw material sourcing to the delivery of the final product.

One example is Provenance, a platform that supports smaller brands by offering traceability tools to verify ethical practices throughout the production process.

Consumers can scan QR codes on products to access detailed information about the product's origin, materials, and environmental impact, building trust and promoting informed purchasing decisions (Provenance, 2023).

In the luxury sector, LVMH's Aura Blockchain Consortium enables customers to authenticate luxury items by tracing each product's journey. This blockchain-based traceability ensures the authenticity of high-end goods while promoting ethical sourcing and sustainable production (LVMH, 2023). Blockchain in fashion supports transparency, encourages ethical consumer choices, and reinforces circular practices by reducing waste and promoting sustainability.

IoT in Manufacturing for Predictive Maintenance

The Internet of Things (IoT) enhances efficiency in manufacturing by enabling predictive maintenance, which extends equipment life and reduces material waste. Siemens uses IoT through its MindSphere platform, which collects real-time data from machines to predict maintenance needs, reducing downtime, preventing unexpected failures, and decreasing energy consumption (Siemens, 2023).

Similarly, General Electric's GE Digital platform integrates IoT with predictive analytics to provide manufacturers with real-time insights into equipment performance, leading to significant cost savings and reduced resource consumption (GE Digital, 2023).

IoT also supports energy conservation, as demonstrated by Schneider Electric, which uses IoT to monitor energy usage across its manufacturing sites. This approach reduces emissions and energy costs, aligning with the circular economy's emphasis on resource efficiency (Schneider Electric, 2023).

AI in Waste Management for Enhanced Recycling

Artificial Intelligence (AI) is transforming waste management by optimizing recycling processes. AI systems equipped with machine learning and computer vision technologies can accurately sort recyclable materials, improving efficiency and reducing contamination in recycling streams.

AMP Robotics, a leader in AI-powered waste management, has developed robots that identify and sort materials such as plastic, metal, and paper with 70% increased efficiency, leading to higher material recovery rates and reduced landfill waste (AMP Robotics, 2023).

In Europe, Tomra Systems uses AI-enhanced sorting systems combined with near-infrared sensors to detect materials in waste streams. These technologies have improved recycling rates and reduced waste processing times, making significant contributions to the circular economy (Tomra, 2023).

Remote Sensing in Agriculture for Sustainable Land Use

Remote sensing and geospatial technologies are critical for promoting sustainable land use, particularly in agriculture. These tools provide detailed data on soil conditions, crop health, and water availability, enabling farmers to make informed decisions that optimize resource use.

SmartFarming, a digital agriculture platform, uses satellite imagery to monitor soil and crop health. This data-driven approach has led to water savings of up to 30% and reduced reliance on fertilizers, supporting regenerative agriculture (SmartFarming, 2023).

The European Space Agency's Sentinel-2 satellites monitor crop growth and forest health, providing insights essential for sustainable land management. Global Forest Watch uses similar technology to track deforestation in real-time, helping governments prevent illegal logging and preserve biodiversity (Global Forest Watch, 2023).

Expanding Circular Business Models in the Digital Economy

The digital economy has facilitated the emergence of circular business models, including Product-as-a-Service (PaaS), which enhances product durability and reduces waste. In this model, firms maintain ownership of items and provide them as a service, promoting durability and lifecycle management.

Philips Lighting's PaaS model provides lighting solutions to businesses under subscription contracts, covering maintenance and recycling. This approach encourages Philips to design long-lasting, durable products, reducing environmental impact and supporting circular principles (Accenture, 2023).

Renault's RE-FACTORY initiative refurbishes and repurposes vehicles, extending their lifecycle and ensuring the recycling of parts. This closed-loop system demonstrates how circular business models can reduce waste, conserve resources, and generate new revenue streams (Renault Group, 2023).

Industry-Specific Digital Innovations for Circularity

Digital innovations provide tailored solutions for industries seeking to enhance circularity.

In electronics, Apple's Daisy robot uses AI to disassemble iPhones, recovering valuable materials such as cobalt, lithium, and aluminum. This process ensures the continuous reuse of rare materials, reducing the need for virgin resources (Apple, 2023).

In fashion, ThredUp, a digital resale platform, facilitates the resale of used clothing, extending the lifespan of garments and reducing the need for new production. ThredUp uses data analytics to track demand trends, promoting a more efficient and sustainable second-hand market (ThredUp, 2023).

Focus on Regulatory Compliance Platforms

With global sustainability regulations becoming stricter, digital platforms for compliance are essential for ensuring environmental accountability. These platforms enable companies to meet regulatory requirements, maintain transparency, and streamline data reporting to support circular practices.

SAP's Environmental Compliance Management platform integrates with IoT and ERP systems to monitor carbon emissions and waste management practices in real-time, ensuring companies meet international environmental standards (SAP, 2023).

Assent Compliance automates data collection and reporting for REACH regulations, which track hazardous substances in Europe. By streamlining compliance processes, Assent Compliance helps companies maintain transparent and sustainable material management across supply chains (Assent Compliance, 2023).

Enhancing Collaboration and Data Sharing for Circularity

The digital economy has facilitated the emergence of circular business models, including product-as-a-service (PaaS), which enhances product durability and reduces waste. In this model, firms maintain ownership of items and provide them as a service, promoting durability and lifecycle management.

The Ellen MacArthur Foundation's Circular Economy 100 (CE100) initiative brings together businesses, policymakers, and academic institutions to share circular economy strategies and best practices, fostering collaboration through a shared data platform (Ellen MacArthur Foundation, 2023).

In the automotive sector, CATENA-X enables secure data sharing between manufacturers and suppliers, promoting transparency across the supply chain. By tracking materials and components, CATENA-X supports reuse and recycling, advancing the industry's shift toward a circular economy (CATENA-X, 2023).

CHALLENGES AND BARRIERS TO DIGITAL IMPLEMENTATION IN THE CIRCULAR ECONOMY

Technical and Integration Challenges

One of the primary barriers to implementing digital tools in the circular economy is the technical complexity of integrating various technologies, such as IoT, blockchain, AI, and geospatial systems, into existing operational frameworks. Each technology often operates with its own data standards and interoperability requirements, creating challenges for industries with complex supply chains like automotive and electronics (Gupta & Chen, 2023). These challenges often result in "data silos," where isolated datasets cannot be shared or analyzed effectively.

For example, the electronics industry faces compatibility issues when integrating blockchain technology for traceability with IoT sensors for real-time monitoring. Without seamless data flow, manufacturers are unable to achieve full transparency across the supply chain, which limits their ability to optimize material use and track product lifecycles (Schwab & Malleret, 2023).

To address these challenges, companies are adopting middleware platforms like Siemens' MindSphere, which centralize data aggregation and enable interoperability across various devices and tools. MindSphere allows manufacturers to connect disparate systems, enabling smooth data flow across supply chains and improving resource tracking (Siemens, 2023).

Additionally, financial constraints are a notable challenge, particularly for SMEs that may struggle with the high costs of installing IoT networks, AI-driven analytics, and other digital infrastructure. For example, setting up IoT sensors across a facility and hiring skilled personnel to manage and analyze the data represent significant expenses that smaller firms often cannot afford (World Economic Forum, 2022).

In summary, overcoming technical and financial integration challenges requires investment in adaptable platforms and interoperable solutions, allowing both large corporations and SMEs to embrace digitalization.

Data Security and Privacy Concerns

As companies adopt digital tools to support circular economy initiatives, concerns over data security and privacy have intensified. Digital platforms like IoT networks and blockchain gather extensive data, including supply chain details and consumer behavior, which are valuable for optimizing resources but vulnerable to cyber-attacks. Each IoT device and blockchain node presents potential entry points for cyber threats, increasing the risk of data breaches that could compromise business operations and consumer privacy (Bhardwaj & Mehta, 2023).

Blockchain's decentralized structure provides some inherent security benefits, such as data immutability and decentralized control. However, blockchain technology is not immune to advanced cyber-attacks, particularly as its use becomes more widespread.

In response to these concerns, companies are exploring AI-based cybersecurity tools to monitor for anomalies and enhance threat detection across digital systems. These tools can detect risks in real-time, securing consumer and operational data and ensuring compliance with regulations such as the GDPR (Accenture, 2023).

Data privacy is another significant challenge, especially for global initiatives. Regulations like the GDPR impose strict guidelines on how personal data is handled, limiting how it can be collected, stored, and used. In industries such as consumer electronics, where IoT devices track usage patterns, companies must balance the need for data collection to improve circular practices with regulatory compliance to protect user privacy (Schwab & Malleret, 2023).

In conclusion, data security and privacy are critical issues in digitalized circular economy models. Companies need robust cybersecurity measures, regulatory compliance strategies, and transparent data-handling practices to build consumer trust and protect sensitive information.

Skill Gaps and Resource Constraints

A significant barrier to the successful adoption of digital tools in the circular economy is the lack of skilled personnel proficient in IoT, AI, blockchain, and supply chain management. Many industries, particularly in emerging markets, face notable skill gaps, where access to technical education and training programs is limited (McKinsey & Company, 2023). Without these skills, companies struggle to effectively deploy digital tools, reducing the potential for optimizing resource use and enhancing circularity.

To address these skill gaps, companies are forming partnerships with educational institutions to offer training programs focused on digital technologies and circular economy practices. For instance, Schneider Electric's "Go Green" program collaborates with universities globally to foster sustainable innovation and train students in digital skills. Such initiatives are equipping the next generation with the knowledge needed to support future circular economy efforts (Schneider Electric, 2023).

In addition to skill gaps, resource constraints are another hurdle, particularly for SMEs, which may lack the financial resources needed to adopt high-quality sensors, AI systems, and cybersecurity tools. For instance, while AI-driven sorting systems are beneficial for increasing efficiency in recycling facilities, their cost can be prohibitive for smaller organizations (World Bank, 2022).

Overall, addressing skill gaps and resource limitations will require targeted investments in education, institutional partnerships, and funding programs that support SMEs in their digital transformation efforts.

Standardization and Regulatory Hurdles

A key challenge in the digital implementation of circular economy practices is the lack of standardization, which complicates the collection, processing, and sharing of data across industries. Standardization is essential for digital interoperability, particularly in sectors where multiple stakeholders rely on consistent data handling. However, varying protocols and frameworks between industries result in inconsistencies that hinder large-scale digital adoption (United Nations Environment Programme, 2022).

For example, while blockchain technology has great potential to enhance supply chain traceability, the absence of standardized protocols across industries limits its effectiveness. Companies may invest in blockchain systems that are incompatible with one another, reducing transparency and undermining the full benefits of circularity. To overcome this, organizations like the World Economic Forum advocate for industry-wide standards that promote data compatibility and seamless resource tracking across supply chains (World Economic Forum, 2022).

Regulatory hurdles further complicate digital implementation. Environmental regulations and data protection laws differ significantly across regions, making it difficult for multinational corporations to adopt uniform digital solutions. For instance, compliance with the GDPR in the European Union requires considerable legal resources, particularly in areas like data sharing through IoT devices (Accenture, 2023).

For example, companies that handle consumer data in the EU must adhere to strict GDPR guidelines, which may differ from regulations in other regions, making global implementation complex. This disparity underscores the need for harmonized international standards that align digital technology with sustainability goals.

In conclusion, overcoming standardization and regulatory challenges is critical for advancing digital implementation in the circular economy. Collaborative efforts among industry leaders, policymakers, and regulatory bodies are necessary to establish unified standards and compliance frameworks for sustainable and scalable digitalization.

EMERGING INNOVATIONS IN DIGITAL CIRCULARITY TRACKING

Integration of 5G and IoT for Enhanced Connectivity

The Internet of Things (IoT) and 5G technologies are transforming communication by providing low latency, high bandwidth, and the ability to link a large number of devices, all of which are critical for promoting circular economy principles. 5G-enabled IoT networks facilitate rapid and dependable data transfer, enabling enterprises to get real-time insights throughout product lifecycles, hence enhancing resource efficiency and minimizing waste (Ruan *et al.*, 2023).

In the manufacturing industry, 5G improves IoT-enabled predictive maintenance by facilitating the instantaneous transmission of machinery data, hence enabling early anomaly detection. This proactive strategy minimizes downtime, prolongs equipment longevity, and decreases material waste, as demonstrated by BMW, where predictive maintenance resulted in a 10% decrease in machine downtime (Accenture, 2023).

In logistics, 5G-enabled IoT enhances dynamic, real-time supply chain management. Facilitating instantaneous data interchange enables organizations to modify inventory levels, enhance transportation routes, and diminish emissions. DHL's deployment of a 5G-enabled IoT system has led to a 15% reduction in fuel usage by dynamically rerouting delivery vans according to traffic circumstances (DHL, 2023).

The influence of 5G on IoT applications is revolutionary, improving real-time monitoring, predictive analytics, and resource efficiency, while facilitating circular economy principles through the encouragement of sustainable production and consumption.

Digital Twins in the Circular Economy

Digital Twin technology, which creates a virtual replica of physical assets, processes, or systems, is transforming the circular economy by enabling companies to simulate, monitor, and optimize resource use and product lifecycles. Digital twins provide real-time feedback, allowing for predictions on maintenance needs, resource recovery planning, and waste minimization, making them particularly valuable in industries such as construction, manufacturing, and energy (Li *et al.*, 2022).

In construction, digital twins monitor building lifecycles by providing detailed data on material usage, energy consumption, and maintenance requirements. Skanska, for example, uses digital twins to plan for sustainable deconstruction, ensuring that materials can be efficiently recycled or reused (Zhang & Hu, 2023).

In manufacturing, digital twins simulate production scenarios, allowing companies to optimize designs and processes before physical implementation. Siemens uses digital twin technology to optimize production lines, leading to a 30% reduction in waste by identifying inefficiencies early in the process (Siemens, 2023).

In the automotive industry, Ford employs digital twins to assess the durability of vehicle components, minimizing material waste from physical prototypes and accelerating product development (Ford Motor Company, 2023).

Overall, digital twins provide companies with predictive and analytical tools to optimize resource use, reduce waste, and support sustainable production strategies, aligning with circular economy goals.

Decentralized Applications (DApps) in Blockchain

Decentralized Applications (DApps) are emerging as key tools within blockchain technology, enhancing transparency, security, and collaboration in circular economy systems. Unlike traditional applications, DApps operate on decentralized blockchain networks, providing tamper-resistant platforms for tracking assets and transactions. This decentralized nature is particularly beneficial for circular systems that require transparency in sourcing, production, and end-of-life management (Gupta & Chen, 2023).

In the fashion and electronics industries, DApps facilitate comprehensive traceability across supply chains, supporting ethical sourcing and lifecycle accountability. Provenance, for example, uses DApps to track materials in fashion production, allowing consumers to verify sustainability claims *via* blockchain records. This scalability benefits smaller brands that lack extensive IT infrastructure (World Economic Forum, 2022).

DApps also support closed-loop systems by enabling secure, real-time data sharing among stakeholders, including suppliers, recyclers, and manufacturers. In the electronics sector, DApps track valuable resources like lithium and cobalt, ensuring their recovery and reintegration into new products, thus preventing resource loss (Bhardwaj & Mehta, 2023).

By fostering transparency and improving resource tracking, DApps enhance trust, accountability, and material recovery, which are essential for circular supply chains.

AI-Enhanced Decision Support for Circular Operations

AI-enhanced decision support systems are increasingly being used to optimize resource allocation, improve waste management, and provide actionable insights within circular economy frameworks. AI systems analyze large datasets from IoT devices, digital twins, and other sources, offering real-time recommendations that improve operational efficiency and support sustainable decision-making.

In waste management, AI algorithms, such as those developed by AMP Robotics, analyze waste composition and optimize sorting processes, significantly increasing recycling efficiency by up to 70% (AMP Robotics, 2023). In manufacturing, AI-based decision support systems recommend optimal production schedules based on demand forecasts, reducing overproduction and waste (Schwab & Malleret, 2023).

AI also enables predictive maintenance in resource-intensive industries. By continuously monitoring machine performance, AI models predict equipment failures, allowing for proactive maintenance. ABB's AI-driven predictive maintenance system, for example, reduced equipment downtime by 25%, contributing to more sustainable operations (ABB, 2023).

Ethical considerations are crucial as AI systems increasingly influence automated decision-making. Ensuring transparency and accountability in AI-driven recommendations is essential, particularly when personal or sensitive data is involved. Establishing ethical frameworks and aligning AI systems with regulatory standards will help balance efficiency with privacy and safety concerns.

In conclusion, AI-enhanced decision support systems provide advanced analytical and predictive capabilities that help companies reduce resource use, streamline operations, and promote ethical circular economy practices.

IMPACT ON POLICY AND REGULATORY COMPLIANCE THROUGH DIGITAL TOOLS

Data-Driven Policy Development

Digital tools are transforming the development of policies aimed at supporting circular economy goals by providing real-time, data-driven insights on resource flows, waste patterns, and emissions across industries. Technologies like IoT sensors, AI analytics, and blockchain systems enable policymakers to access extensive datasets that inform more effective and targeted regulatory frameworks (European Environment Agency, 2023). The integration of digital insights is essential for crafting policies that incentivize sustainability and address specific sectoral challenges.

One key example is the European Green Deal, which incorporates data from digital tracking systems to drive industries toward lower carbon emissions and improved waste management. These insights are used to formulate policies that set stricter standards on energy efficiency, encourage renewable resource use, and reduce waste. By leveraging digital data, the European Union (EU) tailors its regulations to target high-impact sectors such as manufacturing and transportation (European Commission, 2023).

In North America, cities are using data from smart city initiatives to guide environmental policy. For instance, IoT-enabled waste management systems in cities like New York and Los Angeles provide detailed data on waste generation and recycling rates, allowing local governments to create policies that promote recycling, reduce landfill waste, and optimize resource allocation (National Renewable Energy Laboratory, 2023). This data-driven approach enables municipalities to implement impactful regulations that are specific to their environmental needs, setting a precedent for localized circular economy policies.

Enabling Compliance and Efficient Reporting

Digital tools, especially blockchain and IoT systems, significantly streamline regulatory compliance and reporting by providing accurate, immutable records and real-time data updates. Through these technologies, companies can maintain transparent, continuously updated records of their sustainability practices, reducing administrative burdens and facilitating efficient regulatory reporting. This approach enhances transparency by allowing regulators to access verified data on resource use, emissions, and waste management (Schwab & Malleret, 2023).

For example, the waste management industry in the United Kingdom uses digital platforms that simplify compliance with environmental regulations. These platforms track data on waste collection, transport, and recycling activities, ensuring regulatory adherence while providing regulators with reliable, real-time information. This digital approach not only reduces administrative costs but also improves the ability of authorities to monitor compliance (Accenture, 2023).

In the pharmaceutical industry, digital tools streamline compliance with safety and environmental regulations by monitoring and reporting real-time data on chemical use, waste disposal, and energy consumption. Pfizer, for example, utilizes a digital compliance system to record data on material usage and disposal, ensuring compliance with regulatory standards for chemical handling while maintaining product safety and environmental protection (Pfizer, 2023). By providing precise data, these digital systems help companies meet regulatory obligations efficiently without the need for extensive manual audits.

Global Efforts Toward Standardization

To facilitate the global adoption of digital tools in circular economy practices, international organizations are prioritizing the standardization of data protocols and reporting practices. Standardization is essential for ensuring interoperability between digital systems and maintaining consistent, transparent reporting across regions. This harmonization allows multinational corporations to implement uniform circular economy practices and supports accurate cross-border data exchange, which is critical for achieving circularity on a global scale.

The International Organization for Standardization (ISO) is a key player in setting global standards for environmental sustainability and data tracking. The ISO 14000 series, which focuses on environmental management, provides guidelines for organizations to implement effective environmental practices. These standards promote the use of digital tracking tools to monitor and report environmental impacts, ensuring that data is collected in a standardized format that can be interpreted globally (International Organization for Standardization, 2022).

Another significant initiative is the Global Reporting Initiative (GRI), which encourages companies to adopt digital tracking systems for enhanced accuracy and transparency in sustainability reporting. Many companies, particularly in resource-intensive sectors like mining and manufacturing, utilize GRI-aligned digital tools to track emissions, water use, and waste management practices, allowing them to report data consistently and contribute to global circular economy goals (Global Reporting Initiative, 2023).

Additionally, the Ellen MacArthur Foundation, in collaboration with the United Nations, has developed a framework to standardize circular economy reporting metrics. This framework provides guidance on best practices for data collection and reporting, ensuring that digital tools are aligned with circularity objectives and that the data collected is comparable across organizations. These global standardization efforts are crucial in advancing sustainable practices and supporting the implementation of circular economy initiatives worldwide (Ellen MacArthur Foundation, 2023).

COLLABORATION AND DATA SHARING IN THE CIRCULAR ECONOMY

Building Cross-Industry Partnerships

Cross-industry collaboration is essential for achieving circular economy objectives, enabling organizations to share resources, optimize processes, and collectively reduce waste. Digital platforms and networks facilitate these partnerships by providing a space where industries can repurpose by-products and minimize waste. A prime example is the use of digital material marketplaces, where leftover materials from one industry are redirected to another, reducing both waste and costs (McKinsey & Company, 2023).

Platforms like the Circular Economy Marketplace serve as hubs for companies to sell excess materials or by-products to organizations in need, fostering a closed-loop system that optimizes resource use while generating new revenue streams. One notable collaboration between the automotive and construction industries involves repurposing surplus metal from vehicle manufacturing for building materials, resulting in a 25% reduction in waste disposal costs (European Circular Economy Stakeholder Platform, 2023).

The Ellen MacArthur Foundation's Circular Economy 100 (CE100) Network is a prominent example of cross-industry collaboration. It brings together companies from various sectors to collaborate on sustainable projects, exchange best practices, and explore material-looping strategies. For instance, CE100 members in the apparel and recycling industries work together to collect textile waste and transform it into raw materials for new products, promoting a circular textile lifecycle (Ellen MacArthur Foundation, 2023).

Data Sharing for Circularity Across Industries

Data sharing plays a crucial role in tracking resources, monitoring product lifecycles, and enabling efficient material recovery across industries. Secure platforms, particularly those leveraging blockchain technology, facilitate data sharing by creating an immutable, transparent ledger that can be accessed by stakeholders, ensuring accountability in circular supply chains (Gupta & Chen, 2023). This transparency is vital for compliance with sustainability standards and for building consumer trust.

For example, in the fashion industry, brands are using blockchain to trace a garment's journey from raw material sourcing to disposal. This transparency fosters consumer trust and aids recycling facilities in processing items according to their material composition. Companies like H&M and Levi's use blockchain to ensure sustainable sourcing, allowing consumers to make informed choices about environmentally responsible products (Bhardwaj & Mehta, 2023).

In the electronics sector, companies like Dell and Fairphone employ blockchain to track the journey of rare minerals such as cobalt and lithium, ensuring ethical sourcing and efficient end-of-life recycling. This technology enables companies to monitor materials throughout the supply chain, supporting efforts to recover and reuse critical resources (Fairphone, 2023).

Platforms like GS1 and the Global Data Synchronization Network (GDSN) are instrumental in standardizing data for supply chains across sectors. By providing consistent data formats, these platforms enhance interoperability between manufacturers, recyclers, and logistics providers, improving circular collaboration by offering accurate, real-time information on product origin, composition, and lifecycle stages (GS1, 2023).

Challenges in Cross-Border Collaboration

Despite the advantages of cross-industry partnerships and data sharing, global collaboration for circular economy practices faces several regulatory and logistical challenges. Variations in regulatory frameworks and data-sharing standards between countries can hinder seamless cooperation, especially in industries with global supply chains like electronics and fashion. Regulatory differences, such as those related to data privacy, create significant obstacles for companies attempting to implement standardized circular practices on a multinational scale (World Economic Forum, 2022).

Data privacy regulations, such as the European Union's General Data Protection Regulation (GDPR), require companies to implement strict protocols when sharing environmental or personal data. Although GDPR helps protect consumer privacy, it also requires substantial investments in compliance, complicating cross-border data sharing. For instance, companies operating in both the EU and the United States must navigate differences between GDPR and U.S. privacy laws, often necessitating dual compliance measures (European Commission, 2023).

Logistical challenges also arise from varying waste management practices, data formats, and the compatibility of digital infrastructure across countries. International standards like ISO 14001 for environmental management provide a partial solution by establishing consistent protocols that facilitate cross-border data sharing and compliance. However, regional alignment on circular economy regulations is still needed to ensure effective international collaboration (International Organization for Standardization, 2022).

One promising solution for overcoming cross-border data-sharing challenges is the establishment of Mutual Recognition Agreements (MRAs), where countries agree to recognize each other's environmental and data protection standards. These agreements help streamline data sharing and regulatory compliance, particularly when paired with the adoption of ISO standards. Such efforts can help align regional regulations, allowing industries to advance circular economy practices more seamlessly (United Nations Environment Programme, 2022).

In conclusion, cross-industry partnerships and secure data-sharing practices are vital for realizing the potential of the circular economy. Overcoming regulatory and logistical challenges will enable industries and governments to collaborate more effectively on standardized, sustainable, and circular practices at a global scale. As more sectors adopt unified frameworks and technologies, the vision of a global, integrated circular economy becomes increasingly achievable.

SOCIAL AND ETHICAL CONSIDERATIONS IN DIGITAL CIRCULAR PRACTICES

Data Privacy and Ethical Use

The growing integration of digital technology in circular systems necessitates the safeguarding of data privacy and the ethical management of data. Oversight of product lifecycles, analysis of user behaviour, and management of resource flows frequently necessitate comprehensive data collection, potentially involving sensitive customer information. IoT sensors collect real-time data on product utilization, facilitating resource management optimization and guiding future design decisions. The ongoing surveillance and documentation of customer behaviour generate privacy issues, particularly as firms manage substantial amounts of personal information.

To mitigate these issues, firms must adhere to data privacy regulations, such as the General Data Protection Regulation (GDPR) in Europe, which requires transparency in data collection and guarantees that consumers maintain ownership over their data (European Commission, 2023). Implementing ethical data practices, including the anonymization of customer data and securing explicit agreement for data gathering, is crucial for fostering consumer trust.

Studies indicate that consumers are more inclined to participate in circular economy projects when they have confidence in companies' responsible data management practices. A survey by Accenture indicates that 75% of customers are inclined to engage in data-sharing programs, provided they trust that their data will be utilized ethically (Accenture, 2023). Ethical data practices allow firms to utilize data for sustainability objectives while safeguarding consumer privacy, creating a framework where environmental and privacy issues are harmonized (Schwab & Malleret, 2023).

Labor and Fair Practices in Recycling and Data Collection

The adoption of digital circular practices, particularly in waste management and recycling, presents both opportunities and challenges in terms of labour practices. Automated sorting systems and AI-driven waste management technologies have revolutionized recycling facilities, creating new roles for operators while reducing reliance on manual labour. However, in emerging economies where manual labour remains essential, it is crucial to uphold ethical labour standards, ensuring fair wages, safe working conditions, and adequate protections.

In the e-waste recycling industry, for example, workers often handle hazardous materials without sufficient protection, highlighting the need for strict labour standards (International Labour Organization, 2023). Companies must also consider the potential displacement of workers due to automation. Instead of fully replacing manual labour, some companies are investing in upskilling programs that train workers to operate new technologies such as IoT devices and data analytics tools.

For instance, Dell's recycling facilities in India have implemented training programs to equip workers with the skills to manage AI-enabled sorting systems, fostering job security while promoting technological adoption (Dell Technologies, 2023). These initiatives support ethical labour practices by ensuring that technology complements human roles rather than replaces them, contributing to workforce resilience (Bhardwaj & Mehta, 2023).

Equitable Access to Circular Technologies

Ensuring equitable access to circular technologies is vital for building an inclusive circular economy, especially for Small and Medium-sized Enterprises (SMEs) and businesses in emerging economies. High initial costs and the need for specialized skills often prevent these organizations from adopting advanced digital tools, creating a digital divide. According to the World Bank (World Bank, 2022), only 23% of SMEs in low-income regions can afford the digital tools necessary for sustainable resource management, compared to 70% in high-income regions.

To address this disparity, collaborative efforts are needed. The United Nations Global Compact Initiative encourages large corporations to partner with SMEs, providing technical support, training, and digital resources. Companies like Siemens and SAP have developed cost-effective software solutions tailored for smaller businesses, enabling them to implement basic IoT and data management systems at a lower cost (United Nations Global Compact, 2023).

In addition to corporate partnerships, government subsidies and grants for digital infrastructure in developing economies can support the widespread adoption of digital circular technologies. Knowledge-sharing initiatives, such as the World Economic Forum's Knowledge Hubs, further facilitate cross-border exchange of expertise, helping emerging markets adopt circular practices. These collaborative approaches are key to creating a global circular economy that leverages digital tools inclusively, ensuring that all stakeholders benefit from the transition to sustainable practices.

In conclusion, addressing the social and ethical dimensions of digital circular practices, including data privacy, labour rights, and equitable access to technology, is essential for fostering an inclusive and sustainable circular economy. By prioritizing these considerations, companies and governments can ensure that the transition to a digital circular economy supports both resource efficiency and societal well-being.

CONCLUSION AND FUTURE PROSPECTS

Summary of Key Insights

The integration of digital tools into circular economy practices is revolutionizing industries by enhancing transparency, resource efficiency, and waste reduction. Key technologies such as the Internet of Things (IoT), blockchain, Artificial Intelligence (AI), and digital twins enable real-time tracking, optimize resource utilization, and facilitate secure data exchange. These advancements support a shift from linear economic models to more sustainable, circular practices (Gupta & Chen, 2023). For instance, predictive maintenance powered by IoT minimizes resource wastage in manufacturing, while blockchain ensures traceable and ethical sourcing in industries like fashion. Despite the transformative potential, challenges remain, particularly regarding interoperability, regulatory compliance, and equitable access to these technologies (Schwab & Malleret, 2023).

Collaboration across sectors and adherence to data privacy and ethical labour standards have emerged as central themes. Partnerships and data-sharing networks enhance access to digital tools and promote cohesive approaches to resource management. Addressing these challenges will allow industries to scale circular practices, thereby driving sustainability across global markets.

Future Prospects in Circular Economy Technologies

The future of digital circularity is set for significant advancements, driven by emerging technologies that promise new possibilities for scalability and resource optimization. Some key trends likely to shape this future include:

- **Increased Automation and AI-Driven Processes**: AI-enhanced automation will further improve efficiency in circular economy practices. Advanced predictive analytics and decision-making capabilities will help companies reduce overproduction by forecasting consumer demand, a key principle of circularity (Bhardwaj & Mehta, 2023). Additionally, AI-driven platforms will enhance precision in recycling processes, particularly in sectors like electronics, where resource recovery is critical.
- **Expansion of Digital Twins in Product Lifecycle Management**: Digital twins, virtual replicas of physical assets, are expected to play a pivotal role in product lifecycle analysis, resource optimization, and end-of-life management. These digital counterparts allow companies to simulate various lifecycle scenarios, improving resource efficiency and extending product lifespans. In aerospace, for instance, digital twins are used to optimize material use and enhance product durability (Schwab *et al.*, 2023).
- **5G-Enabled IoT Connectivity**: The rollout of 5G technology will enhance IoT connectivity, particularly in complex supply chains. Faster, more reliable connections will enable real-time resource tracking and rapid response to disruptions, reducing waste and energy consumption. Logistics companies like FedEx are already exploring 5G applications for dynamic route management, leading to more energy-efficient deliveries (World Economic Forum, 2023).
- **Blockchain Advancements and Decentralized Applications (DApps)**: Blockchain's role in ensuring transparent supply chains will be bolstered by Decentralized Applications (DApps), which facilitate secure peer-to-peer interactions. DApps are particularly useful in industries that require ethical sourcing, such as fashion and electronics, as they enhance material traceability and promote ethical sourcing practices (Accenture, 2023).

While these advancements offer exciting possibilities, the success of digital circular tools will depend on overcoming technical and regulatory hurdles. Policymakers, industry leaders, and researchers must collaborate to ensure that digital developments align with sustainability and equity goals, fostering a resilient circular economy.

Strategic Recommendations for Policymakers and Businesses

To fully harness digital tools for the circular economy, a proactive approach from both policymakers and businesses is essential. Key recommendations include:

- **Promote Standardization and Interoperability**: Universal standards are necessary for seamless integration of digital tools across industries, reducing costs and facilitating data sharing. Policymakers should advocate for standardization in data formats, sharing protocols, and compliance frameworks (Gupta *et al.*, 2023). Standardized frameworks will streamline collaboration, ensuring more efficient and transparent circular practices.
- **Invest in Workforce Development and Training**: The increasing integration of digital tools into circular operations will demand skilled professionals in AI, IoT, and data analytics. Governments and industry leaders should support training programs to close the skills gap and equip workers to manage digital circular systems effectively (Bhardwaj & Mehta, 2023). Tailoring these programs for SMEs will ensure broader access to digital technologies.
- **Support Data Security and Ethical Practices**: Safeguarding data security and ensuring ethical data management are essential, particularly with the use of consumer information. Policymakers should strengthen data protection regulations, while businesses invest in secure infrastructures to protect privacy and build consumer trust.
- **Foster Public-Private Partnerships**: Collaboration between public entities, industry leaders, and tech innovators is critical for advancing digital circular tools. Governments can incentivize businesses to invest in digital circular technologies through subsidies, tax benefits, or R&D grants, promoting faster, scalable adoption.

These strategic recommendations offer a framework for the effective integration of digital tools within the circular economy, promoting sustainability and resource efficiency across industries.

Call for Ongoing Research and Development

Continuous research and innovation are critical to addressing the current challenges in digital circularity, such as improving technological efficiency, scalability, and ethical practices. Key research areas include:

- **Expand Research in Emerging Technologies**: Future R&D should focus on refining digital twins, blockchain applications, and AI-based optimization tools. Investigating their long-term environmental impact and economic viability will shape sustainable business models that balance profitability with ecological responsibility.

- **Explore Solutions for Equitable Access**: Research should explore ways to make digital tools more accessible for SMEs and emerging economies. Scalable, affordable designs are essential to bridging the digital divide, allowing broader participation in circular practices (Schwab *et al.*, 2023).
- **Integrate Environmental Metrics into Digital Platforms**: Developing comprehensive environmental metrics, such as carbon footprint reductions and waste diversion percentages, would allow for more precise tracking of sustainability impacts. Embedding these metrics into digital platforms would enable businesses to quantify their contributions to sustainability goals more effectively.
- **Encourage Multi-Disciplinary Studies on Digital Ethics**: As digital tools increasingly shape circular systems, the ethical implications of data privacy, labor practices, and environmental impact must be explored. Multi-disciplinary research combining environmental ethics, cybersecurity, and economics can help ensure these technologies adhere to principles of transparency, fairness, and accountability.

Final Thoughts

Digital tools have moved the circular economy from a theoretical framework to a practical pathway for sustainable development. Through data-driven insights, resource management, and transparency, these tools are instrumental in creating a future where economic growth is aligned with ecological preservation. However, achieving the full potential of these technologies will require collaborative efforts from policymakers, businesses, and researchers. Together, they can build a resilient circular economy where sustainability is woven into the fabric of global production and consumption practices.

CONCLUSION

Digital tools have moved the circular economy from a theoretical framework to a practical pathway for sustainable development. Through data-driven insights, resource management, and transparency, these tools are instrumental in creating a future where economic growth is aligned with ecological preservation. However, achieving the full potential of these technologies will require collaborative efforts from policymakers, businesses, and researchers. Together, they can build a resilient circular economy where sustainability is woven into the fabric of global production and consumption practices.

REFERENCES

Accenture. (2023). *Digital Technologies and the Circular Economy.* Available from: https://www.accenture.com

Assent Compliance. (2023). *Global Supply Chain Sustainability and Compliance.* Available from:

https://www. assent.com

ABB. (2023). *AI-Driven Predictive Maintenance for Sustainable Industry.* Available from: https://global.abb

Apple, (2023). Daisy robot and the future of electronics recycling. Available from: https://www.apple.com/environment

Bhardwaj, V., Mehta, S. (2023). Data privacy and cybersecurity challenges in blockchain-enabled circular economy systems. *Comput. Secur., 126*, 103123.

Bressanelli, G., Adrodegari, F., Perona, M., Saccani, N. (2023). The role of IoT in enabling circular business models: A systematic review. *Sustainability, 15*(2), 625.

Bevilacqua, M., Ciarapica, F.E., Giacchetta, G. (2022). Sustainable product design using life cycle assessment: A review. *J. Ind. Ecol., 26*(3), 855-872.

Caterpillar, (2023). Connected Equipment and Predictive Maintenance. Available from: https://www.caterpillar.com

Circle Economy. (2023). *The Circularity Gap Report.* Available from: https://www.circularity-gap.world

CATENA-X.. (2023). *Data Collaboration for the Automotive Industry.* Available from: https://catena-x.net

DHL. (2023). Smart Logistics with 5G-Enabled IoT Solutions. Available from: https://www.dhl.com

Dell Technologies. (2023). *Workforce Development and AI Adoption in Recycling.* Available from: https://www.dell.com

Ellen MacArthur Foundation. (2023). Available from: https://www.ellenmacarthurfoundation.org

European Automobile Manufacturers' Association. (2023). *Vehicle Circularity and Resource Efficiency.*

European Environment Agency. (2023). *Digitalisation and Data-Driven Policy for Circular Economy.* Available from: https://www.eea.europa.eu

European Circular Economy Stakeholder Platform. (2023). *Industrial Symbiosis and Material Exchange Initiatives.* Available from: https://circulareconomy.europa.eu

European Commission. (2023). *The European Green Deal.* Available from: https://ec.europa.eu

Fashion for Good. (2023). *The Future of Circular Fashion.* Available from: https://fashionforgood.com

Food and Agriculture Organization. (2023). Available from: https://www.fao.org

Ford Motor Company. (2023). *Leveraging Digital Twins in Automotive Design.* Available from: https://www.ford.com

Global Reporting Initiative. (2023). *GRI Standards for Sustainability Reporting.* Available from: https://www.globalreporting.org

GS1. (2023). *Global Standards for Circular Supply Chains.* Available from: https://www.gs1.org

Global Forest Watch. (2023). *Real-Time Forest Monitoring.* Available from: https://www.globalforestwatch.org

H&M.. (2023). *Conscious Collection and Consumer Education.* Available from: https://hmgroup.com

International Organization for Standardization. (2022). Available from: https://www.iso.org

International Energy Agency. (2022). *Global Status Report for Buildings and Construction.* Available from: https://www.iea.org

IBM. (2023). *Food Trust and AI Applications in Sustainability.* Available from: https://www.ibm.com/food-trust

IKEA. (2023). *Circular Product Lifecycle and Consumer Engagement.* Available from: https://www.ikea.com

International Labour Organization. (2023). *Safety and Labour Standards in Waste Management.* Available from: https://www.ilo.org

LVMH. (2023). *Aura Blockchain Consortium for Luxury Goods.* Available from: https://www.lvmh.com

McKinsey & Company. (2023). *Blockchain and the Future of Global Supply Chains.* Available from: https://www.mckinsey.com

Nestlé. (2023). *Packaging Sustainability and Consumer Feedback.* Available from: https://www.nestle.com

National Renewable Energy Laboratory. (2023). *Smart Cities and Data-Driven Environmental Policy.* Available from: https://www.nrel.gov

Nike. (2023). Sustainable Innovation and Consumer Engagement. Available from: https://purpose.nike.com

Renault Group. (2023). *RE-FACTORY: A Circular Economy Initiative.* Available from: https://www.renaultgroup.com

SAP. (2023). *Environmental Compliance Management Solutions.* Available from: https://www.sap.com

Schneider Electric. (2023). *IoT and Energy Management in Industry.* Available from: https://www.se.com

SmartFarming. (2023). *Satellite Data for Sustainable Agriculture.* Available from: https://www.smartfarmingtech.com

Tomra. (2023). AI-Enhanced Sorting and Recycling Technologies. Available from: https://www.tomra.com

ThredUp. (2023). *Resale Market and Circular Fashion.* Available from: https://www.thredup.com

United Nations Global Compact. (2023). *Digital Inclusion for SMEs in Emerging Markets.* Available from: https://www.unglobalcompact.org

United Nations Environment Programme. (2022). Available from: https://www.unep.org

World Bank. (2022). *Leveraging Geospatial Technologies for Environmental Monitoring.* Available from: https://www.worldbank.org

World Economic Forum. (2022). *Circular Economy and Global Economic Benefits Report.* Available from: https://www.weforum.org

Digital, G.E. (2023). *Predictive Maintenance and Digital Manufacturing.* Available from: https://www.ge.com/digital

Fairphone, (2023). Responsible sourcing and circular electronics. Available from: https://www.fairphone.com

Geissdoerfer, M., Savaget, P., Bocken, N.M., Hultink, E.J. (2017). The circular economy – a new sustainability paradigm? *J. Clean. Prod., 143*, 757-768.

Gupta, H., Chen, X. (2023). Overcoming barriers to digital circular economy implementation: A Review. *J. Ind. Inf. Integr., 30*, 100385.

Li, Y., Liu, Z., Zhang, Q. (2022). Digital twins for sustainable manufacturing and circular economy. *J. Clean. Prod., 378*, 134540.

Pfizer, (2023). Digital tools for compliance and sustainability in pharmaceuticals. Available from: https://www.pfizer.com

Provenance, (2023). Blockchain for ethical product traceability. Available from: https://www.provenance.org

Ruan, Y., Zhang, X., Wang, C. (2023). 5G and IoT: Enablers for smart circular economy. *IEEE Internet Things J., 10*(4), 2571-2583.

Robotics, A.M.P. (2023). *AI and robotics for recycling efficiency.* Available from: https://www.amprobotics.com

Schwab, K., Malleret, T. (2023). Shaping the future of the fourth industrial revolution.

Saberi, S., Kouhizadeh, M., Sarkis, J., Shen, L. (2023). Blockchain technology and its relationships to sustainable supply chain management. *Int. J. Prod. Res., 61*(4), 1252-1267.

Siemens, (2023). Digital solutions for sustainable manufacturing. Available from: https://www.siemens.com

Unilever, (2022). Sustainable packaging and digital transparency. Available from: https://www.unilever.com

Zhang, H., Hu, X. (2023). Digital twins in construction for material efficiency and waste reduction. *Autom. Construct., 150*, 104891.

CHAPTER 3

Circular Economy and Legal Frameworks for Balancing Ecology and Economy

Amanda Adelina Harun[1,*]

[1] *Faculty of Law, Universitas Negeri Gorontalo, Gorontalo, Indonesia*

Abstract: This research aims to: (1) identify and evaluate the challenges and opportunities of integrating Circular Economy (CE) principles into Indonesia's legal framework; (2) analyze and assess the current legal regulations related to waste management and product durability; (3) propose recommendations for reformulating the legal framework to support CE implementation. This research uses a combination of normative legal and empirical legal studies. The first objective employs a normative approach to analyze existing legislation on resource use and waste management. The second objective adopts an empirical legal approach to evaluate the application of CE principles in practice. The third objective utilizes a comparative approach to draw lessons from international CE models, such as Germany's comprehensive CE regulations. The findings reveal that: (1) Indonesia's legal framework currently lacks specific regulations on product durability and waste management, with existing laws focusing primarily on consumer protection and product quality; (2) CE principles face challenges in practice due to limited infrastructure, low public awareness, and inadequate legal support; (3) reformulating the legal framework for CE requires a holistic approach, integrating regulatory measures, stakeholder participation, and lessons from international CE models. This transition promises ecological sustainability and economic growth by reducing waste and maximizing resource use.

Keywords: Circular economy, Environmental sustainability, Linear economy, Legal regulations.

INTRODUCTION

The ecological crisis is closely related to traditional economic models, also known as linear economics, which tend to follow a "take-use-dispose" pattern. Traditional linear economic models exacerbate ecological problems through unsustainable practices that prioritize short-term economic gains over long-term environmental health (Didenko *et al.*, 2018). The linear economy significantly contributes to environmental degradation. This is because the traditional industrial

[*] **Corresponding author Amanda Adelina Harun:** Faculty of Law, Universitas Negeri Gorontalo, Gorontalo, Indonesia; E-mail: amandaharun@ung.ac.id

Theodore Tarnanidis, Vijaya Kittu Manda, Vivek Gupta (Eds.)

model is based on a "take-use-waste" approach, which does not consider the limited nature of resources (Guo *et al.*, 2010). It was estimated to be around 505kg of Municipal Solid Waste (MSW) per capita income in the European Union (EU) in 2020 (Puntarić *et al.*, 2022). When the industries continue t extract resources without replenishing them, it results in diminished resources (Guo *et al.*, 2010). This unsustainable consumption pattern does not take into account the finite nature of natural resources, leading to exhaustion over time (Didenko *et al.*, 2018).

A significant problem with the linear economy is the emergence of waste. Products are often designed for short-term use and disposal, leading to increased waste and pollution. This waste often ends up in landfills or natural environments, causing further ecological damage. Billions of tons of waste are produced each year, leading to severe but not fully understood consequences for the environment (Kouhihabibi, 2022). In Indonesia, 182.7 billion plastic bags are used every year (Citrarum Harum Juara, 2024). The linear economic model is unsustainable because it heavily relies on the extraction of natural resources and generates a large amount of waste (Kouhihabibi, 2022). The traditional linear economic model can lead to dysfunction in the economic system. As resources become increasingly scarce and pollution rises, the economic system struggles to maintain its functions. This can lead to economic instability and increased costs associated with resource extraction and pollution management (Guo *et al.*, 2010).

The Circular Economy (CE) addressed environmental issues caused by the traditional linear economic model. Learning from experiences, the CE offers a sustainable alternative by promoting reuse, recycling, and material regeneration. By encouraging resource efficiency and waste reduction, the CE helps create an environmentally resilient system (Scheel & Bello, 2022). The CE encourages industries to adopt sustainable practices, such as designing products for longevity and recycling, which can significantly reduce waste and resource consumption (Kouhihabibi, 2022). The CE focused on maximizing resource efficiency by promoting recycling, reuse, and remanufacturing (Scheel & Bello, 2022). This reduced the need to extract new raw materials, conserving natural resources, thereby minimizing environmental degradation (Scheel & Bello, 2022).

Regulation plays a crucial role in the implementation of a CE. The role of law is particularly important in creating a framework and facilitating the transition from a linear economy to a CE. Environmental regulations significantly enhance the performance of the CE by promoting improvements in industrial structure and regional governance (Peng & Shen, 2024). Laws can mandate the use of sustainable materials and processes in manufacturing, encouraging companies to adopt practices that reduce waste and promote recycling (Peng & Shen, 2024).

Without supportive or even mandatory policies, economic actors are reluctant to adopt practices that reduce waste and extend the life cycle of a product due to limited incentives and market pressures.

The linear economic model leads to the formation of significant waste (Kristianto *et al.*, 2023). Indonesia is the second largest producer of food waste globally, which poses significant economic, social, and environmental challenges (Waluyo & Kharisma, 2023). Many cities in Indonesia rely on landfills that have now reached maximum capacity due to the increase in waste volume, such as the Piyungan landfill, which accommodates 600 tons of waste per day and causes environmental and social issues, including unpleasant odors and the potential contamination of groundwater by leachate (Anggraini *et al.*, 2020; Hayuningrat & Rahmadyanti, 2021). The recycling efforts that have been implemented in Indonesia so far have not been sufficient to tackle the massive waste problem in the country. In Indonesia, this is exacerbated by population growth, especially in urban areas, which results in more complex waste management challenges compared to rural areas (Kristianto *et al.*, 2023).

CE has not been widely implemented in Indonesia, even though its application should encompass various aspects such as production, distribution, and consumption of goods. Each of these aspects still faces challenges, such as high waste production and the accumulation of waste in various landfills that have already reached maximum capacity. This is exacerbated by the lack of adequate legal support to encourage the transition from a linear economy to a CE. For example, regarding waste issues, this country does not yet have effective policies guiding the management of existing waste (Waluyo & Kharisma, 2023). Addressing this issue requires a comprehensive approach that involves government, industry, and community stakeholders working together to create a sustainable and economically viable CE.

However, the implementation of the CE in Indonesia remained limited due to several challenges, including inadequate infrastructure, low public awareness, and the absence of comprehensive legal regulations to support waste management, product durability, and the link between population growth and waste production. Current laws focus more on consumer protection and quality standards, neglecting the importance of extending product lifespans to reduce waste. Given these issues, this study seeks to explore how the circular economy can act as a catalyst for ecological preservation amidst the challenges of modern industry. Additionally, it examined how legal regulations can encourage companies to integrate CE principles into their operations, promoting sustainable practices for ecological sustainability in Indonesia.

RESULTS AND DISCUSSION

Environmental and Industrial Challenges in Adopting Circular Economy

Challenges In Adopting the Circular Economy

The transition to a CE presents both significant opportunities and complex challenges. While this model promotes sustainable resource use, waste reduction, and environmental preservation, its implementation is far from straightforward. Adopting a CE requires addressing multiple barriers, including technological, regulatory, and behavioral factors, which impact its effectiveness across various industries.

Product Durability Issues

The integration of product durability in the CE is a complex challenge that involves efforts to extend the lifespan of products while ensuring economic and ecological sustainability. This strategy aimed not only to reduce waste but also to maximize the efficiency of resource use, thereby decreasing the need for new raw materials. By extending the product life cycle, the environmental impact of production and disposal can be minimized (Li *et al.*, 2023) contributing to the balance between economic growth and environmental preservation. Many types of goods are produced with the intention of being used once or for a short period of time. This has an impact on the increase in consumption, which in turn affects the amount of waste.

Single-use items are specifically designed for one-time applications. They are intended to be used once and then discarded, which is why they are often made from inexpensive materials that can be easily produced in large quantities, such as plastic (Di Paolo *et al.*, 2022). Although convenient, single-use items have a significant environmental impact, including contributions to plastic pollution and a high carbon footprint due to the energy-intensive processes involved in their production and disposal (Di Paolo *et al.*, 2022). Single-use products, especially those made from plastic, have a significant environmental impact, as they remain in the ecosystem for a long time, increasing pollution, particularly in marine ecosystems (Di Paolo *et al.*, 2022).

In addition to single-use products, some manufacturers produce items that are not durable. This is a business strategy where products are designed to wear out or become obsolete after a certain period, encouraging consumers to purchase replacements (Savva *et al.*, 2023). Items such as fast fashion clothing, certain electronics, and low-cost household goods are often designed with a shorter lifespan to encourage consumers to purchase new products regularly (Savva *et al.*,

2023). Many products are discarded not due to physical degradation, but because of emotional durability (Chapman, 2009). Many Domestic Electronic Products (DEP) are discarded while still functioning due to a lack of emotional connection with users, resulting in significant waste and environmental impact, as products are not designed to evolve with changing consumer desires (Chapman, 2009). Designing products that foster lasting emotional connections can reduce waste and extend the lifespan of the products (Chapman, 2009).

High Waste Production

The linear economic system that is currently common in Indonesia depletes resources and generates high levels of waste and emissions (Puluhulawa & Harun, 2024). Indonesia adalah salah satu produsen limbah terbesar di dunia, dengan urbanisasi yang cepat dan pertumbuhan penduduk telah berkontribusi pada peningkatan produksi limbah (Abdussamad *et al.*, 2024). Indonesia generates waste in significant amounts, with reports indicating that the waste piles weigh 175,000 tons each day, totaling 64 million tons per year (Puluhulawa & Puluhulawa, 2021a). Of that amount, 15% is plastic waste, which poses severe environmental challenges (Puluhulawa & Puluhulawa, 2021a). Urban residents on Java Island generate around 189,349 tons of plastic waste every month, with only 11.83% of that plastic waste being collected for recycling (Darus *et al.*, 2020). This means that 88.17% of plastic waste, which is not collected, is directly transported to landfills or remains scattered in the environment. In addition to plastic waste, 8.1 million tons of paper waste are produced each year, with an increase of 1% every two years (Saputra & Fauzi, 2022).

Data from 2016 shows that single-use plastics contribute 80% of the 8 million tons of plastic that enter the oceans each year (McDermott, 2016). In India, 43% of plastic consumption is for single-use packaging, contributing to 1.6 million tons of plastic waste generated each year (Dadhe, 2019). In England, it is estimated that 2.5 to 5 billion disposable coffee cups are thrown away each year, most of which are not recycled due to the plastic lining (Allison *et al.*, 2021). The pervasive disposal of single-use plastics exemplifies how the linear economic model fosters unsustainable consumption patterns, emphasizing the urgent need for a transition to a circular economy. In the context of environmental sustainability, the concept of a linear economy presents a fundamental challenge when applied to single-use plastics. A linear economy, characterized by a 'take-make-dispose' model, inherently promotes the continuous extraction of resources and generation of waste, which aligns with the pervasive use of single-use plastics. These plastics are designed for short-term utility and are discarded after a single use, exacerbating the linear model's shortcomings by contributing to an escalating waste crisis. This approach not only depletes natural resources but also fails to account for the long-term environmental impacts, including pollution and biodiversity loss.

Population Growth

Waste management has become a complex issue that requires a multifaceted approach. The interplay of economic, social, and environmental factors necessitates a thorough examination of the current waste management landscape to identify and address underlying obstacles effectively. Indonesia faces significant challenges in waste management, stemming from a combination of environmental, social, and infrastructural issues. These challenges are exacerbated by the country's rapid urbanization, population growth, and economic development, which have led to an increase in waste production. The complexity of waste management in Indonesia is further intensified by the diverse types of waste (Soesilo & Alfarizi, 2024), including garbage, plastic food, and municipal waste, each requiring tailored management strategies.

Population growth leads to higher waste production due to the increased consumption of goods and services, resulting in greater waste generation (Diani & Haniifah, 2024). Urban areas faced unique challenges, with over 65% of organic waste requiring special handling to prevent environmental impacts (Sutisna, 2024). For example, DKI Jakarta (the Capital city of Indonesia), projections indicate that by 2029, the population will reach over 12 million, with daily waste production estimated to exceed 8,400 cubic meters (Diani & Haniifah, 2024). Areas with high population density often face difficulties in waste management due to limited space for adequate facilities, leading to improper waste disposal practices, such as dumping into rivers or other unsuitable locations, which exacerbates the waste problems (Prajati *et al.*, 2017). The increasing population can overwhelm the existing waste management system if it is not improved or expanded (Diani & Haniifah, 2024). This can lead to inadequate waste collection and disposal, resulting in more litter in public spaces.

The increase in waste is not only caused by population growth but is exacerbated by changes in consumption patterns and urbanization. A higher income level can lead to an increase in consumption (Prajati *et al.*, 2017), impacting the high amount of waste (Puluhulawa & Puluhulawa, 2021b). Urbanization, along with economic growth, significantly contributes to the increase in waste production (Prajati *et al.*, 2017), and this will be exacerbated by the state of the public's knowledge. The low level of public knowledge and involvement in waste management practices, such as waste sorting, is largely due to the lack of government efforts in educating the community and promoting waste separation (Saragih *et al.*, 2023). The level of literacy and education in a society can influence waste management behavior, where higher literacy often contributes to greater awareness and better waste management practices, including recycling (Prajati *et al.*, 2017). On the contrary, low literacy levels can lead to improper waste disposal practices due to a lack of understanding of the importance of proper waste management.

Waste Management

In addition to issues related to waste management concerning its processing. The waste management system in Indonesia is often inefficient, leading to the accumulation of waste at final processing sites. Waste processing is ineffective, as seen in Jatibarang, Semarang, leading to environmental and health risks (Harjanti & Anggraini, 2020). The existing waste processing methods often struggle to handle certain types of waste. Electronic waste (e-waste) is still difficult to process in Indonesia, worsening the waste management problem (Rimantho *et al.*, 2022). Various innovations are needed in waste processing. TPST Mustika Ikhlas in Tangerang demonstrates the effectiveness of integrated waste management through community participation, reducing waste by converting it into compost and inorganic materials (Johannes, 2018). Recycling initiatives, such as turning paper waste into industrial raw materials, can significantly reduce waste volume and environmental impact (Saputra & Fauzi, 2022).

B) Economy Circular as a Tool for Ecological Preservation

The CE offers comprehensive solutions to various environmental and economic challenges by promoting sustainable resource management and waste reduction. The CE is a transformative model aimed at decoupling economic growth from environmental degradation by promoting sustainable production and consumption patterns (Yang *et al.*, 2023). The CE model in Indonesia aims to optimize resource utilization by eliminating waste generation and extending the functionality of resources (Fatmawati *et al.*, 2024). This approach reduces production costs and produces products with high market value, contributing to economic growth and environmental sustainability.

The transition to a CE represents a significant change in industrial production models that focuses on enhancing sustainability by reducing waste and maximizing resource use. This transformation necessitates a reevaluation of conventional linear production processes, which typically generate a lot of waste. Instead, a circular business model is adopted that emphasizes resource efficiency, waste reduction, and the recycling of materials within the production cycle. The integration of CE with green chemistry principles can lead to the development of sustainable products and processes that focus on waste reduction and resource conservation, which is crucial for ecological preservation (Ncube *et al.*, 2023).

The Circular Economy Business Model (CEBM) is considered a resilient system that promotes innovation and the integration of sustainability into business practices, making it essential for addressing sustainability challenges and ecological conservation (De Angelis, 2022). A business model that adopts a CE aimed to optimize material flows and reduce production costs while enhancing sustainable development indicators (Marinina *et al.*, 2022). The transition to a CE requires businesses to innovate and rethink their models to align with sustainability goals, considering environmental and social aspects that are crucial for ecological preservation (Koval *et al.*, 2023).

LEGAL REGULATIONS IN PROMOTING CIRCULAR ECONOMY INTEGRATION FOR ECOLOGICAL SUSTAINABILITY

Existing Law in Indonesia that supports the Circular Economy

Regulations and policies play a crucial role in driving the transition to a CE, as they can establish standards, incentives, and enforcement mechanisms that ensure sustainability practices are consistently applied throughout the production and consumption chain (Peng & Shen, 2024). Indonesia's approach to the CE is diverse, involving various sectors and stakeholders, and is influenced by traditional practices and modern regulatory frameworks. Legal policy and support are essential for adopting a CE. Implementing a CE in Indonesia faces challenges such as limited infrastructure, public awareness, and the need for more comprehensive policies. However, there are opportunities for growth in sectors such as recycling, renewable energy, and sustainable agriculture (Maesarini, 2023). Indonesia has several laws and regulations that indirectly support the principles of CE, including laws on waste management, environmental protection, and sustainable development. However, there is yet to be a national law that officially declares the use of CE principles.

Product Durability

Innovation in product design and production processes plays a crucial role in the CE, where design science drives the transition from a linear to a circular model through product life cycle management that encompasses creation to recycling at the end of its lifespan (Pigosso & McAloone, 2017). Durable and reliable products are one of the requirements of a CE, aimed at reducing waste production. In Indonesia, there is currently no law regulating the obligation of producers to create products with long durability. The existing regulations primarily focus on consumer protection and product safety without addressing durability as an important component. However, the aspect of consumer protection sets standards for a product, which can help maintain product quality that indirectly affects the product's durability.

Based on Law No. 8 of 1999 concerning Consumer Protection, Article 7, producers are required to provide accurate information about the quality and condition of the goods/services they produce. Although it does not specifically mention product durability, this regulation can be interpreted as an effort to ensure that consumers receive goods that match the description and quality expectations. Article 8 also prohibits producers from manufacturing and selling goods that do not meet quality standards. This indirectly affects the durability of the product. Products marketed must meet the Indonesian National Standard (SNI) based on Law Number 20 of 2014 concerning Standardization and Conformity Assessment, as well as Government Regulation (PP) 102 of 2000 concerning National Standardization. The Indonesian National Standard (Standar Nasional Indonesia/SNI) related to product quality includes aspects of safety and sometimes durability. However, specifications regarding product durability may vary depending on the type of product regulated. The Indonesian National Standard plays an important role in ensuring the quality and safety of products, including aspects of durability, even though not all SNI standards explicitly mention durability as a primary requirement.

Product durability regulations are very important in CE, because without clear rules, producers tend to create short-lived goods to encourage repeat consumption, which increases waste and hinders sustainability. This regulation plays a key role in promoting product durability and reducing environmental impact. The Ecodesign for Sustainable Products Regulation in Europe shows that standardization can enhance product durability by establishing minimum requirements for resilience and material efficiency, thereby encouraging manufacturers to design more durable products (Schlegel *et al.*, 2024).

High Waste Production

Reducing waste production is one of the key points in a CE. By minimizing waste from the outset, CE strategies can lower costs associated with recycling processes and waste management (Bigdeloo *et al.*, 2021). This approach is very important in sectors such as food waste management, where waste prevention efforts can significantly reduce the amount of waste generated (Bigdeloo *et al.*, 2021). In terms of regulations, there is currently no law that directly governs the limits or amount of waste produced by individuals or companies. However, some existing environmental regulations and policies aim to reduce the amount of waste. Law No. 18 of 2008 on Waste Management serves as the foundation for waste management in Indonesia, promoting the 3R principles (Reduce, Reuse, Recycle) to decrease the amount of waste. Although it does not set limits on the amount of waste produced, this law emphasizes waste reduction through better management at the source, both by the community and industry. Government Regulation No.

81 of 2012 concerning the Management of Household Waste and Similar Household Waste requires local governments to be responsible for the implementation of waste management with the aim of reducing the volume of waste produced.

Although there are several environmental policies, such as Law No. 18 of 2008 and Government Regulation No. 81 of 2012, which promote waste management and the 3R principles (Reduce, Reuse, Recycle), these policies do not explicitly regulate the limits on the amount of waste produced by individuals or companies. The lack of regulations limiting the amount of waste produced by individuals and companies hinders the implementation of a CE, as it allows for excessive waste production without any restrictions or incentives for reduction. Restrictions on waste are not always implemented by directly setting quantity limits, but rather through other mechanisms, such as taxes or bans on certain types of waste. Most countries still implement these partial regulations without fully restricting production or use throughout their entire life cycle (United Nations Environment Programme, 2018). The same thing in the context of Indonesia, restrictions on waste are often implemented through other mechanisms, such as taxes or bans on certain types of plastic, without directly setting quantity limits. For example, the DKI Jakarta Province has implemented Governor Regulation No. 142 of 2019, which mandates the use of environmentally friendly shopping bags in shopping centers and markets. However, this regulation is still partial, and its effectiveness is hindered by unclear definitions regarding the types and prices of eco-friendly bags, indicating the need for a more comprehensive and consistent regulatory framework to limit the production and use of plastic as a whole (Benedicta *et al.*, 2023).

Population Growth

Population growth and the consumption of goods and services are increasing, which puts pressure on natural resources. Urbanization, driven by population growth, leads to an increase in construction activities, which consume a significant quantity of raw materials and generate significant waste (Zhang *et al.*, 2023). Specifically, there is no law that regulates the relationship between population growth and its connection to waste production; however, there are laws that indirectly address this issue. Law no. 32 of 2009 on the Protection and Management of the Environment emphasizes the principle of sustainable development that considers the balance between economic, social, and environmental growth. This principle aligns with the CE, which focuses on the efficient use of resources and reducing environmental impact. Law No. 18 of 2008 on Waste Management emphasizes waste management based on the 3R principles (Reduce, Reuse, Recycle) aimed at reducing waste production and improving efficiency in its management.

Rapid population growth, especially in urban areas, is a significant driver of increased waste production, exacerbated by economic development and modern lifestyles, which contribute to higher waste volumes (Nopiah *et al.*, 2023). The absence of regulations that specifically link population growth to waste production in Indonesia leads to unsustainable consumption and production practices, increasing the risk of a future surge in waste volume that is difficult to manage. To effectively support a CE, specific regulations are needed to govern the relationship between population growth and waste production, in order to ensure that increased consumption and industrial activities do not negatively impact the environment. Regulations that control human populations to prevent practices that are not in line with CE and could harm the environment.

Waste Management

One of the focuses of the CE is in the field of waste management. The legal framework for waste management in Indonesia is still fragmented and does not yet include specific regulations for certain types of waste. For example, Law Number 18 of 2008 on waste management emphasizes waste reduction and promotes recycling and reuse, which are key components of a CE (Maesarini, 2023). Construction waste has not been specifically regulated, leading to inconsistent practices and enforcement across different regions (Hansen, 2024). Law No. 18 of 2008 regulates waste management in Indonesia based on the 3R principles, but it does not yet cover electronic waste, which poses a high risk to the environment and health due to its hazardous materials (Puluhulawa & Harun, 2024). Although Indonesia's Waste Management Law does not explicitly mention electronic waste, Article 2(4) provides a legal basis to interpret e-waste as a form of "specific waste" requiring targeted regulation and handling. Existing laws and policies regarding plastic waste management are insufficient, necessitating improvements to address the issue of plastic pollution (Maskun *et al.*, 2023). Local government policies often lack the necessary commitment and innovation to manage waste effectively, with many cities experiencing a "waste emergency" phase due to inadequate policy implementation (Maesarini, 2023).

Although the legal framework regarding waste management is not yet perfect, various initiatives related to recycling are being carried out by several industries. In the paper industry, recycling paper waste is carried out, with the industry using fibers from paper waste as raw materials, which reduces the need for new resources and minimizes waste (Saputra & Fauzi, 2022). Effective paper waste recycling can reduce overall waste in this country by up to 10.2% per year. Although various efforts have been made to recycle waste, the current practices in Indonesia have not been able to address the waste problem comprehensively, as they are carried out on a small scale. The lack of public interest in the recycling process is due to the fact that the economic benefits of recycling are not always clearly visible (Rizkiah, 2023). The regulations are unclear, and enforcement is lacking, leading to ongoing environmental pollution (Maskun *et al.*, 2023). Aside from regulatory aspects, in various recycling sectors, Indonesia faces significant infrastructure challenges. The lack of modern facilities and integrated systems hinders the effectiveness of recycling efforts, whether in the management of plastic, ship, or electronic waste (Sunaryo & Tjitrosoemarto, 2022).

B) Circular Economy in Germany

The European Union's CE Action Plan, which is part of Germany, was first adopted in 2015 (Duque-Acevedo *et al.*, 2020). This plan has significantly influenced the adoption and implementation of CE practices across member countries, including Germany (Duque-Acevedo *et al.*, 2020). Germany is identified as one of the pioneers in the implementation of the CE model (Roleders, 2023). Germany, the Netherlands, and China are countries that are considered quite successful in implementing the Circular Economy Act (Waluyo & Kharisma, 2023).

The Circular Economy Act in Germany provides a framework that involves the government, the private sector, and society in addressing environmental challenges (Waluyo & Kharisma, 2023). The assessment of CE practices in Germany involves a comprehensive evaluation of various indicators that measure the effectiveness and impact of these practices. At least, there are 13 indicators used to assess CE practices, namely:

1. The level of waste management and recycling, tracking the efficiency of waste reduction and recovery efforts (Banjerdpaiboon & Limleamthong, 2023).
2. The level of use of circular materials is an important measure of how well material is recycled back into the production process (Banjerdpaiboon & Limleamthong, 2023).
3. Consumer behavior and market demand, towards environmentally friendly products, and their willingness to pay more (Priatmojo, 2023).
4. Economic impact indicators, assessing the financial implications of circular strategies, such as cost savings from resource efficiency and the economic value derived from recycling and reuse activities (Kulakovskaya *et al.*, 2023).
5. Environmental impact indicators, evaluation of environmental pressure reduction (Helander *et al.*, 2019).
6. Resource efficiency and productivity (Banjerdpaiboon & Limleamthong, 2023).
7. Design and construction practice, guiding sustainable building design (Nemeth *et al.*, 2022).

8. The integration of new technologies into CE practices, such as anaerobic digestion for waste treatment, is an indicator of innovation and efficiency in resource use (Molina-Moreno *et al.*, 2017).
9. A policy and regulatory framework that supports CE practices (Banjerdpaiboon & Limleamthong, 2023).
10. Social impact and engagement, measuring public awareness, education, and involvement in CE activities (Priatmojo, 2023).
11. Life cycle assessment, evaluating the environmental impact of a product throughout its life cycle, provides a comprehensive view of its sustainability(Moraga *et al.*, 2019).
12. Resource-based trail indicators assess environmental input and output from CE activities, offering insights into overall sustainability (Helander *et al.*, 2019).
13. Sector-specific indicators have specific indicators that measure circularity in their unique context according to sectors (Molina-Moreno *et al.*, 2017).

Although not part of an official regulatory framework, the indicators used in Germany encompass a holistic and comprehensive approach. This set of indicators not only focuses on environmental aspects but also includes economic, social, and policy dimensions (Moraga *et al.*, 2019). Indicators serve as valuable tools for decision-makers by providing relevant information that can guide policies and business decisions, enabling the classification of CE strategies and measurement scope, and offering a standardized way to measure and compare circularity across various sectors and regions (Moraga *et al.*, 2019), help assess the effectiveness of sharing models and practices (Atstaja *et al.*, 2022), help assess the effectiveness of sharing models and practices (Mazur-Wierzbicka, 2021).

For example, the indicator "economic impact" assesses the financial implications of circular strategies, such as cost savings from resource efficiency and the economic value generated from recycling and reuse activities. On the other hand, "social impact and engagement" measures public awareness and participation in CE activities. This multidimensional approach is important because the CE is not just about waste management, but a complex system involving various sectors and stakeholders. The emphasis on resource efficiency and productivity in several indicators reflects the main goal of the CE to maximize the value of every material used. Indicators such as "waste management and recycling rates" and "circular material usage rates" highlight the importance of assessing how materials can be repurposed within the production cycle. Overall, these 13 indicators provide a comprehensive evaluation framework for the CE, covering various relevant dimensions. The approach used by Germany can serve as a model for other countries, including Indonesia, to develop a more comprehensive and effective CE assessment system. By using indicators that encompass resource efficiency, technological innovation, policies, and social aspects, countries can measure their progress in the transition towards a sustainable CE.

The German approach to the CE offers valuable insights into sustainable practices and innovations. The efforts of this country to reach various sectors, including packaging, construction, and business models, showcase a comprehensive strategy to achieve a CE. The manufacturing and automotive industries are increasingly adopting the principles of the CE. In Germany, the CE aims to conserve resources by minimizing the use of materials and energy (Horbach & Rammer, 2019). Germany has established requirements for energy-related product design to enhance its environmental performance, thereby encouraging manufacturers to consider the entire product lifecycle, promoting durability, repairability, and recycling (Whalen, 2020). The construction industry in Germany, particularly in the use of wood and plastic, plays a crucial role in the adoption of a CE, with prefabricated wooden construction recognized as a promising technology for resource efficiency, although it faces challenges in widespread implementation (Schuster & Geier, 2022). The German textile industry is beginning to integrate circular business models, such as recycling, upcycling, and product-as-a-service (Arnold *et al.*, 2023). The agri-food industry applies the principles of the CE by emphasizing the reduction, reuse, and recycling of resources to maximize the value of products throughout their life cycle (Nastari *et al.*, 2022).

For companies, this innovation can lead to cost savings, increased competitiveness, and higher product demand, which positively impacts financial performance and revenue growth (Horbach & Rammer, 2019). Companies that adopt CE innovations tend to experience positive effects on sales growth and job creation, as well as improved financial positions (Horbach & Rammer, 2020). The CE practices in Germany have positive impacts on resource efficiency, economic growth, employment, and financial performance, with variations across sectors and company sizes (Horbach & Rammer, 2020).

In addition to focusing on the production of goods that align with the CE, waste processing is also a concern. The company focuses on designing products for longevity, reusability, and recyclability, including the use of sustainable materials and implementing take-back schemes to recycle products at the end of their life cycle. The recycling rate in Germany is advanced, covering various types of waste with high recycling rates. Even in 2022, the recycling rate for electronic waste and glass reached up to 100%, as shown in the graphic (Statista Research Department, 2024).

The overall German approach to the CE demonstrates how the integration of circularity principles can be effectively applied across various industrial sectors.

The use of holistic and multidimensional indicators allows for a comprehensive measurement of the success of CE practices, ranging from resource efficiency to technological innovation and policy. The application of the CE contributes to environmental sustainability by reducing, reusing, and recycling waste materials, which helps to mitigate the negative impacts of the traditional linear economy (Castro *et al.*, 2022). This achievement demonstrates that the transition to a CE can provide financial benefits for companies while also having a positive impact on the environment.

FUTURE DIRECTIONS FOR CIRCULAR ECONOMY

The linear economy contributes to environmental degradation due to inefficient waste management practices. Unmanaged waste can lead to hazardous pollutants, affecting air and water quality, and ultimately damaging the environment (Kristianto *et al.*, 2023). The linear economy model did not maximize the economic potential of materials, as it does not prioritize recycling or reusing the resources. Improper waste management in a linear economy can pose significant public health risks. The accumulation of waste can lead to water and air pollution, which can cause health issues such as respiratory problems and other diseases.

The government plays a crucial role in developing regulations that support a CE by promoting cleaner production, responsible consumption, and end-of-life management (García-Madurga *et al.*, 2022). This involves the creation of policies that encourage collaboration among stakeholders and the implementation of leadership strategies that promote CE practices. Law also plays a role in promoting circular economic integration for ecological sustainability.

Law can mandate the use of sustainable materials and processes in manufacturing, encouraging companies to adopt practices that reduce waste and promote recycling. Legislation can significantly aid the transition to a CE by establishing standards, providing incentives for sustainable practices, and ensuring compliance, thereby fostering an environment conducive to sustainable economic growth and environmental protection (Peng & Shen, 2024). By establishing clear standards for waste management, recycling, and resource efficiency, the law can provide a framework for businesses and individuals to follow, ensuring that the principles of the CE are applied consistently. Law can facilitate cooperation and regional governance, which is essential for the effective implementation of the CE practices.

One of the main challenges in implementing a CE in Indonesia is the lack of integrated policies that support the transition (Lestari, 2023). Integrating regulations that are interrelated with each other is also important in supporting the CE. Integration of environmental regulation with trade law is essential to fostering sustainable business practices. CE policies are inherently multi-sectoral, requiring the involvement and cooperation of various sectors (Rimantho *et al.*, 2022). Commercial law acts as a catalyst for environmental compliance through contractual obligations and corporate governance standards, which are crucial to inserting environmental responsibility into the Corporate Governance (Liu & Zhen, 2024).

Successful implementation of the CE requires the support of industry and the general public, but without clear policies and incentives, obtaining this support is a challenge (Lestari, 2023). Industry needs to see the real benefits of adopting CE practices to be fully committed to the transition. Through penalties and law enforcement mechanisms, ensure that they adhere to the principles of the CE, thereby reducing environmental impact and promoting sustainable development (Peng & Shen, 2024). The legal framework can support educational initiatives that raise awareness of the benefits of a CE, encouraging wider adoption of its principles.

In the context of electronic waste, the current legal framework in Indonesia, such as Act No. 18 of 2008 on Waste Management, does not specifically address electronic waste management (Puluhulawa & Harun, 2024). These regulatory gaps make it difficult to manage electronic waste effectively, which is vital for the CE. There is a shortage of facilities associated with waste operations and limited temporary waste storage areas. There is a shortage of recycling technology and the infrastructure needed to support the CE. This lack of infrastructure hampers proper disposal and recycling of waste, which is an important component of the CE. Building the necessary infrastructure, such as collection sites and recycling facilities, is a significant challenge. The logistics of collection, disposal, and waste treatment require careful planning and investment.

The integration of Act No. 18 of 2008 on Waste Management with the principles of the CE is a significant step towards sustainable waste management in Indonesia. This integration aims to change waste management practices by emphasizing the reduction of waste, recycling, and the reuse of materials, in line with the broader objectives of the circular economy. The Act No. 18 of 2008 provides a comprehensive legal framework for waste management in Indonesia, emphasizing waste reduction, reuse, and recycling (Hardi *et al.*, 2024). Another problem is that the implementation of this law faces challenges due to the lack of enforcement mechanisms and clear sanctions for non-compliance, which leads to legal uncertainty. Addressing these issues requires a comprehensive approach that includes legislative reform, awareness-raising, and collaboration between governments, producers, and society. Thus, the integration of the principles of the CE with the Waste Management Act can be achieved more effectively.

CONCLUSION

The traditional linear economic models have led to various ecological problems, such as high levels of waste production and unsuitable consumption of natural resources. The Circular Economy (CE) has emerged as an alternative capable of addressing this issue through reuse, recycling, and efficient resource management. However, the implementation of CE in Indonesia still faced many challenges, including a lack of specific regulations related to waste management, product durability, and the relationship between population growth and waste production. Although there are regulations supporting the principles of 3R and sustainable development, their implementation has not been effective due to limited infrastructure, public awareness, and weak law enforcement. Therefore, a comprehensive regulatory framework, support from various stakeholders, and innovation in economic practices are needed to encourage the transition from a linear economy to a circular economy for ecological sustainability.

REFERENCES

Anggraini, N., Apriani, S., Najjah, S., Mataram, U., Mataram, U., Mataram, U. (2020). REPRO (Recycling Project) Sebagai solusi alternatif pengelolaan sampah di era revolusi industri 4.0 Menuju indonesia zero waste. *Jurnal Ilmiah Penalaran Dan Penelitian Mahasiswa, 4*, 80-90.

Abdussamad, Z., Harun, A.A., Muhtar, M.H., Puluhulawa, F.U. Constitutional balance: Synchronizing energy and environmental policies with socio-economic mandates. E3s Web of Conferences ISEEP, vol. 506, 2024, p. 1–15.
[http://dx.doi.org/10.1051/e3sconf/202450606006]

Allison, A.L., Lorencatto, F., Miodownik, M., Michie, S. (2021). Influences on single-use and reusable cup use: a multidisciplinary mixed-methods approach to designing interventions reducing plastic waste. *UCL Open Environ, 3*, 1-11.
[http://dx.doi.org/10.14324/111.444/ucloe.000025]

Atstaja, D., Koval, V., Grasis, J., Kalina, I., Kryshtal, H., Mikhno, I. (2022). Sharing model in circular economy towards rational use in sustainable production. *Energies, 15*, 1-26.
[http://dx.doi.org/10.3390/en15030939]

Arnold, M.G., Pfaff, C., Thomas, P. (2023). Circular business model strategies progressing sustainability in the german textile manufacturing industry. *Sustainability Article, 15*
[http://dx.doi.org/10.1080/13518470903211632]

Bigdeloo, M., Teymourian, T., Kowsari, E., Ramakrishna, S., Ehsani, A. (2021). Sustainability and circular economy of food wastes: waste reduction strategies, higher recycling methods, and improved valorization. *Materials Circular Economy, 3.*
[http://dx.doi.org/10.1007/s42824-021-00017-3]

Benedicta, N.O., Sodri, A., Triaswati, N. (2023). Preferensi dan Kesediaan Membayar Konsumen Terhadap Kantong Belanja Ramah Lingkungan di Provinsi DKI Jakarta. *Jurnal Ilmu Lingkungan, 22*, 155-162.
[http://dx.doi.org/10.14710/jil.22.1.155-162]

Banjerdpaiboon, A., Limleamthong, P. (2023). Assessment of national circular economy performance using super-efficiency dual data envelopment analysis and Malmquist productivity index: Case study of 27 European countries. *Heliyon, 9*, e16584.
[http://dx.doi.org/10.1016/j.heliyon.2023.e16584]

Castro, À.M., Castro, J.M., Burgos, R.Y., Suqilanda, E.M. (2022). Circular economy and its impact on environmental sustainability. *Centro Sur, 6*, 1-29.

Chapman, J. (2009). Design for (Emotional) Durability. *Des. Issues, 25*, 29-35.

Citrarum Harum Juara. (2024). Available from: https://citarumharum.jabarprov.go.id/wow-1827-mili-r-kantong-plastik-dipakai-di-indonesia-setiap-tahun/

Darus, N., Tamimi, M., Tirawaty, S., Muchtazar, M., Trisyanti, D., Akib, R., Condorini, D., Ranggi, K. (2020). An overview of plastic waste recycling in the urban areas of java island in indonesia. *Journal of Environmental Science and Sustainable Development, 3*, 402-415. [http://dx.doi.org/10.7454/jessd.v3i2.1073]

Dadhe, A. (2019). Plastic Waste Management By. *Pezzottaite Journals, 8*, 3218-3223.

De Angelis, R. (2022). Circular economy business models as resilient complex adaptive systems. *Bus. Strategy Environ., 31*, 2245-2255. [http://dx.doi.org/10.1002/bse.3019]

Duque-Acevedo, M., Belmonte-Ureña, L.J., Yakovleva, N., Camacho-Ferre, F. (2020). Analysis of the circular economic production models and their approach in agriculture and agricultural waste biomass management. *Int. J. Environ. Res. Public Health, 17*, 1-34. [http://dx.doi.org/10.3390/ijerph17249549]

Didenko, N.I., Klochkov, Y.S., Skripnuk, D.F. (2018). Ecological criteria for comparing linear and circular economies. *Resources, 7.* [http://dx.doi.org/10.3390/resources7030048]

Di Paolo, L., Abbate, S., Celani, E., Di Battista, D., Candeloro, G. (2022). Carbon footprint of single-use plastic items and their substitution. *Sustainability (Switzerland), 14.* [http://dx.doi.org/10.3390/su142416563]

Fatmawati, F., Ilham, I., Saleh, S., Razak, A.R. (2024). Waste management system: A case study of waste bank management toward a circular economy in maros regency. *Jurnal Borneo Administrator, 20*, 1-14. [http://dx.doi.org/10.24258/jba.v20i1.1206]

García-Madurga, M., Grilló-Méndez, A.J., Delgado-De Miguel, J.F., Esteban-Navarro, M. (2022). Circular economy and public policies in the face of the new normality. *Glob. NEST J., 24*, 576-589. [http://dx.doi.org/10.30955/gnj.004312]

Guo, J., Mao, H., Wang, T. (2010). Ecological industry: a sustainable economy developing pattern. *J. Sustain. Dev., 3*, 239-242. [http://dx.doi.org/10.5539/jsd.v3n3p239]

Hayuningrat, M.A., Rahmadyanti, E. (2021). Analisis kebutuhan lahan dan sarana prasarana pengelolaan sampah (studi kasus : TPA ngegong kota blitar). *Jurnal Teknik Sipil, 2*, 54-64. [http://dx.doi.org/10.31284/j.jts.2021.v2i1.1872]

Harjanti, I.M., Anggraini, P. (2020). Waste management at the jatibarang final disposal site, semarang city. *Jurnal Planologi, 17*, 185.

Hansen, S. (2024). Construction waste management from environmental law perspective in indonesia. *International Journal of Law and Public Policy, 6*, 1-7. [IJLAPP]. [http://dx.doi.org/10.36079/lamintang.ijlapp-0601.578]

Helander, H., Petit-Boix, A., Leipold, S., Bringezu, S. (2019). How to monitor environmental pressures of a circular economy: An assessment of indicators. *J. Ind. Ecol., 23*, 1278-1291. [http://dx.doi.org/10.1111/jiec.12924]

Horbach, J., Rammer, C. (2019). Employment and performance effects of circular economy innovations. *SSRN.*

Horbach, J., Rammer, C. (2020). Circular economy innovations, growth and employment at the firm level: empirical evidence from germany. *J. Ind. Ecol., 24*, 615-625.

[http://dx.doi.org/10.1111/jiec.12977]

Hardi, K.A. (2024). Senastri DrNMJ, Wiryani DrM. Environmental law enforcement regulations regarding producer obligations in waste management in indonesia. *Journal Of Law Theory And Law Enforcement, 3*, 44-58.
[http://dx.doi.org/10.56943/jlte.v3i1.497]

Johannes, H.P. (2018). Waste reduction through integrated waste management modeling at mustika residence (Tangerang). *Journal of Environmental Science and Sustainable Development, 1*, 12-24.
[http://dx.doi.org/10.7454/jessd.v1i1.15]

Koval, V., Arsawan, I. W. E., Suryantini, N. P. S., Kovbasenko, S., Fisunenko, N., & Aloshyna, T. (2023). Circular economy and sustainability-oriented innovation: conceptual framework and energy future avenue. Energies, 16(1), 243..
[http://dx.doi.org/10.3390/en16010243]

Kulakovskaya, A., Knoeri, C., Radke, F., Blum, N.U. (2023). Measuring the economic impacts of a circular economy: an evaluation of indicators. *Circular Economy and Sustainability, 3*, 657-692.
[http://dx.doi.org/10.1007/s43615-022-00190-w]

Kouhihabibi, M. (2022). Linear economy *versus* circular economy: new raw material. *Turk Turizm Arastirmalari Dergisi, 4*, 227-246.
[http://dx.doi.org/10.26677/tr1010.2022.1057]

Kristianto, A.H., Suratman, E., Yani, A., Restiatun, R. (2023). Interlinkage of circular economy in waste management, environmental quality, and public health in indonesia. *International Research in Social Sciences, 1*, 1.
[http://dx.doi.org/10.20849/irss.v1i1.1335]

Li, Y., Xiong, X., Qu, M. (2023). Research on the whole life cycle of a furniture design and development system based on sustainable design theory. *Sustainability (Switzerland), 15.*
[http://dx.doi.org/10.3390/su151813928]

Lestari, E.R. Tax policy reconstruction toward implementation of circular economy in indonesia. *Proc West Mark Ed Assoc Conf.* 2023; 2030: 68.

Liu, M., Zhen, R. (2024). Fostering sustainability through legal integration: A multidimensional analysis of environmental and commercial law synergies. *Lecture Notes in Education Psychology and Public Media, 52*, 7-13.
[http://dx.doi.org/10.54254/2753-7048/52/20241520]

Mcdermott, K.L. (2016). Plastic pollution and the global throwaway culture: plastic pollution and the global throwaway culture: environmental injustices of single-use plastic environmental injustices of single-use plastic. ENV 434. *Environ. Justice, 7*, 1-9.

Marinina, O., Kirsanova, N., Nevskaya, M. (2022). Circular economy models in industry: developing a conceptual framework. *Energies, 15.*
[http://dx.doi.org/10.3390/en15249376]

Maskun, K.H., Pattitingi, F., Assidiq, H., Bachril, S.N., Al Mukarramah, N.H. (2023). Plastic waste management in indonesia: current legal approaches and future perspectives. *Hasanuddin Law Review, 9*, 106-125.
[http://dx.doi.org/10.20956/halrev.v9i1.3683]

Meutia Rin Diani. (2024). Diinii Haniifah FRD. Analisis proyeksi pertumbuhan penduduk dan volume sampah DKI Jakarta terhadap dampak yang ditimbulkan. *Journal of Waste and Sustainable Consumption, 1*, 1-18.

Molina-Moreno, V., Leyva-Díaz, J.C., Llorens-Montes, F.J., Cortés-García, F.J. (2017). Design of indicators of circular economy as instruments for the evaluation of sustainability and efficiency in wastewater from pig farming industry. *Water (Switzerland), 9.*
[http://dx.doi.org/10.3390/w9090653]

Moraga, G., Huysveld, S., Mathieux, F., Blengini, G.A., Alaerts, L., Van Acker, K., de Meester, S., Dewulf, J. (2019). Circular economy indicators: What do they measure? *Resour. Conserv. Recycling, 146*, 452-461 [http://dx.doi.org/10.1016/j.resconrec.2019.03.045]

Mazur-Wierzbicka, E. (2021). Circular economy: advancement of European Union countries. *Environ. Sci. Eur., 33.*
[http://dx.doi.org/10.1186/s12302-021-00549-0]

Ncube, A., Mtetwa, S., Bukhari, M., Fiorentino, G., Passaro, R. (2023). Circular economy and green chemistry: the need for radical innovative approaches in the design for new products. *Energies, 16*, 1-21. [http://dx.doi.org/10.3390/en16041752]

Nastari, R., Pisano, S., Pozzoli, M. (2022). Circular economy disclosure by agri-food companies. *International Online Conference,* 69-74.

Puntarić, E., Pezo, L., Zgorelec, Ž., Gunjača, J., Kučić Grgić, D., Voća, N. (2022). Prediction of the production of separated municipal solid waste by artificial neural networks in croatia and the european union. *Sustainability (Switzerland), 14.*
[http://dx.doi.org/10.3390/su141610133]

Peng, B., Shen, X. (2024). Does environmental regulation affect circular economy performance? evidence from china. *Sustainability (Switzerland), 16.*
[http://dx.doi.org/10.3390/su16114406]

Puluhulawa, F.U., Harun, A.A. (2024). Enabling circular economy: towards sustainable electronic waste management regulation. *Jambura Law Review, 6*, 33-65.

Puluhulawa, F, Puluhulawa, MR Plastic waste: environmental legal issues and policy law enforcement for environmental sustainability. E3S Web of Conferences 2021; 259.

Prajati, G., Padmi, T., Rahardyan, D.B. (2017). Projection of big cities waste management and cost based on economic and demographic factors in indonesia. *IOP Conf. Ser. Earth Environ. Sci., 97.*
[http://dx.doi.org/10.1088/1755-1315/97/1/012014]

Puluhulawa, F, Puluhulawa, MR Plastic waste in modern era: developing plastic waste management for sustainability. E3S Web of Conferences 2021; 259: 1–5.

Pigosso, D., McAloone, T. How can design science contribute to a circular economy? Proceedings of the International Conference on Engineering Design, ICED 2017; 5: 299–307.

Priatmojo, W. (2023). Association of consumer behavior to a circular economy: assessing a variety of perceptions and its correlation in germany. *GMPI Conference Series,* 1-17.

Rimantho, D., Syaiful, S. (2022). Nurfaida, Sulandari U. Electronic waste bank model as a solution for implementing circular economy: Case study DKI Jakarta-Indonesia. *Front. Built Environ., 8*, 1-13.
[http://dx.doi.org/10.3389/fbuil.2022.1030196]

Nopiah, Z.M., Zulkipli, F., Basri, N.E.A., Kie, C.J. (2023). A study of waste generation prediction using correlation and multiple regression analyses. international journal of industrial engineering. *Technology & Operations Management, 1*, 54-57.
[http://dx.doi.org/10.62157/ijietom.v1i2.27]

Nemeth, I., Schneider-Marin, P., Figl, H., Fellner, M., Asam, C. (2022). Circularity evaluation as guidance for building design. *IOP Conf. Ser. Earth Environ. Sci., 1078.*
[http://dx.doi.org/10.1088/1755-1315/1078/1/012082]

Rizkiah, D.D.W.H.M.R. (2023). Cultural influences on waste dump and separation behaviors in future capital of indonesia (study case in sepaku regency, indonesia). *Technium Education and Humanities, 4*, 18-29.
[http://dx.doi.org/10.3389/fpsyg.2018.02447]

Roleders, V. (2023). *Transformation of the EU countries to the circular economy model.* Ekonomičnì Gorizonti.

Scheel, C., Bello, B. (2022). Transforming linear production chains into circular value extended systems. *Sustainability (Switzerland), 14.* [http://dx.doi.org/10.3390/su14073726]

Savva, K., Borrell, X., Moreno, T., Pérez-Pomeda, I., Barata, C., Llorca, M., Farré, M. (2023). Cytotoxicity assessment and suspected screening of plastic additives in bioplastics of single-use household items. *Chemosphere, 313.* [http://dx.doi.org/10.1016/j.chemosphere.2022.137494]

Saputra, A.Z. (2022). Fauzi AhS. Pengolahan sampah kertas menjadi bahan baku industri kertas bisa mengurangi sampah di indonesia. *Jurnal Mesin Nusantara, 5*, 41-52. [http://dx.doi.org/10.29407/jmn.v5i1.17522]

Statista Research Department. (2024). Available from: https://www.statista.com/statistics/1333820/recycling-rate-household-waste-germany/

Soesilo, N.I., Alfarizi, M. (2024). Psycho-social conditions of urban communities in the complexity of waste management: Are awareness and waste banks the main solution? *Socioecon. Plann. Sci., 93*, 101834. [http://dx.doi.org/10.1016/J.SEPS.2024.101834]

Sutisna, M.A.R. (2024). Strategi pengelolaan sampah kota terintegrasi menuju zero waste. *Waste Handling and Environmental Monitoring, 1*, 41-50. [http://dx.doi.org/10.61511/whem.v1i1.2024.631]

Saragih, Y., Hidayat, R., Hadikusuma, R.S. (2023). Community perspective on the waste management system in lambangsari bekasi village based on smart garbage robots. *Jurnal Ilmiah Global Education, 4*, 482-487. [http://dx.doi.org/10.55681/jige.v4i2.570]

Schlegel, M-C., McAlister, C., Rama, M. (2024). *Pioneering durability in electronics - the role of standardisation in policymaking and vice versa. electronics goes green 2024.* EGG.

Schuster, S., Geier, S. (2022). CircularWOOD - Towards circularity in timber construction in the german context. *IOP Conf. Ser. Earth Environ. Sci., 1078* [http://dx.doi.org/10.1088/1755-1315/1078/1/012030]

Sunaryo, Tjitrosoemarto BA. Integrated ship recycling industrial estate design concept for indonesia. *IOP Conf. Ser. Earth Environ. Sci., 972.* [http://dx.doi.org/10.1088/1755-1315/972/1/012042]

United nations environment programme. legal limits on single-use plastics and microplastics: a global review of national laws and regulations 2018.

Wahyu Maesarini, I. (2023). Dynamics of local government policy in waste management in indonesia. *Iapa Proceedings Conference.*

Waluyo, Kharisma DB. Circular economy and food waste problems in indonesia: lessons from the policies of leading countries. *Cogent Soc. Sci., 9.* [http://dx.doi.org/10.1080/23311886.2023.2202938]

Whalen, K. (2020). *Circular business models that extend product value going beyond recycling to create new circular business opportunities..* Lund University.

Yang, M., Chen, L., Wang, J., Msigwa, G., Osman, A.I., Fawzy, S., Rooney, D.W., Yap, P.S. (2023). Circular economy strategies for combating climate change and other environmental issues. *Environ. Chem. Lett., 21*, 55-80. [http://dx.doi.org/10.1007/s10311-022-01499-6]

Zhang, N., Gruhler, K., Schiller, G. (2023). A review of spatial characteristics influencing circular economy in the built environment. *Environ. Sci. Pollut. Res. Int., 30*, 54280-54302. [http://dx.doi.org/10.1007/s11356-023-26326-5]

CHAPTER 4

Government Policies Towards a Circular Economy: The Indian Experience

Mona Mahecha[1], **Sanya Yadav**[2,*] and **Karolina Wilamowska**[3]

[1] *Faculty of Law, Manipal University, Jaipur, Rajasthan, India*

[2] *School of Law, Bennett University, Greater Noida, Uttar Pradesh, India*

[3] *Business Attorney and Mediator, Poland*

Abstract: In today's unsustainable era, the circular economy is the solution to address several pressing and interconnected challenges in sustainable development. The circular economy offers significant potential for advancing various Sustainable Development Goals (SDGs), specifically SDG 7, SDG 8, SDG 11, SDG 12, SDG 13, SDG 14, and SDG 15. The swift economic expansion and urban development in India have resulted in notable challenges, including resource depletion, environmental degradation, and a rise in waste generation. The Indian Government has taken significant measures to tackle this urgent issue by transitioning to a circular economy. Among these measures are the creation of the Circular Economy Cell within NITI Aayog and the introduction of specific policies and plans to increase productivity while decreasing waste. In the process of transitioning to the Circular Economy, which promotes waste reduction, proper disposal, recycling, and sustainable resource management, India has implemented programs such as the Swachh Bharat Mission, Jal Jeevan Mission, and Vehicle Scrapping Policy. A Circular Economy differs from conventional recycling initiatives by focusing on the redesign of products for durability, promoting reuse and remanufacturing, and creating closed-loop systems to reduce waste and resource extraction.

Keywords: Action policies, Circular Economy Cell (CE Cell), Circular economy, Environment, Extended Producer Responsibility (EPR), Indian policies, Linear production, NITI aayog, SDG 12, SDGs, Sustainable consumption, Sustainable development goals, Waste management.

INTRODUCTION

The swift economic expansion and urbanization in India have resulted in considerable challenges, including resource exhaustion, environmental

* **Corresponding author Sanya Yadav:** School of Law, Bennett University, Greater Noida, Uttar Pradesh, India; E-mail: sanyayadav87@gmail.com

degradation, and increased waste generation. A development model that optimizes resource utilization is urgently required. The circular economy is an economic system that organizes production methods around the reuse and recycling of inputs to minimize environmental emissions while promoting sustainable and eco-friendly production practices. It serves as a crucial mechanism in addressing the environmental crisis through the encouragement of material reuse. It additionally promotes the effective use of expired products to mitigate their adverse effects on the environment. It promotes the responsible utilization of natural resources and prolongs the lifespan of environmentally hazardous products, including plastics and various electronic devices. We mostly depend on Linear production models, which consist of extraction, production, consumption, and disposal. However, this model is not sustainable for the planet. In the circular economy, raw materials are kept for longer in production cycles and can be used again and again, which greatly reduces waste and makes production and consumption more sustainable (Mhatre *et al.*, 2020). This model fundamentally aims to retain resources within the economy for extended periods, thereby enabling the utilization of generated waste as raw materials for other industries. Consequently, the CE has emerged as a progressively significant domain within economics in recent years (Alnajem *et al.*, 2020). The circular economy is founded on three core principles: eliminating waste and pollution through design, maintaining products and materials in circulation at their highest value, and restoring natural systems (Knäble *et al.*, 2022).

India is experiencing a significant shift from a linear economic model to one that emphasizes recycling, serving as a precursor to the more advanced concept of a circular economy. This transformation is occurring as a result of various influences, including policy measures, corporate initiatives, technological advancements, and public engagement. Circular Economy is also important for achieving SDG 12, *i.e.*, Sustainable Consumption and Production.

NEED FOR CIRCULAR ECONOMY

The global statistics on domestic material consumption per capita, categorized by type of raw material, indicate that in 2000 it was 9.22 tonnes, while in 2022 it increased to 12.04 tonnes. The consumption rate in India was 3.65 tonnes in 2000 and increased to 5.76 tonnes in 2022 (United Nations Environment Programme, 2024). From 116 million tonnes in 2022, fiber production reached a record 124 million tonnes in 2023. If present trends continue, global fiber production is predicted to reach 160 million tonnes by 2030, up from 58 million tonnes in 2000. The overall proportion of recycled fibers experienced a minor decline in 2023, dropping from approximately 7.9% to 7.7%. This shift is due to the rise in fossil-based polyester production, which was cheaper than recycled polyester. From

2022 to 2023, the amount of fossil-based synthetics made went up from 67 million tonnes to 75 million tonnes. Less than 1% of the global fiber market came from pre- and post-consumer recycled textiles (Textile Exchange, 2024). The major portion of materials extracted for economic use consists of virgin resources, while the contribution of secondary materials has been on a consistent downward trajectory since the inception of the Circularity Gap Report's measurements: decreasing from 9.1% in 2018 to 7.2% in 2023, just five years later (Circle Economy Foundation, 2023). The global consumption of some of the most widely used materials is projected to rise significantly in the coming decades. From 2018 to 2030, global plastic consumption is projected to rise by 4.1 percent. Subsequently, from 2030 to 2050, it is projected that global plastic consumption will rise by 2.4 percent (Statista, 2024) .

UN EFFORTS TOWARDS CIRCULAR ECONOMY

UNEA 4. Resolution 1 (UNEP/EA.4/Res.1) articulates that a circular economy embodies an emerging sustainable economic framework. This framework emphasizes the intentional design of products and materials for reuse, remanufacturing, recycling, or recovery, thereby ensuring their sustained presence within the economy alongside the resources from which they originate. This strategy seeks to eliminate or lessen the production of waste, especially hazardous waste, while simultaneously curbing or diminishing greenhouse gas emissions (United Nations, 2019). UNEA 5. Resolution 11 (UNEP/EA.5/Res.11) promotes the incorporation of innovative methodologies to attain sustainable production and consumption, wherein products and materials are engineered for reuse, remanufacturing, recycling, or recovery, thereby prolonging their presence in the economy alongside their constituent resources. It emphasizes avoiding or minimizing waste generation, particularly hazardous waste, and preventing or reducing greenhouse gas emissions (United Nations Environment Assembly, 2022).

The UNEP circularity platform outlines its scope and how it promotes sustainable consumption and production. UNEP Executive Director Inger Andersen asserts that circularity, along with sustainable consumption and production, is crucial for the realization of all multilateral agreements, including the SDGs, the Paris Agreement, and the post-2020 global biodiversity framework (United Nations Environment Programme, 2024).

In 2015, UN Trade and Development (UNCTAD) began its exploration of the circular economy by collaborating with the Ellen MacArthur Foundation, concentrating on the resource-circularity opportunities within significant economies like India and China. Circularity has been incorporated into various initiatives within UNCTAD, encompassing actions aimed at tackling fossil fuel and fisheries subsidies. UNCTAD supports the circular economy by promoting conversations and projects that aim to find value in waste streams, encouraging dialogue on collaborative economy sectors, looking at new business models, raising consumer awareness, and encouraging them to change their lifestyles. UNCTAD collaborates with various international organizations to advance the circular economy at both national and multilateral levels, thereby serving the international community on this critical issue (UNCTAD, 2025).

SDGS AND CIRCULAR ECONOMY

The Circular Economy (CE) entails advocating for the responsible and cyclical utilization of resources, which may facilitate the attainment of SDGs (Moraga *et al.*, 2019). The CE is increasingly recognized by policymakers, corporations, and governments as a means to attain the SDGs set by the UN in 2015 (Dantas *et al.*, 2020) .

The circular economy aligns with SDG 12 by emphasizing the effective utilization of resources, reducing waste, and encouraging sustainable consumption practices. The manufacturing processes within a circular model focus on enhancing product longevity, reparability, and recyclability, which naturally results in decreased resource extraction and waste generation. In this way, other Sustainable Development Goals can also be achieved, which include clean water and sanitation (SDG 6) and climate action (SDG 13). Through the design of products that prioritize longevity and reusability, industries have the potential to significantly address pressing global issues such as water scarcity, environmental degradation, and greenhouse gas emissions (Sustainable Development Goals Resource Centre, 2025). Other SDGs which can be aligned with the circular economy are SDG 8, as the circular economy has potential for job creation and economic growth, and SDG 9, which is related to Industry, Innovation and Infrastructure. As the circular economy will reduce the carbon footprint, it will also align with the SDG 14 (Life below water) and SDG 15 (Life on Land).

The principles of a circular economy contribute to the attainment of SDG 11 (sustainable cities and communities) by reducing waste, increasing resource efficiency, and strengthening urban resilience. To lessen the negative effects on the environment and reduce emissions of greenhouse gases, the circular economy encourages a transition away from fossil fuels and toward renewable energy sources. This aligns with the goals that were established under SDG 7, which focuses on energy that is both affordable and clean. Since it emphasizes the importance of collaboration, cooperation, and multi-stakeholder partnerships to promote the implementation of circular economy principles, the circular economy plays a significant role in the advancement of Sustainable Development Goal 17 (SDG 17). The circular economy significantly contributes to the advancement of the global agenda for future generations by fostering innovation, generating new job opportunities, and promoting economic growth (Robinson, 2024). Table **1** gives a glimpse of the key factors aligned with SDGs for adopting the Circular Economy (Grant Thornton Bharat LLP, 2024a).

Table 1. Key factors aligned with SDGs for adopting circular economy (Grant Thornton Bharat LLP, 2024b).

Factor	Description	Aligned SDG	Key Points
Environmental	reducing waste and pollution; maximizing the lifespan of products and materials; and restoring natural ecosystems, resulting in a reduction in greenhouse gases.	SDG 6, SDG 7, SDG 13	• The '9R' strategies refuse, rethink, reduce, re-use, repair, refurbish, remanufacture, repurpose, recycle, recover can reduce landfill waste's environmental impact. • Recycling improves energy efficiency compared to primary production. • The Energy Transitions Commission (ETC) estimates a 55% reduction in global carbon emissions from heavy industry and transportation by 2050 through materials recirculation and energy efficiency improvements. • Circular Economy strategies offer a 39% reduction in global greenhouse gas emissions (22.8 billion tonnes). • Recycling reduces fossil fuel use and emissions by reducing virgin plastics and synthetic fibers. • Wearing garments twice as often could reduce textile industry emissions by 44%.
Economic	New Business Opportunities, Cost reduction, job creation, less plastic waste, innovation in industry, and more jobs create opportunities for education.	SDG 1, SDG 2, SDG 4, SDG 6, SDG 8, SDG 9, SDG 11, SDG 12, SDG 14, SDG 17	• Adopting the Circular Economy can increase resource efficiency, create value from byproducts and waste, and lower treatment and disposal costs. • Compliance with ISO Standards and the EU Circular Economy Action Plan encourages material circulation, efficiency, and sustainable growth. • The Circular Economy presents a USD 4.5 trillion opportunity by reducing waste, fostering innovation, and creating jobs. • Circular business offers innovation opportunities. • Reducing plastic pollution benefits fishing, tourism, affordable healthcare, and climate change mitigation. • Shifting to a Circular Economy could generate a net addition of 6 million jobs by 2030. • Employment opportunities in recycling, repair, rental, and novel secondary material utilization. • Formalizing employment and enhancing conditions for informal laborers (*e.g.*, waste pickers) yields safer and more secure job opportunities.

(Table 1) cont.....

Factor	Description	Aligned SDG	Key Points
Market	Recognition of ecological concerns among consumers and the increasing demand for circular or sustainable products	SDG 12	• increased consumer awareness of environmental issues and demand for green initiatives. • Consumers demand products that adhere to Circular Economy principles, shaping market trends and prompting companies to embrace sustainable practices.
Regulatory	Legislation and regulations that promote the implementation of a Circular Economy	SDG 16	• EPR holds manufacturers accountable for their products' entire lifespan. • Product design and eco-design regulations encourage longer lifecycles, easy disassembly, and recyclable or renewable materials. • Waste management regulations integrate Circular Economy goals by setting targets for waste reduction, recycling, and proper disposal.
Population	Trends in population growth and urbanization	SDG 15	By 2050, the world's population will reach 9 billion, with 55% living in densely populated cities. A Circular Economy emphasizes the need for sustainable resource management and waste reduction solutions.
Resource Efficiency	Optimising the utilisation of limited resources	SDG 12	• Using recycled and recyclable materials in textiles can reduce land, water, and fossil fuel usage. • Promoting second-hand and rental markets to reduce new clothing purchases and extend their use. • Recycling or reusing old clothes.
Health and Biodiversity Protection	Safeguarding human health and biodiversity	SDG 3	• Shifting to a Circular Economy reduces pollution from waste and resource extraction, protecting human health and biodiversity. • Proper collection and processing protect workers and the environment from hazardous materials. • Recycling conserves natural resources and reduces pollution.

INDIAN POLICIES TOWARDS CIRCULAR ECONOMY

India, the third-largest global consumer of raw materials, anticipates substantial material demand projections of nearly 15 billion tonnes by 2030 and potentially exceeding 25 billion tonnes by 2050. Recognizing this challenge, India is advancing towards a circular economy, anticipating considerable economic advantages: an estimated $218 billion annually by 2030 and a notable $624 billion by 2050. The Government of India is actively pursuing its net-zero objectives, with circular economy strategies being crucial (Jain, 2024). The major policies implemented by the Indian Government towards the circular economy are outlined as follows:

Regulatory Actions

1. **Solid Waste Management Rules 2016** The Government has comprehensively revised the Municipal Solid Wastes (Management and Handling) Rules 2000, subsequently notifying the updated Solid Waste Management Rules, 2016 on April 8, 2016. The 2016 regulations require the segregation of waste at the source to facilitate waste conversion into wealth through recovery, reuse, and recycling (Sambyal, 2018). The SWM Rules 2016 delineate comprehensive criteria for establishing solid waste processing and treatment facilities, managing solid waste in mountainous regions, implementing waste-to-energy processes, developing sanitary landfills, selecting sites, constructing facilities at sanitary landfills, specifying landfilling operations, and executing closure upon completion of landfilling, as well as pollution prevention, and the closure and rehabilitation of obsolete dumps (Ministry of Environment, Forest and Climate Change, 2016a).
2. **E-Waste (Management) Rules, 2016** The Ministry of Environment, Forest, and Climate Change notified the E-Waste (Management) Rules, 2022 on November 2, 2022. The new regulations replaced the E-waste (Management) Rules, 2016. The Rules 2022 establish an Extended Producer Responsibility (EPR) framework for recycling electronic waste. The rules are applicable to all manufacturers, producers, refurbishers, dismantlers, and recyclers. All manufacturers, producers, refurbishers, and recyclers must register on the CPCB portal. The E-Waste Management Rules reduce hazardous substances in Electrical and Electronic Equipment (EEE) manufacturing. EEE and component manufacturers must ensure that their products do not exceed the maximum allowable concentration of lead, mercury, or other hazardous substances. The E-Waste (Management) Rules enable recognition, registration, skill development, monitoring, and safety and health for e-waste dismantling and recycling workers. No entity may conduct business without registration and must refrain from engaging with any unregistered entity (Ministry of Environment, Forest and Climate Change, 2022a).
3. **Plastic Waste Management Rules** The Government introduced the Plastic Waste Management Rules in 2016, which replaced the earlier Plastic Waste (Management and Handling) Rules in 2011. The Plastic Waste Management Rules, 2016, outline the responsibilities of producers and generators within the plastic waste management framework and create a collection system for plastic waste by producers and brand owners, which is in line with extended producer responsibility. The collection of a plastic waste management fee is required through the pre-registration of producers, importers of plastic carry bags and multilayered packaging, and vendors selling these items to support the waste management system. Furthermore, the regulations promote the use of plastic waste in road construction in accordance with Indian Road Congress guidelines

or for energy recovery and conversion to oil, thus tackling waste disposal issues. Additionally, there are increased obligations placed on waste producers, which encompass the payment of user fees as established by local governing bodies, as well as the collection and transfer of waste by institutional generators and event coordinators. Manufacturers of plastic products and packaging must fulfill their Extended Producer Responsibility (EPR) commitments, including recycling targets and integrating recycled plastic materials (Ministry of Environment, Forest and Climate Change, 2016b). The Plastic Waste Management Amendment Rules, 2021, have established a legal framework for the Guidelines for Extended Producer Responsibility, which are currently being formulated to ensure the successful execution of EPR (Ministry of Environment, Forest and Climate Change, 2021). On February 16, 2022, the Plastic Waste Management (Amendment) Rules 2022 issued the Guidelines on Extended Producer Responsibility (EPR) for plastic packaging. The Guidelines set mandatory targets for EPR, plastic packaging waste recycling, rigid plastic packaging reuse, and recycled plastic content. The guidelines encourage sustainable plastic packaging and reduce its plastic footprint. Under the Swachh Bharat Mission, the Indian Government provides supplementary central assistance to States and Union Territories for solid waste management, including plastic waste management, in urban and rural areas (Ministry of Environment, Forest and Climate Change, 2023a).

4. **Batteries (Management and Handling) Rules** The Battery Waste Management Rules, 2022, were published by the Ministry of Environment, Forest and Climate Change, Government of India, on August 24, 2022, aiming to ensure the environmentally sound management of waste batteries. This represents a significant advancement in the genuine promotion of a Circular Economy. The regulations established in 2022 superseded the Batteries (Management and Handling) Rules from 2001. The regulations operate under the principle of Extended Producer Responsibility (EPR), which mandates that producers, including importers, of batteries take on the responsibility for the collection and recycling or refurbishment of waste batteries, as well as the incorporation of recovered materials from these wastes into new batteries. The regulations encourage establishing new industries and fostering entrepreneurship in the collection and recycling or refurbishment of waste batteries (Ministry of Environment, Forest and Climate Change, 2022b). The rules were again amended on October 25, 2023, and March 14, 2024. The amended rules provide the minimum percentages of recycled materials mandated in the total dry weight of different battery types for the forthcoming fiscal years. These standards are intended to progressively elevate, propelling the industry towards enhanced sustainability (Ministry of Environment, 2024).

5. **Mines and Minerals Development & Regulation Act 1957** The MMDR Act, 1957, underwent significant amendments in 2015 aimed at reforming the mineral sector. Key changes included the introduction of an auction method for granting mineral concessions to enhance transparency in resource allocation, the establishment of the District Mineral Foundation (DMF) to support the welfare of communities impacted by mining, and the creation of the National Mineral Exploration Trust (NMET) to promote exploration, alongside implementing strict penalties for illegal mining activities. The Act underwent additional amendments in 2016 and 2020 to tackle specific emerging issues, with the most recent changes made in 2021. These reforms eliminated the distinction between captive and merchant mines, transferred statutory clearances to maintain mining operations despite lessee changes, lifted mineral concession transfer restrictions, and allowed non-auctioned concession holders' rights to lapse if they have not led to mining leases. Private sector concessions are only awarded through auction. The Act promotes effective and accountable mining methods, facilitating the recycling of minerals (Ministry of Mines, 2023).

The Ministry of Environment, Forest and Climate Change has introduced waste management regulations pursuant to the Environment (Protection) Act, 1986, aimed at the environmentally sound management of waste, these includes - "(i) Solid Waste Management Rules, 2016; (ii) Plastic Waste Management Rules, 2016; (iii) Bio-medical Waste Management Rules, 2016; (iv) Construction and Demolition Waste Management Rules, 2016; (v) Hazardous and Other Wastes (Management and Transboundary Movement) Rules, 2016. (vi) E-Waste Management Rules, 2022, (vii) Battery Waste Management Rules, 2022." Of the total waste generated, approximately 150,000 metric tons per day in urban areas, around 76% is processed. In 2022, pursuant to applicable waste management regulations, Extended Producer Responsibility (EPR) utilizing a market mechanism was implemented for the environmentally sound management of plastic packaging waste, electronic waste, waste tires, battery waste, and used oil (Ministry of Environment, Forest and Climate Change, 2023b).

EPR represents a strategic framework that reallocates the duty of addressing the environmental consequences of products across their entire lifecycle, from consumers to producers. The Ministry of Environment, Forest and Climate Change (MoEFCC) has implemented Extended Producer Responsibility (EPR) regulations for multiple waste categories, such as electronics and electrical equipment, plastics, batteries, tyres, and pharmaceuticals. The purpose of these regulations is to ensure that producers take responsibility for managing the waste generated by their products after consumption. This initiative promotes the adoption of sustainable practices and supports the development of a circular economy (Corpzo, 2023). The regulatory framework for EPR in India involves a range of policies, rules, and guidelines that delineate the roles and responsibilities of various stakeholders. Important policies and guidelines have been discussed above.

Action Policies

1. **Efforts by NITI Aayog** As mentioned in the press release of NITI Aayog on 18th March 2021, to facilitate the shift of the country from a linear to a circular economy, eleven committees have been established. To speed up India's transition from a linear to a circular economy, eleven separate committees are formed under the leadership of the appropriate line ministries. These committees comprise representatives from the MoEFCC and NITI Aayog alongside domain experts, academics, and business representatives. The focal points include – "municipal solid and liquid wastes, scrap metal (ferrous and non-ferrous), lithium-ion (Li-ion) batteries, tyre and rubber recycling, gypsum, end-of-life vehicles, electronic waste, toxic and hazardous industrial waste, used oil waste, agriculture waste, and solar panels" (NITI Aayog, 2021). The Circular Economy Cell (CE Cell) was established in NITI Aayog in September 2022 as a specialized unit focused on advancing the principles of the Circular Economy. The main activities involve coordinating with stakeholder Ministries and Departments to implement the Circular Economy action plans. In collaboration with the Ministry of Road Transport and Highways (MoRTH), CE Cell has undertaken various initiatives, including the operationalization of the Vehicle Scrapping programme and the formulation of a strategy for the disposal of unfit and outdated Central and State Government Vehicles. The planned initiatives for the next financial year include the creation of a detailed Mission Document focused on Circular Economy, the development of an interactive Dashboard to track progress across various aspects of Circular Economy, and enhancing collaboration with States (NITI Aayog, 2025). NITI has developed a Circular Economy Action Plan for Li-ion Batteries. The action plan has considered the different lifecycles of batteries, encompassing manufacturing, usage, collection, dismantling, reuse, and recycling processes (NITI Aayog, 2022).
2. **Swachh Bharat Mission** In India, approximately 55 million tonnes of Municipal Solid Waste is produced each year by 377 million individuals living in urban regions. The urban population of India is projected to reach 600 million by 2030 and 814 million by 2050. India is projected to produce 165 million tonnes of waste by 2030 and 436 million tonnes by 2050. The annual greenhouse gas emissions from Municipal Solid Waste are projected to reach 41.09 million tonnes by 2030 (Mitigation Action Facility, 2024). The Government has been diligently developing policies and advancing projects to

propel the nation towards a circular economy. In the domain of municipal solid and liquid waste, numerous policies and regulations (like Solid Waste Management Rules 2016, Plastic Waste Management Rules 2016, Construction and Demolition Waste Management Rules 2016, Policy on Promotion of City Compost, National Faecal Sludge and Septage Management Policy 2017) have been established to promote the scientific processing of waste and facilitate resource recovery. The circular economy agenda concerning municipal solid and liquid waste gained substantial momentum at the national, state, and city levels following the initiation of the Swachh Bharat Mission-Urban (SBM-U) in 2014. The initiative, grounded in the 3R principles (reduce, reuse, recycle), has effectively enhanced urban India's solid waste treatment capacity from 18% in 2014 to 68% in 2021 (including recycling). Numerous success stories exist, with states such as Chhattisgarh achieving zero-landfill status and cities like Indore implementing 100% source segregation of waste (Ministry of Housing & Urban Affairs, 2022a). The Swachh Bharat Mission has notably enhanced the circular economy in India. Household waste is being transformed into compost, biogas, electricity, and materials such as charcoal for road construction. Numerous biogas plants have been established in various villages as part of the Gobardhan Yojana, utilizing animal waste for biogas production (Prime Minister's Office, 2024).

3. **Jal Jeevan Mission (Urban)** Jal Jeevan Mission (Urban) is announced in the Union Budget 2021-22, with the aim to ensure universal water supply coverage to all households *via* functional taps in all 4,378 statutory towns, in alignment with Sustainable Development Goal 6. JJM(U) is advocating for a circular economy of water by formulating a city water balance plan for each municipality, emphasizing the recycling and reuse of treated sewage, the restoration of water bodies, and the conservation of water resources. Twenty percent of water demand is satisfied through the utilization of reclaimed water, facilitated by the establishment of an institutional framework (Ministry of Housing and Urban Affairs, 2021). This model aligns with the Five "R"s framework for water management reduce, reuse, recycle, restore, and recharge and encompasses the complete water value chain, from supply to consumers to the disposal of wastewater. The JJM-U emphasizes the formulation of three plans: the City Water Balance Plan, the City Wastewater Recycling Plan, and the City Aquifer Management Plan (Jainer, 2021).
4. **AMRUT Scheme** The Atal Mission for Rejuvenation and Urban Transformation (AMRUT) was initiated on June 25, 2015, targeting 500 selected cities and towns nationwide. The initiative emphasizes the enhancement of fundamental infrastructure in designated cities and towns, targeting areas such as water supply, sewerage and septage management, stormwater drainage, green spaces and parks, as well as non-motorized urban

transport. The Mission incorporates a series of Urban Reforms and Capacity Building initiatives. AMRUT Mission has been integrated into AMRUT 2.0, which commenced on 01st October 2021. The initiative aims to enhance the circular economy of water by developing a City Water Balance Plan (CWBP) for each city, emphasizing the recycling and reuse of treated sewage, the rejuvenation of water bodies, and water conservation efforts. This initiative will assist urban areas in pinpointing opportunities for initiatives aimed at achieving universal access to functional water tap connections, conserving water sources, revitalizing water bodies and wells, recycling and reusing treated wastewater, and implementing rainwater harvesting practices. Drawing from the projects outlined in CWBP, the Mission aims to achieve 'water security' in cities by implementing a circular economy approach to water management (Ministry of Housing & Urban Affairs, 2022b).

5. **Vehicle Scrapping Policy** The Vehicle Scrappage Policy was introduced on August 13, 2021. The policy aims to mitigate vehicular air pollution in India, where the transport sector accounts for 14%, by systematically phasing out outdated and unfit vehicles in a sustainable way (Law, 2021). In August 2024, the Ministry of Road Transport and Highways introduced the Voluntary Vehicle Modernization Program, also known as the Vehicle Scrapping Policy, aimed at establishing a framework for the systematic removal of unfit, polluting vehicles nationwide. This initiative will be supported by a network of Registered Vehicle Scrapping Facilities (RVSFs) and Automated Testing Stations (ATSs). Currently, there are over sixty RVSFs operating across 17 States and UTs, along with more than seventy-five ATSs in 12 States and UTs, with additional facilities planned for the future (Ministry of Road Transport & Highways, 2024). The Central Government has issued certain policies for Vehicle Scrappage (Paul, 2023a). "Automotive Industry Standard–129 on End-of-Life Vehicles (AIS-129) b. Guidelines for Environmentally Sound Facilities for Handling, Processing, and Recycling of End-of-Life Vehicles (ELV), 2019 c. Motor Vehicles (Registration and Functions of Vehicle Scrapping Facility) Rules, 2021.
6. **Steel Scrap Recycling Policy, 2019** The Government announced the Steel Scrap Recycling Policy in November 2019. The policy establishes a framework to encourage the creation of metal scrapping centres in India for the scientific processing and recycling of ferrous scrap from diverse sources and to promote the circular economy in the steel sector (Ministry of Steel, 2019). The establishment of scrapping centres by Public Sector Units or Private Sector entities is determined by commercial factors. The Ministry of Road Transport and Highways (MoRTH) and the Ministry of Environment, Forest and Climate Change (MoEF and CC) play a significant role in the execution of the Steel Scrapping Policy. The Ministry of Road Transport and

Highways (MoRTH) has established the Vehicle Scrapping Policy, which incorporates a framework of incentives and disincentives aimed at developing an ecosystem for the decommissioning of older, unfit, and polluting vehicles. The Ministry of Environment, Forest and Climate Change (MoEF and CC) has issued the Hazardous and Other Wastes (Management and Transboundary Movement) (HOWM) Rules, 2016, to guarantee the secure storage, treatment, and disposal of hazardous and other wastes in an environmentally sound manner, preventing detrimental impacts on the environment and human health (Ministry of Steel, 2023).

7. **Financing for MSMEs** The Ministry of Micro, Small, and Medium Enterprises inaugurated two sub-schemes under the RAMP Programme on December 20, 2023: (i) the MSE Green Investment and Financing for Transformation Scheme (MSE GIFT Scheme) and (ii) the MSE Scheme for Promotion and Investment in Circular Economy (MSE SPICE Scheme). The MSE Green Investment and Financing for Transformation Scheme (MSE GIFT Scheme) aims to assist MSMEs in adopting green technology through interest subvention and credit guarantee support. The primary aim of the initiative is to assist Micro and Small Enterprises (MSEs) in obtaining institutional financing at preferential rates for the adoption of clean and green technologies, thereby facilitating their transition to environmentally sustainable business practices. The MSE Scheme for Promotion and Investment in Circular Economy (MSE SPICE Scheme) is the inaugural initiative by the Government of India to endorse circular economy projects. The principal objective of the initiative is to foster resource efficiency, mitigate environmental impact, and augment the competitiveness of micro and small enterprises in India (Ministry of Micro, Small & Medium Enterprises, 2024).
8. **The National Solar Mission** To advance the development of solar energy in the nation, the National Solar Mission (NSM) was initiated in January 2010, under which the Government has periodically introduced various schemes (Ministry of New and Renewable Energy, 2023). This is a significant governmental initiative involving state participation to foster ecologically sustainable development while tackling India's energy security issues. The objective of this mission is to position India as a global leader in solar energy by formulating policy conditions that facilitate the dissemination of solar technology nationwide (Yadaw & Umar, 2024).
9. **SEBI ESG Reporting** SEBI has mandated that companies disclose their Environmental, Social, and Governance (ESG) performance to reduce greenwashing. These guidelines require organizations to disclose their environmental and social policies, performance metrics, risks, and operational framework and practices. These principles aim to help investors understand a

company's ESG performance and make better investments. These regulations provide transparency and accountability, helping organizations improve ESG results (Rao, 2024).

10. **Sovereign Green Bonds** The Indian Government plans to issue Sovereign Green Bonds (SGrBs) as a component of its larger market borrowings aimed at funding green initiatives. The generated revenue will be designated to fund public sector initiatives focused on decreasing the economy's carbon intensity (Sharma *et al.*, 2023).
11. **India Circular Economy Forum (ICEF) 2024** The India Circular Economy Forum (ICEF) 2024 is an annual knowledge platform designed to facilitate significant advancements in the Circular Economy sector in India. The forum aims to enhance awareness of circular economy practices among policymakers, industry leaders, and the general public. It functions as a platform for collaboration among enterprises, governmental bodies, and academic institutions to promote circular economy initiatives. Annually, the forum emphasizes a particular theme; this year's concentration was on Innovation, Technology, and business models that foster circularity, showcasing successful case studies and exemplary practices. The forum promotes policy frameworks that enable the transition to a circular economy, in accordance with SDGs (Leleu, 2024). The Government of India has joined the Global Alliance for Circular Economy and Resource Efficiency (GACERE), which seeks to collaborate with governmental and non-governmental organizations to promote a global and equitable transition to a circular economy and enhance the sustainable management of natural resources. The Government of India is a participant in the Steering Committee of the International Resource Panel (IRP). The Panel seeks to deliver independent, cohesive, and authoritative scientific evaluations pertinent to policies regarding the sustainable utilization of natural resources (Ministry of Environment, Forest and Climate Change, 2024).

In the past decade, startups have established themselves as essential catalysts in transforming the Indian circular economy through digitization and technological innovations, effectively addressing challenges and promoting societal growth. Additionally, there is an intensified emphasis on creating novel materials, technologies, and business models that enhance sustainability and mitigate environmental impact (Jain *et al.*, 2024). Governments have access to a range of tools to promote the swift adoption of circular economy principles. These encompass regulatory mandates, market-driven incentives like subsidies, taxes, or cap and trade systems, compensation for the improvement of vital ecosystem services such as soil recarbonization, and informational campaigns aimed at promoting voluntary actions (Fiksel *et al.*, 2020).

CHALLENGES IN TRANSITIONING TO CIRCULAR ECONOMY

A major issue is the technological gap, which obstructs the implementation of innovative solutions for sustainable practices. There is an absence of comprehensive data to guide and facilitate strategic decisions during this transition. Another concern is the inefficiency within the waste management sector. India possesses a substantial informal sector engaged in waste collection and disposal, with many participants lacking awareness of circular economy principles. Consequently, numerous waste collectors and recyclers resort to the most rudimentary and frequently contaminating methods of waste disposal, including incineration or landfill dumping. Principles of the circular economy must be incorporated into the waste management sector, and waste collectors and recyclers should be educated on circular practices and their contributions to the circular economy (Sarma *et al.*, 2023).

The regulatory framework is essential in influencing the circular economy. Despite India's advancements in regulations such as Plastic Waste Management and e-Waste Management, regulatory obstacles continue to exist. Effective execution of streamlined regulations is crucial for promoting the economy (Dematdive, 2023). Organisations that operate according to the linear business model receive subsidies, taxes, and other forms of government assistance. Regrettably, the situation is the opposite when an organisation attempts to implement the principles of the circular economy (Gechbaia *et al.*, 2023).

Lack of awareness in respect of the circular economy is also a key issue. A circular economy necessitates a collaborative endeavor among all stakeholders to effectuate systemic transformation in the design, production, consumption, and disposal of goods and services. The lack of a multi-stakeholder approach may hinder knowledge dissemination and the exchange of best practices. In the absence of collaboration, businesses and government entities may lack the resources necessary to invest in circular infrastructure, technologies, and research and development. Insufficient collaboration at the policy level may lead to contradictory policies and regulations, thereby undermining circular practices and obstructing the transition to a circular economy. Conversely, a lack of connection with consumers and NGOs may restrict consumer participation in circular practices.

Personnel constitute the biggest barrier to the transition process. Presently, they lack understanding of the circular economy's principles. Also, they lack the necessary skills for this process. They are unable to participate in the process unless the organizations provide pertinent support for CE during the initiation and implementation phases. This is the sole method by which it is feasible to implement novel business models. This process is even more challenging for small businesses, as they require additional financial resources and organizational support. When it comes to environmental concerns, companies are primarily motivated by rationality (Brendzel-Skowera, 2021).

Culture is also a significant challenge. The perceptions of individuals are diverse, and this perception is further influenced by their life experiences and the skills they have acquired. The market is undergoing such rapid transformations that it is exceedingly challenging to make predictions. The pandemic served as the most illustrative example of the potential for unforeseen circumstances to alter the course of events. In these circumstances, adaptation is proceeding at a glacial pace. The issue of a decrease in the number of highly qualified employees is being confronted, which can be regarded as one of the primary obstacles. Additionally, seasonality is the most significant obstacle to the circular business model, particularly in agriculture and related sectors. The second issue that warrants attention is the absence of collaboration between rural Small and Medium-sized Enterprises (SMEs) and other sectors. While there are states and organizations that encourage innovation, their primary focus is on medium and large companies, rather than Small and Medium-sized Enterprises (SMEs). Consequently, they are experiencing financial difficulties. This situation is primarily experienced by non-agricultural companies (Atstaja *et al.*, 2022). Lack of “green” suppliers is another issue (Rizos *et al.*, 2016).

CONCLUDING REMARKS

India's swiftly advancing market and significant developmental potential can confer a competitive edge over established economies. The Indian market's strengths and stakeholder collaboration could accelerate sustainable and resilient prosperity in the circular economy's long-term vision. The advancements that are made in the circular economy will not only make urban and agricultural economies more resilient, but they will also offer several benefits, such as the reduction of climate change, the assurance of food and water security, the enhancement of biodiversity, the creation of jobs, and the empowerment of marginalized communities. It is necessary to execute a roadmap in a methodical and comprehensive manner to make the transition to a circular economy. The net-zero future is an imperative that will influence every facet of our daily existence. Start-ups will have various opportunities while integrating waste management in the design phase to support a circular economy and enhance sustainability.

The circular economy in India is predominantly in its infancy. Industries may struggle to identify suitable partners for collaboration and to successfully transition to a circular business model without a comprehensive strategy and planning. Pioneering organizations are surmounting the challenges of this transformation by employing an experimental methodology alongside substantial investments, commitments, and partnerships. Resultantly, these organizations, aided by cross-sector collaborations, will become pioneers, acquiring valuable experience and facilitating informed decision-making for sustainable circular growth. Corporations must engage in cross-learning within their industry while also supporting academia to foster the innovation essential for this transition. Moreover, the industry must collaborate with the Government, which is prioritizing India's transition to a circular economy. Ultimately, the Government and industry must promote and integrate circular consumption and service approaches within society. This will ultimately facilitate the transition of businesses and the nation towards a circular economy.

REFERENCES

Alnajem, M., Mostafa, M.M., ElMelegy, A.R. (2020). Mapping the first decade of circular economy research: a bibliometric network analysis. *Journal of Industrial and Production Engineering, 38*(1), 29-50. [http://dx.doi.org/10.1080/21681015.2020.1838632]

Alhilali, S., Arora, R., Chowdhury, N., Creyts, J. Ruiz, Mrs., Vesper, H., Jääskeläinen, A., Verri, Sr., Perez, C. I., Steinmann, J., Veldhoven, S. V., Rijn, D., & Rivas, M. (2023). The Circularity Gap Report, 2024. In Circularity Gap World. Circle Economy Foundation. Retrieved December 9, 2024, from https://reports.circularity-gap.world/cgr-global-2024-37b5f198/CGR+Global+2024+-+Report.pdf

Aayog, N.I.T.I. (2021, March 18). Govt Driving Transition from Linear to Circular Economy [Press release]. https://pib.gov.in/PressReleasePage.aspx?PRID=1705772#:~:text=To%20expedite%20the%20transition%20of,focus%20areas%20(Annexure%201)

Aayog, N.I.T.I. (2022). Annual Report 2022–23. https://www.niti.gov.in/sites/default/files/2023-02/Annua--Report-2022-2023-English_1.pdf

Atstaja, D., Cudecka-Purina, N., Hrinchenko, R., Koval, V., Grasis, J., Vesere, R. (2022). Alignment of circular economy business models for framing national sustainable economic development. *Acta Innovations, 42*, 5-14.
[http://dx.doi.org/10.32933/actainnovations.42.1]

Brendzel-Skowera, K. (2021). Circular economy business models in the SME sector. *Sustainability, 13*(13), 7059.
[http://dx.doi.org/10.3390/su13137059]

Circular Economy, (2025). Sustainable Development Goals - Resource Centre. https://sdgresources.relx.com/circular-economy-0

Corpzo, (2023, October 11). The Role of EPR in India's Circular Economy Journey. Corpzo. https://www.corpzo.com/extended-producer-responsibility-epr-in-india-paving-the-way-for-a-circular-economy#:~:text=The%20implementation%20of%20EPR%20has,the%20use%20of%20hazardous%20materials

Circular Economy Cell | NITI Aayog. (2025.) https://www.niti.gov.in/circular-economy-cell

Dematdive. (2023, December 13). Indian Circular Economy: Key Challenges and Opportunities in 2024 and Beyond. Dematdive. https://dematdive.com/circular-economy/

Dantas, T., De-Souza, E., Destro, I., Hammes, G., Rodriguez, C., Soares, S. (2020). How the combination of Circular Economy and Industry 4.0 can contribute towards achieving the Sustainable Development Goals. *Sustainable Production and Consumption, 26*, 213-227.
[http://dx.doi.org/10.1016/j.spc.2020.10.005]

Fiksel, J., Sanjay, P., Raman, K. (2020). Steps toward a resilient circular economy in India. *Clean Technol. Environ. Policy, 23*(1), 203-218.
[http://dx.doi.org/10.1007/s10098-020-01982-0]

Gechbaia, B., Maisuradze, T., Paresashvili, N., Goletiani, K., Gvarishvili, L. (2023). Challenges and barriers in transition to circular economy business models. E3S Web of Conferences, 408, 01016.

Grant Thornton Bharat, L.L.P. (2024). *Envisioning Future of Circular Economy in India.* https://campaign.grantthornton.in/l/991702/2024-08-01/393n2/991702/1722503629NoJgNiS7/Envisioning_Future_of_Circular_Economy_in_India_7727_v2.pdf

India – Waste Solutions for a Circular Economy - Mitigation Action Facility. (2024). Mitigation Action Facility. https://mitigation-action.org/projects/india-waste-solutions-for-a-circular-economy/

Jain, P. (2024). https://www.outlookbusiness.com/opinions/india-embraces-circular-economy-for-sustainable-future-news-418241

Jainer, S. (2021). *Parched Cities of India: Jal Jeevan Mission as a Ray of Hope for.* https://wri-india.org/pt/blog/parched-cities-india-jal-jeevan-mission-ray-hope-urban-water-resilience

Jain, A., Trivedi, A., Kapoor, P., Deb, A., Gupta, D., Mahan, K., Bhalla, S.G. (2024). *Startups Accelerating Circular Economy for Sustainable Bharat.* https://www.chase-india.com/media/qqfc0xyh/startu--accelerating-circular-economy-report-revised.pdf

Knäble, D., De Quevedo Puente, E., Pérez-Cornejo, C., Baumgärtler, T. (2022). The impact of the circular economy on sustainable development: A European panel data approach. *Sustainable Production and Consumption, 34*, 233-243.
[http://dx.doi.org/10.1016/j.spc.2022.09.016]

Law, I. (2021). https://www.mondaq.com/india/rail-road-cycling/1111528/national-vehicle-scrappage-policy-advancing-automotive-circular-economy-in-india#:~:text=What%20is%20the%20National%20Vehicle,in%20an%20environment%2Dfriendly%20manner

Leleu, G. (2024). *The Road to Circularity: Key Insights on the Transition to a Circular Economy in India.*

Mhatre, P., Panchal, R., Singh, A., Bibyan, S. (2020). A systematic literature review on the circular economy initiatives in the European Union. *Sustainable Production and Consumption, 26*, 187-202.
[http://dx.doi.org/10.1016/j.spc.2020.09.008]

Moraga, G., Huysveld, S., Mathieux, F., Blengini, G.A., Alaerts, L., Van Acker, K., De Meester, S., Dewulf, J. (2019). Circular economy indicators: What do they measure? *Resour. Conserv. Recycling, 146*, 452-461.
[http://dx.doi.org/10.1016/j.resconrec.2019.03.045]

Paul, A. (2023). *Vehicle Scrappage Policy in India.* https://www.teriin.org/sites/default/files/2023-08/1692266855Policy%20Brief%20Vehicle%20Scrappage%20in%20India.pdf

Rao, A. (2024). *ESG Reporting Mandates in India: Guidelines for Businesses.* https://www.india-briefing.com/news/esg-reporting-mandates-in-india-guidelines-for-businesses-34217.html/

Rizos, V., Behrens, A., Van Der Gaast, W., Hofman, E., Ioannou, A., Kafyeke, T., Flamos, A., Rinaldi, R., Papadelis, S., Hirschnitz-Garbers, M., Topi, C. (2016). Implementation of Circular Economy Business Models by Small and Medium-Sized Enterprises (SMEs): Barriers and Enablers. *Sustainability, 8*(11), 1212.
[http://dx.doi.org/10.3390/su8111212]

Robinson, C. (2024). *Advancing the Global Agenda through adopting Circular Economy.* https://sdg-action.org/advancing-the-global-agenda-through-adopting-circular-economy/

Sambyal, S.S. (2018). *Government notifies new solid waste management rules.* https://www.downtoearth.org.in/waste/solid-waste-management-rules-2016-53443

Sharma, A., Sharma, N. (2023). https://globalcompact.in/wp-content/uploads/2023/08/Sustainable-Circul-r-Economy-1.pdf

Sarma, S.P., Bhalla, S.G., Kumar, M. (2023). https://eacpm.gov.in/wp-content/uploads/2023/07/17-Indis-Tryst-with-a-Circular-Economy.pdf

Statista, (2024, May 24). *Global consumption growth rate of selected materials 2018-2050.* https://www.statista.com/statistics/1114860/global-consumption-growth-rate-selected-materials/

Yadaw, P.K., Umar, M.M. (2024). Unleashing India's Solar Potential: A Review of the National Solar Mission and the Path to Sustainable Energy in India. *Journal of Technology Innovations and Energy, 3*(2), 49-63.
[http://dx.doi.org/10.56556/jtie.v3i2.930]

Ministry of Environment. (2016). *Forest and Climate Change.* https://pib.gov.in/newsite/printrelease.aspx?relid=138591k

Ministry of Environment. (2022). *Forest and Climate Change.* https://pib.gov.in/PressReleasePage.aspx?PRID=1881761

Ministry of Environment. (2016). *Forest and Climate Change.* https://pib.gov.in/newsite/printrelease.aspx?relid=138144

Ministry of Environment. (2021). *Forest and Climate Change.* https://pib.gov.in/PressReleaseIframePage.aspx?PRID=1745433

Ministry of Environment. (2023). *Forest and Climate Change.* https://pib.gov.in/PressReleasePage.aspx?PRID=1909909

Ministry of Environment. (2022). *Forest and Climate Change.* https://pib.gov.in/PressReleasePage.aspx?PRID=1854433

Ministry of Environment. (2024). http://www.indiaenvironmentportal.org.in/content/476868/ battery-wast--management-amendment-rules-2024/

Ministry of Mines. (2023). https://pib.gov.in/PressReleasePage.aspx?PRID=1945102#:~:text=The%20Act%20was%20further%20amended,operations%20even%20with%20change%20of

Ministry of Environment. (2023). *Forest and Climate Change.* https://pib.gov.in/PressReleaseIframePage.aspx?PRID=1986203

Ministry of Housing & Urban Affairs. (2022). https://pib.gov.in/PressReleasePage.aspx?PRID=1885837

Ministry of Road Transport & Highways. (2024). https://pib.gov.in/PressReleasePage.aspx?PRID=2049367

Ministry of Steel. (2019). https://pib.gov.in/newsite/PrintRelease.aspx?relid=194359

Ministry of Steel. (2023). https://pib.gov.in/PressReleaseIframePage.aspx?PRID=1907157

Ministry of Micro. (2024). *Small & Medium Enterprises.* https://pib.gov.in/PressReleseDetail.aspx?PRID=2035103&reg=3&lang=1

Ministry of New and Renewable Energy. (2023). https://pib.gov.in/PressReleasePage.aspx?PRID=1983208#:~:text=The%20Union%20Minister%20for%20New,schemes%20from%20time%20to%20time

Ministry of Environment. (2024). *Forest and Climate Change.* https://www.pib.gov.in/PressReleasePage.aspx?PRID=2003989

Ministry of Housing and Urban Affairs. (2021). https://pib.gov.in/Pressreleaseshare.aspx?PRID=1694420

Prime Minister's Office. (2024). https://pib.gov.in/PressReleasePage.aspx?PRID=2061052

Textile Exchange. (2024). *Materials Market Report.* https://textileexchange.org/app/uploads/2024/09/Materials-Market-Report-2024.pdf

United Nations. United Nations. (2019). *Resolution adopted by the United Nations Environment Assembly on 15 March 2019. In United Nations Environment Assembly of the United Nations Environment Programme.* https://documents.un.org/doc/undoc/gen/k19/010/42/pdf/k1901042.pdf

United Nations Environment Assembly. (2022). https://wedocs.unep.org/bitstream/handle/20.500.11822/39920/ENHANCING%20CIRCULAR%20ECONOMY%20AS%20A%20CONTRIBUTION%20TO%20AC

HIEVING%20SUSTAINABLE%20CONSUMPTION%20AND%20PRODUCTION.%20English.pdf?sequence=1&isAllowed=y

United Nation Environment Programme. (2025). https://www.unep.org/circularity

UNCTAD. (2025). *Circular Economy*. https://unctad.org/topic/trade-and-environment/circular-economy

United Nations Environment Programme. (2024). *Domestic material consumption per capita.* https://ourworldindata.org/grapher/domestic-material-consumption-per-capita

CHAPTER 5

Community-based Waste Management and Societal Impact: Utilizing Demand Side Management for Sustainable Transformation of Solid Waste Management

Ankit Tiwari[1,*], **Akash Kumar Shukla**[1], **Tej Singh**[2] and **Deepak Rathod**[3]

[1] *Department of Electrical Engineering, Madhav Institute of Technology & Science, Gwalior, Madhya Pradesh, India*

[2] *Centre of AI, Madhav Institute of Technology & Science, Gwalior, Madhya Pradesh,India*

[3] *Department of Electrical and Electronics Engineering, Shri Vaishnav Institute of Technology and Science, Shri Vaishnav Vidyapeeth Vishwavidyalaya, Indore, Madhya Pradesh, India*

Abstract: Solid waste management is a global issue due to urbanization and changing lifestyles. Current solutions are inefficient, especially in developing countries like India. Demand Side Management (DSM) can help control waste production. A multidisciplinary approach, including reduction campaigns, recycling programs, variable waste collection charges, and smart waste monitoring systems, can reduce environmental impact and promote sustainable practices. Mathematical analysis can evaluate the efficacy of these DSM-inspired interventions. This paper explores the application of Demand-Side Management (DSM) principles in Solid Waste Management (SWM), focusing on strategies like waste reduction campaigns, incentivized recycling programs, variable waste collection charges, and smart waste monitoring systems. The study evaluates the efficacy of these DSM-inspired interventions, highlighting their potential to revolutionize SWM by optimizing resource use, minimizing environmental impact, and promoting responsible consumer behavior.

Keywords: Circular economy, Demand-side management, Recycling, Smart cities, Societal impact, Solid waste management, Waste collection.

INTRODUCTION

The everyday creation of wasted products has emerged as one of the most pressing worldwide concerns in light of the aspirational reimagining of humanity,

* **Corresponding author Ankit Tiwari:** Department of Electrical Engineering, Madhav Institute of Technology & Science, Gwalior, Madhya Pradesh, India; E-mail: ankittiwariiitb@gmail.com

Theodore Tarnanidis, Vijaya Kittu Manda, Vivek Gupta (Eds.)

particularly when a significant portion of it is improperly managed. Approximately 2 billion tree-sized masses are produced annually by the planet. On a yearly basis, the municipal solid waste commodity reaches up to 1 billion tonnes, with at least 33% of this considered environmentally mishandled (World Bank, 2018). It is predicted that this volume shall multiply up to a million in the next few years. About 40 billion tonnes estimated for 2050 raises a huge problem, which poses a major threat to various aspects of human life. A lot of researchers have indicated the destructive public health effects of wrong and unwise ways of dealing with waste management.

Proper waste management *via* disposal and recycling methods is essential to avoid air, water, and land pollution. Overall, solid waste-related emissions can grow up to 2%. According to the World Bank (World Bank, 2018), such commitment could double the releases of CO_2 till 2050 (2 billion tons of CO_2 by 2050). What is more, air pollution and dialectical groundwater and ocean plastics are caused by the inappropriate waste processing ways (Skenderovic *et al.*, 2015). Very often, this disorder of poor drainage is accompanied by an undefined pollution of surfaces, which is usually due to the uncontrolled passing of liquid wastes and sewage facilities (Lestari & Trihadiningrum, 2019).

There are adjacent issues with waste management that follow from this, once the wastes are left unattended. Problems related to improper waste collection sites, like laborers who work for their living, navigating waste, are the most vulnerable groups. These people are exposed to a variety of infections from parasites and enteric infections, which may occur as a result of waste being mishandled. The health of these people therefore deteriorates with a rise in some diseases that are associated with waste processing (Giusti, 2009).

Lastly, in a way that is similar to the influence of the absence of efficient waste disposal systems, the economy suffers losses as well. Inappropriate waste handling of some sort immediately affects the tourism and hospitality industry (Zorpas *et al.*, 2015), due to the stress it places on the landscape and on the tourist sites. Sustainable waste management through conventional and unsuitable methods in the long run will dedicate the usable land areas, making it possible to build structures, resulting in a high level of economic losses to the countries concerned (Skenderovic *et al.*, 2015).

Sustainable waste management offers an interesting solution, which not only considers but also helps solve the problems caused by the illegal disposal of waste. Proper management of waste can catch such a valuable resource, since the major role of the solid waste is the recovery of energy for recycling and production purposes (Demirbas, 2011). Besides, energy recovery, frequently known as waste-to-energy, prevents waste and supports environmental and human condition associations by the usage of waste energy as fuel (Brunner & Rechberger, 2015). In matters of ecology and the well-being of human beings, however waste management is managed, a properly chosen waste management has proven to be an indispensable tool when it comes to environmental protection and working towards the maximum utilization of resources (Izvercian & Ivascu, 2015).

The current approach to waste management in the circular economy is limited and fragile, with resource recovery primarily through global recycling networks. The potential of the circular economy to move from a linear to a circular economy is highlighted, with fruit by-products being valorized through antioxidant extract production. The circular economy can reduce food loss and waste, contribute to resource conservation, and optimize the consumption chain of materials and waste. However, there are knowledge gaps, including empirical research on practical implementation and social, economic, and policy implications of transitioning to a circular economy approach. Thus, the current experience with waste management in a circular economy does present a range of difficulties and missed opportunities, and the dependence on the global recycling network for resource utilization is certainly a significant part of them. Although it is a relatively recent development, the circular economy is already revealing its potential to transform various approaches prescribed by the linear model of "take-make-dispose", while there remains a lot to be explored and improved as well. Digitalization's potential for waste prevention, reduction, reuse, and recycling is also explored. Here are some areas in waste management and the circular economy that require further study and development:

1. **Resource Recovery and Valorization**: Think about the possibility of applying the novel methods for upcycling, *i.e.*, obtaining antioxidants from the vegetable by-products. This converts a wasted facility into a revenue generator and economic resources stream and promotes conservation.

2. **Food Loss and Waste Reduction**: The Circular economy offers a route to improve the system of input and waste production by optimizing material and resource circulation. These responsibilities can be best achieved by bringing up the levels of supply chain efficiency, distribution of excess food, and setting sustainable patterns of consumption.

3. **Knowledge Gaps and Practical Implementation:** In addition to the advantages, there are many issues that need to be addressed along the way to shift towards the circular economy model. An experimental investigation is necessary

to get insight into the problems associated with the real implementation of this step change, as well as the social, economic, and policy issues it is connected to.

4. **Digitalization and Waste Management:** With digitalization solutions, there is a great possibility to turn waste management upside down by efficient planning and implementation of waste avoidance, waste reduction, recycling, and waste re-use. Yet, innovations like IoT, keeping track of waste, optimization of routes and incline, even material recovery and recycling, will continue with the blockchain.

On the whole, implementing the circular economy style will offer an opportunity to handle challenges and promote resource efficiency. In order for the circular model to be effective, challenges have to be addressed, and solutions implemented. Therefore, it thinks of work across all the disciplines, investment in development and research department, concern for the policies and regulations, and implementation of innovations and technologies sectors, as well as business models. By doing problem-solving and creating opportunities, we can achieve a close to eco-friendly and robust waste management system within this circular economy framework.

Demand-Side Management (DSM) strategies can be applied to waste management to optimize resource utilization, reduce environmental impact, and improve efficiency. Demand-Side Management (DSM) has always had a pivotal position in current energy systems, as it largely provides us with the ability to use energy resources in a proper and economical manner. DSM provides energy consumers with an opportunity to manage their energy consumption in ways that can be adjusted when there are specific circumstances (for example, the energy prices are experiencing some fluctuations or the energy supply is stressed) The DSM will move the energy consumption into non-peak hours and also reduce the energy demand completely during the high grid stress-time in a way that the energy use will be optimized and the waste will be largely minimized. Often, in an electricity system, the balance between demand and supply needs to be kept to maintain the security of the electricity grid and its reliability. DSM promotes the capability of adjusting the demand of less expensive electricity to more expensive times to reduce the cost of purchase. In this type of situation, the buyer will benefit because they purchase electricity at less expensive times. Therefore, the distribution of energy supply when many different sources are involved reduces the risk of congestion in the grid, prevents blackouts, and facilitates the use of existing infrastructure, as no excess capacity is needed. The integration of variable renewables (solar and wind) actually becomes more challenging with their accelerated deployment. As DSM techniques are implemented, such as demand response, energy storage, and smart grid technologies, these are all tools that aid in addressing the intermittency and variability of renewable energy generation by coupling energy consumption with moments of high renewable output. The demand for electricity is normally at its highest during the peak periods, and the price of the energy and the stress on the grid are usually at their highest. Consumers can buy at lower prices and also save themselves from further costs, leading to the building of new expensive generation plants through the deployment of DSM strategies such as demand response programs and time-of-use pricing, which aim to reduce peak demand. Through DSM, energy efficiency measures are articulated and overseen, from consumers' energy efficiency endeavors such as buying energy-efficient appliances, effective building energy management systems, and adopting energy-saving practices. The process of DSM mitigates overall consumption of energy, which consequently cuts down emissions of greenhouse gases; thus, it improves air quality and impacts climate change negatively. Using the information provided through real-time usage data, energy saving tips, or incentives for demand response programs are some of the ways in which consumers' informed choices on when and how they use the energy lead to increased energy savings. Predominantly, DSM is meant to be an essential factor of the implementation of an advanced, steady, and eco-friendly energy system for the sake of both customers and society. Through DSM Strategies, technologies, and investments, we can attain a sustainable, reliable, and secure energy future while simultaneously providing environmental reductions, promoting a sustainable economy, and improving quality of life.

DSM helps consumers increase their energy consumption, resulting in cost savings and consumer engagement. These strategies include peak load shifting, variable pricing, waste reduction incentives, smart technologies, education and outreach, collaboration, policy support, and regular monitoring and evaluation. Incentives for waste reduction include source reduction, reuse, composting, and purchasing products with minimal packaging. Smart technologies like IoT sensors and data analytics can optimize waste collection routes and schedules. Education campaigns, collaboration with businesses and local governments, and policy support can also help promote sustainable waste management practices. Similarly, as the DSM systems have already worked wonders in managing and controlling consumer energy assets, the same holds great potential for learning in managing the optimum generation and disposal of solid wastes. The actions applied in DSM are preventive, with the achievement of a constant enhancement of energy efficiency. SWM concerns can therefore be handled by applying DSM techniques, which are connected with energy management. There are two main types of DSM mechanisms:

1. Demand-Response (DR): DR techniques are post activities designed to ensure users change their electricity consumption in a variable manner and in response to information obtained from utilities or the grid. These signals could be changes in price or calls for help in an emergency due to problems in the grid. DR strategies are indispensable to mitigate exigencies as blackouts and avoid overcrowded demand at a certain period by negotiating user behavior.

2. Demand-Side Management (DSM): While DSM strategies are aimed at Demand-Side Reduction (DSR), DSM techniques are more about convincing consumers to use electricity more efficiently over a longer period. These methods are designed to create consistent, more permanent behavioral modifications regarding energy usage rates. DR and DSM strategies are often combined with each other in order to fulfill more general energy management goals.

This brings some reasons why the DSM program should be implemented and promoted. Among them are:

1. Cost-Cutting: DSM activities are known to reduce the operating costs of a facility by a significant percentage through the reduction of energy costs and trash disposal fees. By applying the best energy practices and the approved waste management systems, companies are able to solve their energy bill problems and therefore eliminate the problems associated with the implementation of the waste disposal polices.

2. Environmental and Social Improvement: The society gets an added advantage in that DSM initiatives can be entrusted with waste management strategies that minimize further negative impact on the environment, and at the same time foster bonding of the society. DSM has provided users with a platform to spend less energy and then recollect and regenerate constituents, which is vital for the reduction of pollution, the conservation of resources, and finally, better environmental characteristics.

3. Reliability and Network Optimization: The DSM could be used effectively in enhancing the reliability and efficiency of energy networks for end-use since it has the potential to achieve the maximum energy for appropriate waste management. By controlling the peak demand, DSM managers contribute to the reduction of the load on the grid, and increase its stability to prevent failures such as blackouts or other mistakes in the frequencies.

4. Market Enhancement: With the means of DSM measures, we offer an opportunity for ideas to develop and competitions to be constructive, and we enhance the energy and waste management sectors. Therefore, by subsidizing various energy conservation measures, the democratization of the use of renewable energy technologies, as well as performance improvement of the DSM providers, the market both deepens and is made more secure.

DSM can, thus, be said to be effectively grounded on sound policy that is indispensably useful given overall resource utilization, sustainability, and significant waste and energy concerns. Such organizations can gain the fruits of DSM, like cost-cutting, protection of the environment, website functionality, and market reach that will finally ensure that they are part of creating a better future, which is not only sustainable but also resistant.

Literature Review

Due to the impacts associated with S.W.M., both on the natural environment and human health, it has received international attention. Recyclable waste and emission of greenhouse gases are just a few environmental issues caused by the conventional waste management practices. Thus, sustainable and environmental methods of managing solid wastes to sustain the earth's environment should be searched for intensively. In order to discuss the current tendencies and investigate further directions in the sphere of solid waste management research, the current literature review tries to include and briefly discuss recent works concerning waste management and DSM.

The Approach of the Circular Economy

A promising way of reducing the environmental impacts of solid waste is through the application of the circular economy. The net benefits of a waste reduction programme include the following: Implementing methods of saving the environment from pollution, encouraging the development of sustainable civilization, and building an efficient society through eradicating water and land pollution (GHG emissions) and saving natural resources (Wilson *et al.*, 2007; Tchobanoglous, 2009). Introducing new approaches for the selection of the solid waste disposal sites, (Kahraman *et al.*, 2017) emphasize the application of the intuitionistic fuzzy EDAS method. Also, (Campos *et al.*, 2020) presented a case on circular economy solution to the management of fruit industrial by-products showing that waste materials can be beneficially reused in the industry. According to (Gregson *et al.*, 2015), the circular economy waste management is narrow and fragile in the current Anglophone context, and the management of wastes as ›resources‹ is dominated by international recycling networks. This result stresses that there is a need to develop better and comprehensive strategies for the enhancement of resource utilisation within the circular economy concept. To their credit, (Rosenboom *et al.*, 2022) successfully demonstrate how a shift from a linear to a circular economy can be accomplished by producing antioxidant extracts to further enhance the value of fruit by-products. This describes a new way of disposing of waste within the ambit of the circular economy and opens up the idea of actually making value out of waste products. (Singh & Ordóñez, 2016) focused on how the circular economy leads to saving natural resources and reducing greenhouse gas emissions when reducing food loss and waste in the food supply chain. This research raises awareness of further impacts on sustainability and the environment consequent of amalgamating circular economy concepts to waste management regimes. Moreover, it has the potential to metamorphose the circle of consumption for technical and biological material and redesign the industrial supply chain, as quoted by (Fatimah *et al.*, 2020). This means an integrated approach to waste management corresponding to the principles of the circular economy.

New opportunities for optimizing solid waste management procedures arise with the help of the latest technologies, including nanotechnologies. In a dialogue with the European Commission about nanotechnology uses in agriculture and farming, Fraceto *et al.* have described how nanomaterials may help to promote diverse concepts of sustainable agriculture and improve the methods of waste treatment (Fraceto *et al.*, 2016). Martín-Ríos *et al.* opined that open innovation efforts can be both strategically and economically improved in a company through technological improvement that will enable the calculation and minimisation of wastes in collaboration with other companies (Martín-Ríos *et al.*, 2018). Voluntary initiatives also serve a long-term explicit public interest of enhancing the sustainability of the food service industry and help in minimizing wastage. In addition, writing about advancements in the field of smart technologies for managing food waste, Martín-Ríos, Hofmann, and Mackenzie underscored the importance of focusing on sustainability in changes that occur in the management of food waste, pointing out that there are still many practical and affordable solutions to be found in the field of waste management (Martín-Ríos *et al.*, 2020). That is why the research results by Martín-Ríos, Hofmann, and Mackenzie (Martín-Ríos *et al.*, 2020) and Martín-Ríos *et al.* (Martín-Ríos *et al.*, 2018) show the effectiveness of outsourcing partners and collaborations with other organizations to benefit from changes in technology in waste management. Such kinds of alliances provide firms with technologies and information on novel ways of enhancing waste management.

Sustainable food systems cannot be totally understood without referring to waste management, with innovation being the key aspect. As mentioned by Herrero *et al.*, to mitigate waste generation and disposal in the food production and supply chain requires a systems approach (Herrero *et al.*, 2020). They also embraced innovation as a way of advancing the change for a sustainable food system. Food losses and waste have received a lot of attention and are recognized as being important both for the future sustainability of the planet and food security. Crippa *et al.* stated that the environmental consequences of food loss or food waste account for one-third of the food produced for human consumption globally

(Crippa *et al.*, 2021). This shows why it is important to reduce FLW to enhance food security as well as reduce the impact of food systems on the environment. In addition, Connolly-Boutin and Smit call for the integration of ecologically sound waste management systems as part of an adequate food system by pointing out that while sewage/sludge/biosolids can be regarded as polluted, they can also be a good source of organic materials to enrich the soil and enhance crop productivity (Connolly-Boutin & Smit, 2016). Hence, strategies from circular business models have emerged as answers to challenges created by food loss and waste. According to Zucchella and Previtali, circular principles are important to develop sustainable food systems as well as for appropriate waste management (Zucchella & Previtali, 2018). They stress the centrality of the circular economy networks where the focal actor is embedded, and in particular, multi-stakeholder networks, such as suppliers, customers, research institutions, and public agencies. According to Tripathi *et al.*, control of biomass waste in food processors and the use of agro-wastes from different producers to produce carbon-free products are emphasized (Tripathi *et al.*, 2019).

Knickmeyer pointed out that sustainably feeding the world's growing population is not possible without compromising the three pillars of sustainable development goals and Global Food Safety Partnership: sustainable, availability, and quality (Knickmeyer, 2020). This underlines the need to enhance the output of food production while trying to reduce wastage in order to enhance food security, as well as to develop goals of sustainable development. To enhance the profile of food security and environmental sustainability, Shafiee-Jood and Cai passionately support the reduction of food loss and waste (Shafiee-Jood & Cai, 2016). They also shed light on how the formal organizations that seek to handle waste and the informal sector address this challenge. Circular economy approaches are now being increasingly adopted as measures towards the standardization of climate change and various issues of solid waste management. Several scholars, including Yang *et al.* (Yang *et al.*, 2023) and Tiwari and Sharma (Tiwari & Sharma, 2024), have pointed out that circular economy approaches can help in the overall aim of resources and waste management and should therefore be of major concern in addressing environmental problems. In their subsequent detailed discussion of the strategies regarding building design and construction for a circular economy, Eberhardt *et al.* discuss how sustainable architectural practices contribute to resource utilisation and the minimisation of waste. Strategies for the circular economy based on digitalization provide new possibilities to reconsider the approaches to solid waste management (Eberhardt *et al.*, 2019). Following the lead of authors such as Kurniawan *et al.*, the use of technology in supporting sustainable and circular approaches toward waste management can be ascertained, with the possibility of digitalization acting as a catalyst in the enhancement of the SWM in China (Kurniawan *et al.*, 2022).

Demand Side Management Review

Demand side management, or DSM for short, is an important element in the overall management of energy resources and ensuring that there will be efficient use of energy in several areas, such as residential, commercial, and industrial. Another crucial aspect of the system in modern energy systems is linking energy storage systems and variable behind-the-meter renewable energy systems with demand side management (Bird *et al.*, 2013). In the present literature review, we endeavour to review and compile the current research findings on demand side management strategies and technologies to emphasize the future research directions.

Today, the smart grid is based on Demand-Side Management (DSM) programs that enable energy providers to mitigate the peak load demand and redesign load patterns, as well as support consumers in making an adequate decision regarding electricity consumption (Mohsenian-Rad *et al.*, 2010). Thanks to the increase in the demand for electricity and the advanced concept of smart grids, Home Energy Management Systems (HEMS) can further reduce electricity consumption today (Pop *et al.*, 2018). Nevertheless, interactions between the utility company and its consumers are at the center of the current DSM programs, and more user-drivers are demanding decentralized and self-organized demand-side systems (Mohsenian-Rad *et al.*, 2010). Energy management aims at controlling the complexity of energy, the demand side of which has been gaining more attention from industry and research over the supply side (Mohsenian-Rad *et al.*, 2010). Similarly, among the important targets of the research community in recent years is another effective technique of energy management known as Model Predictive Control (MPC) (Zenginis *et al.*, 2018). Moreover, heuristic optimization has also been studied to obtain a solution for demand-side management for smart grids (Logenthiran *et al.*, 2012).

In addition, Pop *et al.* have identified a promising area for future research: the possibility of decentralized management of demand response programs in smart energy grids through blockchain technology (Pop *et al.*, 2018). However, there are still gaps in our knowledge regarding the best ways to incorporate blockchain technology into demand-side management systems and how it might affect reliability and energy efficiency. According to Vardakas *et al.*, future studies should concentrate on creating and assessing sophisticated algorithms and pricing strategies for demand response programs in smart grids (Zenginis *et al.*, 2018). To address the growing demand for electricity and the difficulties presented by smart grid technologies, more research into autonomous and distributed demand-side energy management systems among users is also required, as is the development of HEMS (Mohsenian-Rad *et al.*, 2010; Pop *et al.*, 2018).

Demand Side Management (DSM) plays an important part in today's energy frameworks; it helps manage the precise use of paraphernalia. In doing so, this literature review aims at systematising and, thereby, synthesising prior research findings on a broad range of topics associated with DSM and to generate an overview that underlines the significance and challenges of DSM research alongside research topics that could be investigated in the future. In conclusion, the research outlets on DSM provide utilitarian data on a variety of tactics, challenges, and opportunities in order to intensify energy efficiency and enhance the reliability of the systems. For the development of DSM further, further research should focus on closing the gap in knowledge and on how the combination of DSM with new technologies and regional factors could be achieved. Based on the literature review, the paper finds that demand-side management is also a vital component for smart grid future planning. It also highlights possible directions for continued research, such as the development of distributed and automated demand response systems, the use of advanced algorithms and innovative pricing models, and the exploration of the applicability of distributed ledger technology to the operation of demand response programs on a decentralized basis using blockchain. These directions for further study will allow for maximizing the energy system and deploying demand-side management in smart grids in the optimum manner.

Circular Economy Gaps and DSM as a Strategic Complement

Through material reduction, reuse, and recycling, the 7 (CE) encourages resource efficiency. Nevertheless, it frequently underestimates the dynamics of trash generation and consumer behaviour. By providing control over consumption patterns through pricing signals, feedback systems, and smart technology, DSM enhances CE. A strong framework for flexible, community-focused SWM systems is produced by coordinating CE and DSM, which addresses inefficiencies as well as sustainability objectives.

By providing proactive control over consumption habits through pricing signals, feedback systems, and smart technology, DSM enhances CE. DSM techniques, such as demand response and time-of-use pricing, were first created in energy systems and can be similarly used for the production and handling of solid waste. Waste output can be modulated, for instance, by offering incentives for waste reduction, dynamic pricing for waste pickup, and real-time bin monitoring.

New developments in Solid Waste Management (SWM) have not received much attention in the literature, especially when it comes to the environmental effects and hazards of cutting-edge technologies like nanotechnology. The development of sophisticated multi-criteria decision-making models that Integrate Demand-

Side Management (DSM) strategies, circular economy concepts, and sophisticated digital technologies is urgently needed. SWM systems can be made much more sustainable by including circular economy techniques like resource valuation, waste-to-energy conversion, and closed-loop production systems. Furthermore, particularly in developing nations, there is a clear knowledge vacuum about the socioeconomic effects of switching to SWM practices driven by the circular economy. Thus, in order to support effective, fair, and ecologically conscious waste management, future research should also investigate the creation of integrated mathematical models that incorporate DSM tactics with circular economy frameworks.

Methodology

The creation of mathematical models to evaluate and enhance different facets of waste management procedures is part of the Demand Side Management (DSM) integrated solid waste management mathematical modelling framework. The Description of the Mathematical Modelling Framework for DSM-Integrated Solid Waste Management:

The methodology for developing the mathematical model for DSM-integrated solid waste management involves several key steps:

Defining the Model

We suggested two mathematical models, and these model takes into account variables including population density, waste generation rates, pricing schemes, and incentives in order to optimize the waste collection, recycling, and disposal processes and technical innovation. The model aims to optimize waste management efficiency, encourage recycling, and minimize costs through the creation of mathematical formulas and algorithms.

Model 1:

Let's define the following variables:

a. Total waste generated at time t in the city: w (t) (in tons).

b. Total waste collected at time t in the city: cl(t) (in tons).

c. Total waste recycled at time t in the city: r(t) (in tons).

d. Total waste disposed of at time t in the city: d (t) (in tons)

e. Price of waste disposal/recycling at time t in the city: p(t) (in rupees per ton).

f. Incentive provided for waste reduction or recycling at time t in the city: i(t)

g. Time Period: T (*e.g.*, hours, days, months, years)

Mathematical Modelling:

The following equations can be used to represent the mathematical model:

The rate of waste generation over time is represented by the function f(t), and it is represented by Equation (1). This function might be dependent on economic activity, population growth rates, historical data, *etc.*

(i) Waste Generation:

$$\frac{dw(t)}{dt} = f(t) \tag{1}$$

(ii) Waste Collection:

$$cl(t) = x \times w(t) \tag{2}$$

where,

The fraction of waste generated that is collected is denoted by x. This is predicated on an ongoing collection efficiency.

(iii) Waste Recycling:

$$r(t) = y \times cl(t) \tag{3}$$

where y is the recycling rate, or the percentage of waste collected that is recycled.

(iv) Waste Disposal:

$$d(t) = (1 - y) \times cl(t) \tag{4}$$

The remainder of the waste that has been collected is disposed of.

(v) Cost of Waste Management:

$$C(t) = p(t) \times d(t) - i(t) \times r(t) \tag{5}$$

The difference between the money received from the disposal of waste and the incentives offered for recycling is the cost of waste management at time t.

The goal is to optimize waste management strategies like pricing, incentives, and recycling rates in order to maximize the total cost savings over the entire duration of the project.

Therefore,

$$Maximize \int_0^t C(t)dt \tag{6}$$

This mathematical model offers a framework for evaluating the efficacy of various DSM waste management techniques. It can be expanded upon and improved upon in accordance with particular requirements, limitations, and goals pertinent to the waste management system under study.

Model 2 (Fragmented modelling):

Extended parameters

h. Number of waste collection zones(transfer station):n

i. Total waste collected in zone z at time t (in tons): clz(t)

j. Total waste recycled in zone z at time t (in tons): rz(t)

k. Total waste disposed of in zone z at time t (in tons): dz(t)

l. Price of waste disposal in zone z at time t (in currency per ton): pz(t)

m. Incentive provided for waste reduction or recycling in zone *z* at time *t* (in currency per ton): iz(t)

n. Area of zone z (in square kilometers): az

o. Density of population or waste generators (in persons or businesses per square kilometer): Dz

p. Maximum capacity for pricing adjustment: kc

q. Maximum capacity for incentive adjustment: kr

Let's now determine the waste management factors for every zone (fragmented model/modified model):

(vi) Waste Generation:

$$\frac{dw(t)}{dt} = \sum_{z=1}^{n} Dz \times az \tag{7}$$

The area of each zone and the population density both affect the rate of waste generation.

(vii) Waste Collection:

$$clz(t) = x \times w(t) \times \frac{az}{\sum_{z=1}^{n} az} \tag{8}$$

Each zone's waste collection is based on the overall amount of waste produced and its area.

(viii) Waste Recycling:

$$r(t) = y \times clz(t) \tag{9}$$

Each zone's collected waste has some recycled material.

(ix) Waste Disposal:

$$d(t) = (1 - y) \times clz(t) \tag{10}$$

Each zone's residual portion of collected waste is disposed of.

(x) Pricing and Incentives:

$$\mathrm{pz(t)} = \mathrm{p(t)} \times \left(\frac{clz(t)}{kc}\right) \tag{11}$$

$$\mathrm{iz(t)} = \mathrm{p(t)} \times \left(\frac{rz(t)}{kr}\right) \tag{12}$$

The goal is to optimize waste management strategies like pricing, incentives, and recycling rates in order to maximize the total cost savings over the entire duration of the project.

Therefore,

(xi) Objective Function:

$$Maximize \int_0^t \sum_{z=1}^{n} Cz\,(t)dt \tag{13}$$

A framework for examining DSM tactics adapted to waste management in the context of smart cities is provided by this mathematical model. It can be improved and expanded to include more elements, limitations, and goals particular to the city's waste management program and sustainability objectives.

These sets of equations offer a foundational structure for expressing the DSM-integrated solid waste management mathematical model. To fully capture the intricacy of the waste management process, more equations and parameters might be added, contingent upon particular goals, limitations, and system dynamics.

DISCUSSION

By applying the concept of Demand Side Management (DSM), which has previously been successfully applied in the field of utilities and energy systems, the problems associated with solid waste management can be solved. However, unlike utilities, where demand is dictated by patterns of usage, goods that become solid waste are consumed and later deemed useless or discarded. Hence, accurate, quick prediction of solid waste generation is a critical factor in planning and designing the MSWM systems of any municipality or urban area. A realistic approach for achieving accurate prediction, design, and planning of solid waste generation is through the use of the DSM methodologies. Since waste generators have the most control over solid waste management decisions, waste policies and price signals are then potent shapers of consumer choice. Some of the DSM tools, such as Time of Use rates and Real/Dynamic Time Pricing, are useful when implemented in solid waste management. The implementation of DSM approaches into SWM can be eased by integrating market-like decision-making into the activity. Furthermore, DSM also offers smart metering and decision-making characteristics that could apply to optimise solid waste management processes. For informing and expressing feedback on the current tariff systems, new and structured tariff systems, including the frequency-based tariffs, variable can tariffs, and pre-paid bag or sticker tariffs, varieties can be used with Web-based or communication solutions. These models and DSM techniques will help municipalities to progress sustainability, optimise resources, and enhance the management of solid wastes. Such actions conform to the concept of smart cities. In order to integrate DSM into solid waste management and to maximize equations 6 and 13, a number of models can be taken into consideration:

A. Waste Generator Type Model:

Description: Considering the style of living, income, family size, job status, *etc.*, it categorizes the waste generators into several types by using social and demographic attributes.

Goal: Knowledge about waste generator groups' traits and behaviors will help to tailor waste management strategies to each group and serve their needs and desires. This makes it possible to start collection and removal activities of wastes geared to targeted target groups and also targets the diffusion of information, and awareness creation activities.

B. Model of Waste Generated Type:

Description: The waste generated type model is intended to classify the waste by categories according to the type of waste and its composition. They include organic waste, recyclable waste, special waste, and non-recyclable waste.

Goal: The purpose of this model is to assist the waste management authorities in scheduling the collection, recycling, and disposal procedures by categorizing wastes. It also allows the efficient development of departmentalized plants and recycling methods aimed especially at recycling certain types of waste to increase the resource yield and minimize the hazardous effects on the external environment.

C. Model of Waste Repository Type:

Description: This model is intended to seek, distinguish, recognize, or categorize several kinds of dump-like, landfill, recycling, composting, and transfer stations.

Goal: Local waste management authorities could develop strategies for utilizing these structures effectively by applying parameters determined with this model, promoting the knowledge of capacities and peculiarities of various kinds of waste repositories. It enables efficient resource provision and efficient determination of waste transportation channels to ensure efficient implementation of the waste management protocols.

D. Waste Collection Type Model:

Description: The waste collection type model defines the routes and exact dates for waste collection based on such parameters as population density, geographic location, and the rates of waste production.

Goal: This model reduces vehicle emissions, the utilization of fuel, and costs associated with waste collection through enhancing efficiency in route picking and schedules. It reduces noise from homes and businesses whilst ensuring proper, reliable, and timely waste collection services.

E. Waste Transportation Model:

Description: The aim of this model is to provide a means of cheap and effective transport of waste from the collection centre to processing or disposal centres.

Goal: The aim of this model is to reduce waste haulage expenditure, carbon footprint, and traffic nuisance by improving the efficiency of waste transport networks. It minimizes the chances of full collection points with waste that may take a long time before it is collected and moved to the processing or disposal centre.

F. Model of Waste Disposal Type:

Description: The waste disposal type model provides strategies for the disposal of waste while at the same time considering some factors such as cost and the law, as well as the effects on the environment.

Goal: This model helps the waste management authorities to compare different disposal options and thereby to make the right decision on the kind of disposal strategies that can be adopted for different kinds of wastes, like composting, incineration, and landfilling. It ensures that business organizations meet the stipulated legal requirements while minimizing the amount of damage pollution causes to the environment.

DSM in relation to solid waste management comprises of the following strategies of Demand Side Management: These are ICT and artificial intelligent tools to educate the waste generators on the available waste management methods, financing mechanism for the private sectors for waste to energy projects, schemes and incentives to encourage institutions to embrace waste management programs and incentives for new inventions and technologies on waste management innovations. The use of these methods is thus to enhance awareness, investment, and overall advancement in technological innovation in waste management. Most of these strategies entail the offering of financial incentives, thus increasing energy recovery and decreasing the use of MSW in landfills and greenhouse gas emissions. If such methodologies are embraced, can they be utilised to enhance the sustainable waste management system?

These models incorporate variables including population density, price methods, incentive programs, and trash generation rates. Maximising recycling and resource efficiency while reducing waste management expenses is the goal of the objective functions. To operationalise DSM techniques at different stages of the waste management process, six conceptual models are also presented. These frameworks for strategic planning, rather than mathematical models, offer valuable insights into the design and implementation of systems. Their extent and connection to the primary DSM goals are summed up in Table **1** above.

Table 1. Scope and Linkage to the Main DSM Objectives

Related to Math Model	Conceptual Model	Purpose	DSM Link
Model 1	Waste Generated Type	Classify waste types (organic, recyclable, *etc.*)	Targeted recycling strategies
	Waste Collection Type	Optimize routes/schedules using density and volume	Smart logistics, fuel savings
	Waste Disposal Type	Assess disposal options by cost/environmental impact	Optimal method selection
Model 2	Waste Generator Type	Categorize generators by behavior/socioeconomics	Tailored incentives, outreach
	Waste Repository Type	Map and optimize the use of landfills and composting sites	Infrastructure efficiency
	Waste Transportation	Streamline movement from source to treatment	Emission reduction, cost savings

CONCLUSION

A workable approach to solid waste management, Demand-Side Management (DSM) emphasises resource optimisation, waste reduction, and behavioural modification. It improves stakeholder collaboration and the responsiveness of the waste system. Real-time data sharing and integration with digital infrastructures are two of DSM's advantages. However, grassroots empowerment and active local engagement are necessary for DSM to be successful. DSM may greatly improve planning, forecasting, and optimisation when incorporated into SWM systems using conceptual and mathematical models. Future plans should encourage self-governance in local trash management and broaden the channels for participation. Enhancing transparency and promoting ecological responsibility can be achieved by integrating DSM with community-driven digital platforms. DSM is therefore a transformative governance model for urban sustainability as well as a technical tool.

REFERENCES

Brunner, P.H., Rechberger, H. (2015). Waste to energy: A key element for sustainable waste management. *Waste Manag., 37*, 3-12.
[http://dx.doi.org/10.1016/j.wasman.2014.02.003]

Bird, L., Milligan, M., Lew, D. (2013). *Integrating variable renewable energy: Challenges and solutions (No. NREL/TP-6A20-60451). National Renewable Energy Laboratory.* NREL.

Campos, D., Gómez-García, R., Vilas-Boas, A.A., Madureira, A., Pintado, M.M. (2020). Management of fruit industrial by-products: A case study on a circular economy approach. *Molecules, 25.*
[http://dx.doi.org/10.3390/molecules25020320]

Crippa, M., Solazzo, E., Guizzardi, D., Monforti-Ferrario, F., Tubiello, F., Leip, A. (2021). Food systems are responsible for a third of global anthropogenic GHG emissions. *Nat. Food, 2*, 198-209.
[http://dx.doi.org/10.1038/s43016-021-00225-9]

Connolly-Boutin, L., Smit, B. (2016). Climate change, food security, and livelihoods in sub-Saharan Africa. *Reg. Environ. Change, 16*, 385-399.
[http://dx.doi.org/10.1007/s10113-015-0761-x]

Demirbas, A. (2011). Waste management, waste resource facilities, and waste conversion processes. *Energy Convers. Manage., 52*(2), 1280-1287.
[http://dx.doi.org/10.1016/j.enconman.2010.09.025]

Eberhardt, L.C.M., Birgisdóttir, H., Birkved, M. (2019). Life cycle assessment of a Danish office building designed for disassembly. *Build. Res. Inform., 47*, 666-680.
[http://dx.doi.org/10.1080/09613218.2018.1517458]

Fatimah, Y.A., Govindan, K., Murniningsih, R., Setiawan, A. (2020). Industry 4.0-based sustainable circular economy approach for smart waste management systems to achieve SDGs: A case study of Indonesia. *J. Clean. Prod., 269*, 122263.
[http://dx.doi.org/10.1016/j.jclepro.2020.122263]

Fraceto, L.F., Grillo, R., de Medeiros, G.A., Scognamiglio, V., Rea, G., Bartolucci, C. (2016). Nanotechnology in agriculture: Which innovation potential does it have? *Front. Environ. Sci., 4*, 20.
[http://dx.doi.org/10.3389/fenvs.2016.00020]

Giusti, L. (2009). A review of waste management practices and their impact on human health. *Waste Manag., 29*(8), 2227-2239.
[http://dx.doi.org/10.1016/j.wasman.2009.03.028]

Gregson, N., Crang, M., Fuller, S., Holmes, H. (2015). Interrogating the circular economy: The moral economy of resource recovery in the EU. *Econ. Soc., 44*, 218-243.
[http://dx.doi.org/10.1080/03085147.2015.1013353]

Herrero, M., Thornton, P.K., Mason-D'Croz, D., Palmer, J., Benton, T.G., Bodirsky, B.L. (2020). Innovation can accelerate the transition towards a sustainable food system. *Nat. Food, 1*(5), 266-272.
[http://dx.doi.org/10.1038/s43016-020-0074-1]

Izvercian, M., Ivascu, L. (2015). Waste management in the context of sustainable development: Case study in Romania. *Procedia Econ. Finance, 26*, 717-721.
[http://dx.doi.org/10.1016/S2212-5671(15)00841-3]

Kahraman, C., Keshavarz Ghorabaee, M., Zavadskas, E.K., Cevik Onar, S., Yazdani, M., Oztaysi, B. (2017). Intuitionistic fuzzy EDAS method: An application to solid waste disposal site selection. *J. Environ. Eng. Landsc. Manag., 25*(1), 1-12.
[http://dx.doi.org/10.3846/16486897.2017.1308618]

Knickmeyer, D. (2020). Social factors influencing household waste separation: A literature review on good practices to improve the recycling performance of urban areas. *J. Clean. Prod.*
[http://dx.doi.org/10.1016/j.jclepro.2019.118605]

Kurniawan, T.A., Othman, M.H.D., Hwang, G.H., Gikas, P. (2022). Unlocking digital technologies for waste recycling in Industry 4.0 era: A transformation towards a digitalization-based circular economy in Indonesia. *J. Clean. Prod., 357*, 131911.
[http://dx.doi.org/10.1016/j.jclepro.2022.131911]

Logenthiran, T., Srinivasan, D., Shun, T.Z. (2012). Demand-side management in smart grid using heuristic optimization. *IEEE Trans. Smart Grid, 3*(3), 1244-1252.
[http://dx.doi.org/10.1109/TSG.2012.2195686]

Lestari, P., Trihadiningrum, Y. (2019). The impact of improper solid waste management on plastic pollution in the Indonesian coast and marine environment. *Mar. Pollut. Bull., 149*, 110505.
[http://dx.doi.org/10.1016/j.marpolbul.2019.110505]

Martín-Ríos, C., Demen-Meier, C., Gössling, S., Cornuz, C. (2018). Food waste management innovations in the foodservice industry. *Waste Manag., 79*, 196-206.
[http://dx.doi.org/10.1016/j.wasman.2018.07.033]

Martín-Ríos, C., Hofmann, A., Mackenzie, N. (2020). Sustainability-oriented innovations in food waste management technology. *Sustainability*.
[http://dx.doi.org/10.3390/su13010210]

Mohsenian-Rad, A.H., Wong, V.W., Jatskevich, J., Schober, R., Leon-Garcia, A. (2010). Autonomous demand-side management based on game-theoretic energy consumption scheduling for the future smart grid. *IEEE Trans. Smart Grid, 1*(3), 320-331.
[http://dx.doi.org/10.1109/TSG.2010.2089069]

Pop, C., Cioara, T., Antal, M., Anghel, I., Salomie, I., Bertoncini, M. (2018). Blockchain-based decentralized management of demand response programs in smart energy grids. *Sensors (Basel), 18*(1), 162.
[http://dx.doi.org/10.3390/s18010162]

Rosenboom, J-G., Langer, R., Traverso, G. (2022). Bioplastics for a circular economy. *Nat. Rev. Mater., 7*, 117-137.
[http://dx.doi.org/10.1038/s41578-021-00407-8]

Singh, J., Ordóñez, I. (2016). Resource recovery from post-consumer waste: Important lessons for the upcoming circular economy. *J. Clean. Prod., 134*, 342-353.
[http://dx.doi.org/10.1016/j.jclepro.2015.12.020]

Shafiee-Jood, M., Cai, X. (2016). Reducing food loss and waste to enhance food security and environmental sustainability. *Environ. Sci. Technol., 50*(16), 8432-8443.
[http://dx.doi.org/10.1021/acs.est.6b01993]

Skenderovic, I., Kalac, B., Becirovic, S. (2015). Environmental pollution and waste management. *Balkan Journal of Health Science, 3*(1), 2-10.

Tchobanoglous, G. (2009). Solid waste management.*Environmental engineering: Environmental health and safety for municipal infrastructure, land use and planning, and industry.* Wiley.

Tripathi, N., Hills, C., Singh, R., Atkinson, C. (2019). Biomass waste utilization in low-carbon products: Harnessing a major potential resource. npj Climate and Atmospheric Science, 2, 1–10.

Tiwari, A., Sharma, P. (2024). Preference-based grey theory model and its application in waste disposal selection A case study. *Sadhana, 49*(1), 1-14.
[http://dx.doi.org/10.1007/s12046-023-02097-9]

Wilson, D.C., Smith, N.A., Blakey, N.C., Shaxson, L. (2007). Using research-based knowledge to underpin waste and resources policy. *Waste Manag. Res., 25*(3), 247-256.
[http://dx.doi.org/10.1177/0734242X07080755]

World Bank. (2018). *Trends in solid waste management.* https://datatopics.worldbank.org/what--waste/trends_in_solid_waste_management.html

Yang, M., Chen, L., Wang, J., Msigwa, G., Osman, A.I., Fawzy, S. (2023). Circular economy strategies for combating climate change and other environmental issues. *Environ. Chem. Lett., 21*(1), 55-80. [http://dx.doi.org/10.1007/s10311-022-01408-6]

Zorpas, A.A., Voukkali, I., Loizia, P. (2015). The impact of the tourist sector on waste management plans. *Desalination Water Treat., 56*(5), 1141-1149. [http://dx.doi.org/10.1080/19443994.2014.940223]

Zucchella, A., Previtali, P. (2018). Circular business models for sustainable development: A "waste is food" restorative ecosystem. *Bus. Strategy Environ.* [http://dx.doi.org/10.1002/bse.2216]

Zenginis, I., Vardakas, J., Mekikis, P.V., Verikoukis, C. (2018). Cooperative energy management in microgrids.*Transportation and Power Grid in Smart Cities.* Communication Networks and Services.

CHAPTER 6

Empowering Community-Led Waste Management: Lessons from the Haritha Karma Sena (HKS) Initiative

Renju Chandran[1,*], Sarath Chandran M.C.[2], Padma Rao Sahib[3] and Krishnashree Achuthan[4]

[1] *School of Contemporary Knowledge Systems, Chinmaya Vishwa Vidyapeeth (Deemed to be University), Ernakulam, Kerala, India*

[2] *Amrita School of Arts, Humanities and Commerce, Amrita Vishwa Vidyapeetham, Amritapuri, Kerala, India*

[3] *Faculty of Economics and Business, University of Groningen, Groningen, The Netherlands*

[4] *Center for Cybersecurity Systems and Networks, Amrita Vishwa Vidyapeetham, Amritapuri, Kerala, India*

Abstract: This chapter enlists the transformational possibilities that the decentralized, community-led initiative called Haritha Karma Sena holds in sustainable rural waste management. It has to do with its operating framework, the impact of environmental sustainability, and its role in socio-economic empowerment. It brings all such critical elements to the forefront as participation by communities, capacity building, and integrating advanced technologies along with improvements in the collection, segregation, and processing of waste. The report has found that the program has been successful in engaging households and institutions, reducing social stigma, and improving the livelihoods of waste workers, though with some gaps, such as infrastructure gaps and income instability. Discussion on policy implications involves investment in infrastructure, targeted training programs, and innovative financial mechanisms that can ensure scalability and sustainability of the program in the long run. This chapter addresses the initiative of Haritha Karma Sena and underlines that decentralized models are useful to tackle the global problem in waste management while simultaneously developing community resilience and stewardship of the environment.

Keywords: Community waste management, Haritha Karma Sena (HKS), Socio-economic empowerment, Sustainable environment.

* **Corresponding author Renju Chandran:** School of Contemporary Knowledge Systems, Chinmaya Vishwa Vidyapeeth (Deemed to be University), Ernakulam, Kerala, India; E-mail: renju.chandran@cvv.ac.in

Theodore Tarnanidis, Vijaya Kittu Manda, Vivek Gupta (Eds.)

INTRODUCTION

Ridding rural India of all types of waste is marred with several problems, such as infrastructure deficit, lack of awareness, and community participation deficits. The increasing population, thereby growing waste generation, has intensified these problems and posed adverse environmental, social, and economic consequences. Segregation at the source and efficient waste disposal mechanisms and recycling mechanisms are not adequate and add to the worsening situation.

In this respect, one such beacon of hope from the district of Ernakulam is the HKS initiative. In fact, it was a community-driven program that solved these problems by incorporating grassroots efforts in the waste management processes. It was also a means of socio-economic development for the marginalized population, besides environmental sustainability.

This program is decentralized because local people, primarily women, collect, sort, and process the waste. It empowers its members by providing them with an employment opportunity and skill building, and makes them own the waste management process and increase community participation. HKS further emphasizes awareness creation and changing behaviors among residents, ensuring the principle of sustainability is deeply in place in community practices (Equator Initiative, 2024). This chapter explores the multi-dimensional impacts of the Haritha Karma Sena program, focusing on their model of operation, the experience and challenges of members, and the implications for rural sustainability. Discussion of these issues puts forth the relevance of community-led approaches to waste management in India toward meeting the country's needs as well as the global sustainability agenda.

THE HARITHA KARMA SENA PROGRAM AND ITS DECENTRALIZED APPROACH

The Haritha Karma Sena program is predicated on the principle of decentralization, which is an aspect relatively well known in the annals of academic literature as having a significant impact on managing solid waste at the local level. Decentralized waste management puts a premium on local solutions; collection, segregation, and processing usually take place either within the community that generated the waste or close by. Thus, the environmental footprint on transportation of waste is low, and community ownership can be fostered for local waste management practices (Vinti & Vaccari, 2022).

According to research, community-based waste management can significantly improve source segregation of waste, which is a critical factor in the achievement of efficient recycling and composting (Abubakar *et al.*, 2022). The Haritha Karma

Sena fits into this finding because it integrates local communities into the chain of waste management, thus creating a sense of responsibility and participation among residents. Studies in similar contexts have revealed that with the active involvement of the community, there is a marked improvement in waste collection efficiency and reduction in waste-related environmental hazards (Ferronato & Torretta, 2019).

Second, employment generation for most of these groups, mainly comprising women and low-income households, aligns the objectives with SDGs (Shevelkova *et al.*, 2023). Indeed, by incorporating vulnerable populations into initiatives targeting waste management, this contributes to better improvement of livelihoods while offering improvements in social equity (Suresh *et al.*, 2024). The work of Haritha Karma Sena's model of working supports the same by means of creating job opportunities alongside giving specific skill development skills aligned to the requirements for their workers.

Another strong support for the compatibility of this initiative with global sustainability goals lies in promoting organic farming practices. Organic farming is highly dependent on the compost produced from biodegradable waste, and it has been identified in recent research that decentralized systems for managing waste can ensure the smooth supply of high-quality compost in agriculture (Ayilara *et al.*, 2020). The Haritha Karma Sena promotes local farming use of compost, thus supporting the sustainable environment while improving rural area soils and agricultural productivity (Shameerdas & S. B., 2024).

EXAMPLES OF SIMILAR PROGRAMS GLOBALLY

Many programs globally share the same rationale and goals as the HKS. These programs establish that community-led waste solutions can be effective:

- Waste Wise Cities (Kenya), launched under the auspices of the UN-Habitat, Waste Wise Cities involves working with cities in less-developed countries to improve conditions through community-based and capacity-building services (Ozoike-Dennis *et al.*, 2019). It focuses on sorting at source, recycling, and composting, similar to the HKS model.
- Green Dot Program (Germany) This is one of the very successful decentralized waste management schemes in Germany. The local businesses and communities are engaged in segregating and recycling the packaging waste, and it helps to reduce their dependence on landfills. (Ramasubramanian *et al.*, 2023).
- Barangay Solid Waste Management (Philippines) This program enables the barangays, which are the village-level administrative divisions, to manage their own waste within their communities. The program aims to educate residents on

segregation and recycling, while at the same time providing livelihood opportunities through composting and recycling activities (Atienza, 2011).

- Kampala Waste Management Initiative (Uganda). Decentralized waste management has been embraced in Kampala in association with local community groups. Most of the waste collectors, being from poor families, are organized into cooperatives, ensuring environmental and economic benefits at once (Kiggundu, 2024).
- Zero Waste Scotland (Scotland). The goal of this initiative is to create a circular economy through the reduction of waste generation and the maximization of recycling and resource recovery. This initiative engages local communities and businesses in sustainable waste practices, emphasizing the significance of local participation (Wishart & Bebbington, 2020).
- Eco Citizen World Map Project (Global) Supported by various organizations, this project fosters grassroots action in waste management by mapping local initiatives and sharing best practices (Boostani *et al.*, 2024). It underscores the importance of community-driven solutions in attaining global sustainability goals.

While each global case operates within its unique socio-political context, common lessons emerge that are directly applicable to the HKS model. For instance, the Philippines' barangay-level waste governance aligns with Kerala's ward-level decentralization, offering a peer-level comparison in community accountability. Germany's Green Dot system, although industry-driven, emphasizes institutional partnerships a potential pathway for HKS to enhance participation from private entities. Meanwhile, the Kampala initiative shows the viability of cooperative models among economically disadvantaged groups, akin to the livelihood focus of HKS. These comparative insights highlight pathways through which the HKS can improve compliance, scale sustainably, and increase institutional engagement.

RESULTS AND DISCUSSIONS

An extensive survey with HKS members in the Ernakulam district gave interesting insights about the functioning and challenges of the initiative and about its impact. The following is a brief analysis based on the collected data.

HOUSEHOLD AND INSTITUTIONAL PARTICIPATION

The Haritha Karma Sena program has reached more than 50,000 households and 1,600 institutions in its waste management activities. Such figures indicate how the program has been generally accepted by communities and institutions in participating in decentralized waste management practices. However, a significant improvement area is still compliance with user fee payments.

Although 68% of households pay user fees, the other 32% is a big gap in participation. This participation gap likely stems from multiple interrelated factors. Financial constraints, especially in economically weaker rural households, play a central role. Additionally, inconsistent waste collection services may erode user trust, while inadequate community sensitization campaigns leave many unaware of how their fees directly contribute to program sustainability and local environmental benefits. Addressing these issues through flexible fee schemes, consistent service delivery, and targeted outreach is essential for improving compliance (Table **1**). Likewise, 65.6% of institutions contribute to user fees, but that leaves 34.4% that do not contribute to user fees, thus becoming a challenge for sustainable operations.

Table 1. Household and institutional participation.

Metric	Count	Percentage
Households that are part of the HKS facilities	**50,000**	-
Households paying user fees	34,000	68%
Households not paying user fees	16,000	32%
Institutions that are part of the HKS facilities	**1,600**	-
Institutions paying user fees	1,050	65.6%
Institutions not paying user fees	550	34.4%

Source: Primary data

The dual perception of Haritha Karma Sena workers 67% feeling socially recognized and 13% experiencing stigma highlights the complex societal attitudes toward waste work. These findings suggest the need for structured public recognition programs and awareness campaigns that reframe waste work as a vital contribution to public health and sustainability.

ADDRESSING THE GAP IN HOUSEHOLD PARTICIPATION

The gap in user fee compliance among households calls for targeted interventions in order to improve participation. Educational campaigns that emphasize the environmental and health benefits of efficient waste management can be implemented to increase awareness about how user fees directly fund reliable waste collection services. Another avenue through which this can be facilitated is flexible payment mechanisms for households at different income levels, for example, reduced rates for Below Poverty Line (BPL) families or even deferred payment options for residents during times of temporary financial difficulties. An efficient and consistent waste collection service will be an added determinant for developing trust and confidence among the residents. In addition, incentive programs, such as lower fees for early payments or discounts on local goods and services, can encourage households to participate consistently.

The 34.4% non-compliance rate of institutions also requires specific strategies to improve compliance. Facilitating stakeholder dialogues with institutional representatives can help identify barriers to compliance and co-create tailored solutions. Recognition programs that publicly highlight and reward institutions adhering to user fee requirements through certificates of excellence can foster positive reinforcement. Other things, such as monitoring systems that could track compliance rates and further follow-ups for noncomplying institutions, would ensure a better enforcement mechanism. Coupled with this, through collaboration with local governing bodies and forming policies that mandate user fees contributing to institutions and using funds in a transparent way, would bring more institutional participation.

Community engagement is crucial in filling the gaps in participation. The setting up of local committees of neighbourhood groups can play the role of an intermediary between the households, institutions, and the Haritha Karma Sena, ensuring uniform service delivery and user fee payment compliance. Participatory budgeting, whereby the community participates in deciding on the use of funds collected, enhances transparency and increases trust. Sharing success stories of compliant households and institutions within the community through peer learning programs can also inspire others to follow suit.

Leverage technology and have an effective way to deal with participation gaps. It is possible to make payment and service tracking smooth and fee payment by creating a friendly user digital payment platform. Providing a real-time feedback mechanism enables immediate reporting of missed collections or any problem with services, resulting in quick resolutions and increasing user satisfaction. Data analytics can even complement these by pointing out non-compliance trends that allow for the design of tailored interventions. By implementing these targeted and innovative approaches, the Haritha Karma Sena programme would bring in wider acceptance and sustainability and contribute towards the creation of a cleaner, efficient waste management system.

TRAINING AND SKILL DEVELOPMENT

The success of the Haritha Karma Sena initiative is embedded in the training and skill development of its members. Basic training ensures that participants meet minimum competency standards; however, there is an obvious and increasing demand for advanced modules to address the emerging challenges in waste management. As indicated by survey data, 65% of members expressed interest in waste management awareness programs, 56% emphasized the need for training in the use of Material Collection Facilities (MCFs), and 43% highlighted the importance of developing driving and technical skills. These figures underline the necessity of enhancing the current training framework to better align with the program's expanding scope and complexities.

Currently, training modules are mainly targeting basic waste segregation techniques, education on the environment, and operational procedures in waste collection. However, despite training modules in these areas enabling HKS members to satisfactorily perform their job, the current rapid growth of waste and the sophistication of technological waste management require specialized education. Therefore, advanced modules must focus on these matters. For example, techniques of segregating waste may involve emerging technology such as automated sorting equipment and AI-driven classification, ensuring members remain ahead of the curve in the execution of efficient recycling. Correspondingly, training on operating MCFs efficiently should comprise detailed handling of equipment and safety procedures as well as maintenance schedules to ensure long-term use of resources.

Technical skills for drivers are also important for waste collection operations. Specialized driving courses, especially those designed for e-autos and smart garbage vehicles, would greatly improve efficiency. Training in basic vehicle maintenance would reduce downtime and lower repair costs. Health and safety training is equally important, especially considering the risks of handling hazardous materials. The health and safety of members would best be ensured through the correct use of personal protective equipment and exposure mitigation through suitable methods to biohazardous waste in the conducted workshops.

To implement these advanced training initiatives effectively, collaboration with technical institutions and industry experts is essential. Partnering with these entities would ensure that the training programs are both comprehensive and up to date with the latest industry standards. Hands-on workshops should complement theoretical sessions to equip members with practical skills that translate seamlessly into their daily tasks. Also, certification programs conducted on successful completion of the training modules would not only improve their credibility but also make them even more employable both in and outside this sector.

Focus areas on more advanced trainings with potent strategies enable Haritha Karma Sena's constituents to mitigate challenges experienced presently and enable its constituency to meet the potential requirements that shall surface in the future by effective and sustainable waste management systems. In short, focusing on this will allow this program and its members to sustain, therefore make their own crucial change for waste management, with cleanliness.

INCOME DISTRIBUTION AND ECONOMIC CHALLENGES

Income generation remains a big issue for members of Haritha Karma Sena. Most members depend on the initiative as their primary source of livelihood, though earnings are usually not enough to meet their basic needs.

Income instability is one of the most challenging problems the members of the Haritha Karma Sena initiative face. Almost 45% of the members have an income below ₹5,000 per month, indicating economic vulnerability (Table **2**). This weak earning capacity further exacerbates their vulnerability due to low revenue from user fees, which cannot adequately finance their members. Many members are without additional sources of income generation and are forced to rely entirely on the business venture as a means of survival. More than that, such reliance, coupled with delayed remittance of waste collection fee collections, makes them exposed to greater risks of an economic nature, and quicker remedies for this economic factor have to be discovered.

Table 2. Income distribution.

Income Range	Percentage of Respondents
Below ₹5,000	45%
₹5,000–₹10,000	38%
Above ₹10,000	17%

Source: Primary data

Diversification of income streams is the way forward in addressing such challenges. Production and sale of compost will ensure that the members have a steady income stream through converting organic waste into high-quality compost for local farmers. Similarly, providing a source of employment can be derived from facilitating partnerships with local businesses to establish recycling units for processing non-biodegradable waste. Government agencies and private sector players also need to be collaborated with. Financial incentives, such as subsidies or grants for active HKS members, can reduce economic stress, while sponsorships from private companies for the waste management projects can be an added advantage to the job.

Microfinance provision is the other possible option through which members can be made economically empowered. Through designing microfinance schemes, members can secure the respective capital to commence small-sized businesses related to waste collection, such as swap shops or repair centres. Potential to transform them is also capable of developing skills for other living beings. Training members to produce environmentally friendly products such as cloth bags and recycled paper, or consultancy services in waste management, will open new opportunities for generating income and gradually reduce the reliance on the program itself.

This can also involve having a fair wage policy. Fair wage policies ensure the members are paid fairly and enough for their work. When this is advocated for and set up, the program's workforce is provided with the stability required financially to improve their living standards. Holistically addressing these income-related issues will improve the financial condition of the members of the Haritha Karma Sena, and the program shall be sustainable in the long run, meaning it can continue to make meaningful impacts in waste management and community development.

STATISTICAL INSIGHTS

The success of the HKS initiative in addressing waste management challenges is, however, dampened by massive hurdles, especially in household compliance, social perceptions of waste work, and infrastructural deficiencies. Household compliance rates, though moderately high at 68% for households and 65.6% for institutions, show gaps rooted in financial constraints and inconsistent service delivery, especially in rural and peri-urban areas. Social perceptions further blur the impact of the program as it is being carried out in the duality of recognition and stigma. However, it is reported that 67 percent of HKS members are recognized in society for contributing to cleanliness and public health, while 13 percent are stigmatized due to deep prejudices. Furthermore, infrastructural inadequacies, which include limited MCF availability with the necessary amenities, hinder the smooth operation of business and the satisfaction of employees. Only 43% of the wards have MCFs that are functioning; this creates logistical bottlenecks that strain the efficacy of the program. Interconnected issues point towards some targeted strategies to make improvements in compliance, in social standing, and a structural foundation for the program's long-term sustainability and impact.

HOUSEHOLD COMPLIANCE ANALYSIS

The mean compliance rate for user fee payments by households is 68% and 65.6% for institutions. The level of compliance here represents the readiness of a significant number of people to partake in the waste management system, though a wide gap between the compliant and non-compliant households and institutions is also brought out. Variations in the compliance rates are observed between rural and peri-urban wards. The main challenges rural areas face include lower household incomes and a lack of awareness regarding the significance of waste management services, which decreases the compliance rate. Peri-urban areas, on the other hand, might experience issues such as irregular service delivery or mistrust in the fee collection process. These challenges need to be specifically addressed in order to improve overall compliance.

SOCIAL STATUS CHANGES

With respect to social status, it is both positive and negative concerning Haritha Karma Sena (HKS). In 67%, it was observed that the impact is positive because it provides society recognition to the members for the reason that they contribute to the cleanliness of the environment and the health of everybody. The negative one observed was 13% which stigmatized waste collection. Such stigma is often associated with perceptions of waste work as menial or undesirable. These contradictory experiences need social education campaigns to raise society's understanding of the critical role these waste workers play in attaining their sustainable development goals. In this regard, increasing public recognition will further elevate the social status while removing the stigma.

INFRASTRUCTURE GAPS

The major challenge facing the initiative is the lack of proper infrastructure. Only 43% of wards have fully established Material Collection Facilities MCFs with basic amenities such as toilets, drinking water, and washrooms. This limitation affects the operational efficiency of the program and the satisfaction of its members. Further, inappropriate infrastructure burdens the workers because sometimes they may spend a long time reaching central facilities or inefficient processing mechanisms for waste. Such a step would call for tremendous investments in the construction and later maintenance of decentralized MCFs in all wards.

SCALABLE TECHNOLOGIES

Within the HKS framework, scalable technologies offer direct, actionable benefits. For instance, AI-powered segregation systems could be piloted at existing Material Collection Facilities (MCFs) to enhance efficiency and reduce manual sorting. Mobile applications tailored for the HKS ecosystem can streamline user fee payments, offer real-time service feedback, and support route optimization for collection teams. Moreover, blockchain can be applied to HKS operations for secure tracking of waste processing and payment flows, thereby increasing transparency and stakeholder trust. These technological integrations would not only address current logistical and operational inefficiencies but also make the HKS model more replicable in other regions.

Advanced innovations in areas such as waste tracking systems, AI-driven waste segregation, data analytics, and energy recovery solutions can enhance the operational efficiency and sustainability of these models to a significant extent. These technologies provide timely information, automate labour-intensive processes, and optimize the use of resources. In the system of waste management, additional resources such as blockchain ensure more transparent and accountable actions of stakeholders, which again increases the trust among those stakeholders, while mobilizations and drones improve easy accessibility, engagement, and better monitoring capabilities. All such activities are aligned with circular economic principles, which enable changing wastage into valuable products, thereby reducing the environmental degradation factors.

WASTE TRACKING AND MONITORING SYSTEMS

The Improvements in the scalability of decentralizing waste management models can come through integrating tracking and monitoring systems for waste. Such integrated information and communication technologies can even be deployed into waste-collecting vehicles and their bins to track the exact live quantity of waste, which aids in optimizing routes and hence reduces operational costs. Utilizing GPS, proper utilization of resources with reduced delayed times, and enhancing accountability on the grounds of accurate reporting of vehicle movement and efficiencies of service shall be managed.

SMART WASTE SEGREGATION TECHNOLOGIES

Advanced technologies such as AI-powered sorting machines can automate the segregation of recyclable, organic, and hazardous waste, significantly improving processing efficiency. Robotics with computer vision can further enhance the precision of sorting at MCFs, reducing manual labour and increasing throughput. These technologies not only increase efficiency but also enhance the quality of segregated materials, thus boosting recycling rates and resource recovery.

DATA ANALYTICS AND PREDICTIVE MODELLING

Data analytics can be an essential component of waste management. It will be possible to predict patterns of waste generation through the analysis of historical and real-time data. Such information would ensure that collection and processing resources are better planned for, and where there is more demand for their services. Additionally, predictive modelling through AI predicts equipment failures in MCFs and collection vehicles so that maintenance happens in advance, with no resulting downtime.

MOBILE APPLICATIONS

Mobile applications can enhance access and participation for both the service providers and users. Through community engagement platforms within the application, it is possible to develop resident-friendly fee payment systems; support the scheduling of waste collection activities for better household clean-up; and provide different avenues for reporting on quality aspects of services.

ENERGY RECOVERY TECHNOLOGIES

The production units of biogas help to process biodegradable waste into a renewable source of energy for cooking or generating electricity. Waste-to-energy plants can handle non-recyclable waste, reducing reliance on landfills and contributing to energy security. These technologies align with the principles of the circular economy by transforming waste into valuable resources.

BLOCKCHAIN FOR TRANSPARENCY

Blockchain technology can enhance transparency and trust in waste management through a tamper-proof ledger that tracks waste from origin to disposal. This system can ensure accountability and build trust among stakeholders, including residents, local authorities, and waste workers.

COMPOSTING TECHNOLOGIES

In-vessel composting systems speed up the decomposition of organic waste, and the compost produced is of high quality in shorter periods. Aerated static pile systems, which require minimal labour and infrastructure, can handle large volumes of organic waste efficiently, making them suitable for decentralized models of waste management.

DRONES FOR SURVEYING

Drones can be used to monitor illegal dumping sites, conduct area-wide waste surveys, and determine the efficacy of the installed infrastructure. They help enhance the capabilities for monitoring, reduce manual efforts, and provide accurate data that helps plan and enforce.

POLICY IMPLICATIONS

The policy framework is crucial in tackling the complex issues of waste management and ensuring the scalability and sustainability of community-driven initiatives such as the HKS. Strong policies would have to be in place to build stronger compliance mechanisms, upgrade infrastructure, and improve the economic status of waste workers. Other, more targeted interventions can be seen through subsidies and flexible payment schemes to make the organization more inclusive, while better-structured training and capacity-building programs would prepare them to address changing needs in the sector (Teigiserova *et al.*, 2019). Good infrastructure and effective, working Material Collection Facilities are necessary for efficient operation and higher worker satisfaction, along with policies to end social stigma by employing public awareness and recognition programs that raise the dignity of workers handling waste and further enhance social equity (Szpilko *et al.*, 2023). Decentralization and active community involvement can supplement this, fashioning solutions to local needs for better effectiveness and adaptability (Ma *et al.*, 2017). This chapter thus provides an insight into the policy implications of the HKS initiative and how strategic interventions may lead to long-lasting economic, social, and environmental benefits.

STRENGTHENING COMPLIANCE MECHANISMS

Targeted awareness campaigns and subsidies to low-income households can promote policies encouraging user fee payments. Flexibility in the payment scheme in terms of the household income level may further improve compliance and make the waste management services more inclusive.

INVESTMENT IN TRAINING AND CAPACITY BUILDING

Structured training programs with comprehensive knowledge of advanced waste management practices, such as good driving habits, waste segregation practices, and safe handling techniques of hazardous materials, can be instituted by the governments for such workers. Ties with educational institutions and NGOs will strengthen and enhance the quality as well as reach of these programmes, so that the waste worker meets the emerging challenges.

IMPROVING INFRASTRUCTURE

A huge investment for full-fledged MCFs in all wards with the minimum provision of amenities such as toilets, drinking water, and a washroom. This would facilitate better infrastructure, leading to increased operational efficiency and high worker satisfaction, which in turn would help make waste management more sustainable.

ECONOMIC EMPOWERMENT OF WORKERS

Policies should encourage supplementary income generation for waste workers through government-sponsored recycling units, composting, and eco-product manufacturing. This will enable the stabilization of the financial status of the workers and, consequently, ensure long-term economic advantages.

SOCIAL STIGMA

Public awareness campaigns about the role of waste workers in ensuring environmental sustainability will change society's perception. Inclusive recognition and community dialogues also help to reduce stigma and promote greater social equity.

DECENTRALIZATION AND COMMUNITY PARTICIPATION

Replication of decentralized models like Haritha Karma Sena in other places and policy measures to fortify the community groups with grants, technical support, and capacity building should be promoted. Solutions for waste management also need to take care to provide suitable solutions for every community and involve local communities. Only after this, by dealing with the policy implications, can the initiative of Haritha Karma Sena become a model for sustainable waste management, bringing economic, social, and environmental benefits with it.

CONCLUSION

The Haritha Karma Sena initiative is a great example of what transformation can take place with decentralized and community-driven approaches to rural waste management in India. This is a centralized system that often cannot cater to the diversity of needs in the rural areas, but it is based on local participation, making it adaptable and responsive to the unique challenges of each community. It enables integrating waste management in the social fabric of rural regions and allows people and societies to take ownership of their environment. The common sense of responsibility emerges from this.

The biggest strength of the HKS program is that it bridges the gap between infrastructure and services in waste management. In several rural regions of India, the system for waste collection, segregation, and disposal does not exist. The HKS model, through its decentralized approach, in which waste management operations take place locally, mitigates such challenges. This, on one hand, ensures a reduction in environmental and economic costs associated with long-distance waste transportation while ensuring practices of waste management are tailored to local needs. Such programs help in the community-driven development of solutions, thereby enabling the program to enhance both its operational efficiency and increase resilience in rural waste management (Vinti & Vaccari, 2022).

It is essential to address these gaps and challenges in that regard before replicating the same model in other regions, and the focus area of it would be on infrastructure building, such as Building Material Collection Facilities in each ward-toilets along with available drinking water sources and tools for segregation and separate collection (Petit-Boix *et al.*, 2021). Advanced technologies, such as AI-driven waste segregation systems, IoT-enabled waste tracking, and energy recovery solutions, would enhance the scalability and efficiency of the HKS model. Such technologies not only enhance operational efficiency but also follow the trend across the world set in sustainable waste management (Leknoi *et al.*, 2024).

Scaling the initiative requires training and skill development. Advanced waste management practices, health and safety protocols, and entrepreneurial skills through these training programs will enable HKS members to handle more complex roles and responsibilities. Such programs should be followed by practical workshops and certifications that increase member credibility and employability. Advanced skills empowerment will benefit the program and enhance workers' personal economic growth and social mobility (Nižetić *et al.*, 2020).

It's still community engagement in the model that runs deep in HKS. Ensuring participatory governance and decision-making processes would really include the voices and concerns of local residents in matters at the grassroots level, particularly in the issues involved. Community ownership can even be further strengthened by organizing for community-led monitoring, ensuring participatory budgeting is allotted for user fee distribution, and public recognition in recognizing compliant households and institutions. This shall breed trust and accountability, which could ensure sustained participation and compliance.

The HKS model in other regions requires mutual collaboration between governmental bodies, NGOs, and the private sector. The friendly legislation in place, incentives through funds, and assistance from technologists can ensure this setting (Petit-Boix *et al.*, 2021). Private sector partnerships help with more inputs and technology, such as recycling units or the conversion of waste into energy resources (Arkorful *et al.*, 2022). It ensures the project is kept in a financially solvent and technology-intensive state.

This makes the HKS initiative a replicable model for changing the face of waste management in Indian rural areas since decentralization, local empowerment, and sustainability remain at the heart of focus (Bui *et al.*, 2022). Through improvement in training, infrastructure, and community engagement, the program can further raise rural economies while working on broader goals related to sustainability within India (Manda & Jitta, 2024). It promotes cleaner and healthier environments, at the same time offering economic opportunity and social equity. Therefore, it forms a perfect solution to one of the most important challenges that India is confronting.

FUTURE OUTLOOK

Implementation of high-tech solutions to the HKS will highly boost its effectiveness and scalability. Such apps on waste tracking offer real-time information regarding schedules for collection, compliance rates, and service feedback, thus providing detailed and timely management (Ayob *et al.*, 2017). The use of IoT devices in bins and collection vehicles will monitor the level of waste and optimize the route, which saves on operational costs and impacts the environment. These technologies enhance not only the productivity of waste collection but also the clarity and integrity of the program.

AI-based waste segregation systems are a revolutionary method of sorting recyclable, organic, and hazardous materials. The automation of these processes minimizes the reliance on manual labour and improves the quality and speed of segregation (Silva *et al.*, 2018). Improved segregation rates contribute directly to higher recycling yields and better resource recovery. Biogas production units and waste-to-energy plants can amplify the sustainability of this program, as these will be turning wastes into useful energy sources (Pitkänen *et al.*, 2016). Thus, both environmental and economic benefits have to be gained by the community and other stakeholders through technological innovation.

Blockchain technology will further ensure that the origin, processing, and disposal of waste are tracked in a secure manner. This creates confidence among participants and provides a framework that is easy to track program outcomes. Efficient organic waste management can be achieved through composting technologies such as in-vessel systems and aerated static piles (Rossi *et al.*, 2022). These give high-quality compost for use in the local agricultural sector. All this put together provides an all-inclusive upgrade for the HKS initiative with long-term operational success and sustainability.

The HKS initiative will require comprehensive longitudinal studies for assessing socio-economic and environmental benefits. Such studies will be helpful in evaluating the effectiveness of the program toward reducing waste-related pollution, increasing recycling rates, and improving community health (Levoso *et al.*, 2019). Economic evaluations will be useful in assessing the contribution of the initiative toward job creation, income generation for HKS members, and cost savings for local governments (Sharma *et al.*, 2020). These studies can identify areas where the program is doing well or experiencing challenges, such as infrastructure needs or gaps in community engagement. Findings can be used to refine existing strategies and establish best practices for future implementation. Impact studies also allow for tracking long-term outcomes, such as changes in community attitudes toward waste management or the sustained effectiveness of technological interventions. The HKS initiative can, through the use of advanced technologies and long-term impact evaluations, solidify its position as a leading model for sustainable waste management. These measures are likely to ensure that the programme will always be adaptable and capable of addressing the evolving challenges posed by waste management while contributing toward environmental and socio-economic progress.

REFERENCES

Available from: https://www.equatorinitiative.org/2024/11/12/haritha-karma-sena/

Available from: https://www.ijsdr.org/papers/IJSDR2407088.pdf

Abubakar, I.R., Maniruzzaman, K.M., Dano, U.L., AlShihri, F.S., AlShammari, M.S., Ahmed, S.M.S., Al-Gehlani, W.G., Alrawaf, T.I. (2022). Environmental Sustainability Impacts of Solid Waste Management Practices in the Global South. *Int. J. Environ. Res. Public Health, 19*(19), 12717.
[http://dx.doi.org/10.3390/ijerph191912717]

Ayilara, M., Olanrewaju, O., Babalola, O., Odeyemi, O. (2020). Waste Management through Composting: Challenges and Potentials. *Sustainability, 12*(11), 4456.
[http://dx.doi.org/10.3390/su12114456]

Atienza, V. (2011). Available from: https://www.nswai.org/docs/Review%20of%20the%20Waste%20Management%20System%20in%20the%20Philippines.pdf

Arkorful, V.E., Shuliang, Z., Lugu, B.K. (2022). Investigating household waste separation behavior: the salience of an integrated norm activation model and the theory of planned behavior. *J. Environ. Plann. Manage., 66*(10), 2195-2221.
[http://dx.doi.org/10.1080/09640568.2022.2063112]

Ayob, S.F., Sheau-Ting, L., Jalil, R.A., Chin, H. (2017). Key determinants of waste separation intention: empirical application of TPB. *Facilities, 35*(11/12), 696-708.
[http://dx.doi.org/10.1108/f-06-2016-0065]

Bui, T., Tseng, J., Tseng, M., Wu, K., Lim, M.K. (2022). Municipal solid waste management technological barriers: A hierarchical structure approach in Taiwan. *Resour. Conserv. Recycling, 190*, 106842.
[http://dx.doi.org/10.1016/j.resconrec.2022.106842]

Boostani, F., Golzary, A., Huisingh, D., Skitmore, M. (2024). Mapping the future: unveiling global trends in smart waste management research. *Results in Engineering, 103485*
[http://dx.doi.org/10.1016/j.rineng.2024.103485]

Ferronato, N., Torretta, V. (2019). Waste mismanagement in developing countries: a review of global issues. *Int. J. Environ. Res. Public Health, 16*(6), 1060.
[http://dx.doi.org/10.3390/ijerph16061060]

Kiggundu, A.T. (2024). Assessing solid waste management in kampala city, uganda: a case study of nakawa

urban division. *Current Urban Studies, 12*(03), 419-439.
[http://dx.doi.org/10.4236/cus.2024.123021]

Levoso, A.S., Gasol, C.M., Martínez-Blanco, J., Durany, X.G., Lehmann, M., Gaya, R.F. (2019). Methodological framework for the implementation of circular economy in urban systems. *J. Clean. Prod., 248*, 119227.
[http://dx.doi.org/10.1016/j.jclepro.2019.119227]

Leknoi, U., Painmanakul, P., Chawaloesphonsiya, N., Wimolsakcharoen, W., Samritthinanta, C., Yiengthaisong, A. (2024). Building Sustainable Community: Insight from successful waste management initiative. *Resources Conservation & Recycling Advances, 200238*
[http://dx.doi.org/10.1016/j.rcradv.2024.200238]

Manda, V.K., Jitta, M.R. (2024). Research themes on green infrastructure for smart cities. Available from: https://www.researchgate.net/publication/386020170_Research_Themes_on_Green_Infrastructure_for_Smart_Cities

Ma, J., Hipel, K.W., Hanson, M.L., Cai, X., Liu, Y. (2017). An analysis of influencing factors on municipal solid waste source-separated collection behavior in Guilin, China by Using the Theory of Planned Behavior. *Sustain Cities Soc., 37*, 336-343.
[http://dx.doi.org/10.1016/j.scs.2017.11.037]

Nižetić, S., Šolić, P., González-De-Artaza, D.L., Patrono, L. (2020). Internet of Things (IoT): Opportunities, issues and challenges towards a smart and sustainable future. *J. Clean. Prod., 274*, 122877.
[http://dx.doi.org/10.1016/j.jclepro.2020.122877]

Ozoike-Dennis, P., Spaling, H., Sinclair, A.J., Walker, H.M. (2019). SEA, urban plans and solid waste management in kenya: participation and learning for sustainable cities. *J. Environ. Assess. Policy Manage., 21*(04), 1950018.
[http://dx.doi.org/10.1142/s1464333219500182]

Petit-Boix, A., Apul, D., Wiedmann, T., Leipold, S. (2021). Transdisciplinary resource monitoring is essential to prioritize circular economy strategies in cities. *Environ. Res. Lett., 17*(2), 021001.
[http://dx.doi.org/10.1088/1748-9326/ac44c6]

Pitkänen, K., Antikainen, R., Droste, N., Loiseau, E., Saikku, L., Aissani, L., Hansjürgens, B., Kuikman, P., Leskinen, P., Thomsen, M. (2016). What can be learned from practical cases of green economy? –studies from five European countries. *J. Clean. Prod., 139*, 666-676.
[http://dx.doi.org/10.1016/j.jclepro.2016.08.071]

Rossi, M., Papetti, A., Germani, M. (2022). A comparison of different waste collection methods: Environmental impacts and occupational risks. *J. Clean. Prod., 368*, 133145.
[http://dx.doi.org/10.1016/j.jclepro.2022.133145]

Ramasubramanian, B., Tan, J., Chellappan, V., Ramakrishna, S. (2023). Recent advances in extended producer responsibility initiatives for plastic waste management in germany and UK. *Materials Circular Economy, 5*(1)
[http://dx.doi.org/10.1007/s42824-023-00076-8]

Shevelkova, V., Mattocks, C., Lafortune, L. (2023). Efforts to address the sustainable development goals in older populations: a scoping review. *BMC Public Health, 23*(1)
[http://dx.doi.org/10.1186/s12889-023-15308-4]

Suresh, K., Anbalagan, S., Yaashikaa, P.R., Sundaram, V.A. (2024). An in-depth analysis of sustainable approaches, conventional techniques, and policy frameworks for managing municipal solid waste in india. *Journal of Renewable Energy and Environment, 11*(2), 102-117.

Szpilko, D., De La Torre Gallegos, A., Naharro, F.J., Rzepka, A., Remiszewska, A. (2023). Waste management in the smart city: current practices and future directions. *Resources, 12*(10), 115.
[http://dx.doi.org/10.3390/resources12100115]

Silva, B.N., Khan, M., Han, K. (2018). Towards sustainable smart cities: A review of trends, architectures,

components, and open challenges in smart cities. *Sustain Cities Soc., 38*, 697-713.
[http://dx.doi.org/10.1016/j.scs.2018.01.053]

Sharma, S., Basu, S., Shetti, N.P., Kamali, M., Walvekar, P., Aminabhavi, T.M. (2020). Waste-to-energy nexus: A sustainable development. *Environ. Pollut., 267*, 115501.
[http://dx.doi.org/10.1016/j.envpol.2020.115501]

Teigiserova, D.A., Hamelin, L., Thomsen, M. (2019). Towards transparent valorization of food surplus, waste and loss: Clarifying definitions, food waste hierarchy, and role in the circular economy. *Sci. Total Environ., 706*, 136033.
[http://dx.doi.org/10.1016/j.scitotenv.2019.136033]

Vinti, G., Vaccari, M. (2022). Solid waste management in rural communities of Developing Countries: An Overview of Challenges and opportunities. *Cleanroom Technol., 4*(4), 1138-1151.
[http://dx.doi.org/10.3390/cleantechnol4040069]

Wishart, L.J., Bebbington, J. (2020). Zero waste governance: a Scottish case study. *Int. J. Sustain. Dev., 23*(1/2), 128.
[http://dx.doi.org/10.1504/ijsd.2020.10034394]

CHAPTER 7

Economic and Social Implications of the Circular Economy

Wasswa Shafik[1,2,*], **Ali Tufail**[1], **Rosyzie Anna Awg Haji Mohd Apong**[1], **Liyanage Chandratilak De Silva**[1] and **Abdallah Namoun**[3]

[1] *School of Digital Science, Universiti Brunei Darussalam, Bandar Seri Begawan, Brunei Darussalam*

[2] *Dig Connectivity Research Laboratory (DCRLab), Kampala, Uganda*

[3] *AI Centre, Faculty of Computer and Information Systems, Islamic University of Madinah, Madinah, Saudi Arabia*

Abstract: Circular Economy (CE) is the long-term economic model that guarantees environmental sustainability and resource efficiency. The main goal of the value shift from the existing model to the circular one is to achieve responsible consumption and production across different sectors. The changes regarding industrial processes, increasing reuse, repair, remanufacturing, and recycling will bring many business opportunities in the case of products, as well as certain shortcomings, such as changes in business models. CE represents a transformation from a linear value chain into "closed" loops, and as one of the primary expressions, it emphasizes cooperation among different industrial stakeholders, also sparing post-sales services. Rethinking patterns of production and consumption has become a critical priority to assure sustainable development, particularly for food, textiles, synthetic and chemical products, electrical and electronic equipment, and waste management, which together represent around two-thirds of solid waste in most countries. There are at least three claimants to regard several aspects of CE. From the economic point of view, teams of professionals try to redefine the existing economic model. One of the reasons to enrich the prism through this sector, even though a CE can have positive effects on aspects other than income, is that successful implementation relies strongly on management decisions made by trained economists. Also, different principles of CE are well known under the umbrella of integral ecology, which should be seen from the perspectives of economic, social, and environmental imperatives compatible with sustainable development. The third aspect embedded in the CE concept is the one related to the degree of economic development, as economic domains show some quantitative estimations, such as sustainability, economy, financing, consumer prices, industrial domain, transportation, waste, agriculture, fishery, food industry, tourism, and marketing. This list can be a reasonable basis for periodical multi-disciplinary empirical studies that should strive to improve the existing index, identify other

* **Corresponding author Wasswa Shafik:** School of Digital Science, Universiti Brunei Darussalam, Bandar Seri Begawan, Brunei Darussalam & Dig Connectivity Research Laboratory (DCRLab), Kampala, Uganda; E-mail: wasswashafik@ieee.org

Theodore Tarnanidis, Vijaya Kittu Manda, Vivek Gupta (Eds.)

essential variables, and validate the existing index by using different methods. In the first part of this study, the social and economic implications are discussed separately, regardless of the existing close relationships between them, among others.

Keywords: Circular Economy (CE), Models and strategies, Recovery and efficiency, Strategies and regulations, Sustainable development, Technology and policy.

INTRODUCTION

Today, we live within an economic model that is based on a continuous supply of raw materials to sustain constant growth in production and consumption. Nevertheless, physical resources are finite, and it is apparent that the current use of the world's resources is beyond sustainable levels. The logic of a linear economy enables global consumerism. The shift from a linear economy to a CE[1] is therefore seen as the new narrative to frame sustainability through the core economic model in a globalized world. The vision and evidence are growing that the building of this narrative is critical for the transition to sustainable economies and societies. A CE represents an economic model of production and consumption, which involves sharing, leasing, reusing, repairing, refurbishing, and recycling existing materials and products as long as possible. In this way, the life cycle of products is extended (Kandpal *et al.*, 2024). Materials are recovered from products, sometimes hybrid and composite materials, and can return to the economy instead of being "consumed" and left as waste. A circular approach can thus reduce both the need for using new raw resources and the total system waste. 1. It can contribute to a shift of the fragile balance of the world back towards long-term equilibrium in sustainable levels of production and consumption. Conducting a transition from a linear to a CE model involves rethinking production systems, consumption patterns, and adaptation of business models, and may result in a reorientation of renewed economies. These changes have social, economic, and ecological implications. Household and consumer behavior have begun to shift towards a preference for sustainable products and services tangentially (Serrano-Arévalo *et al.*, 2024).

Over the past decade, a number of cornerstones have emerged that have informed civil economy development. In the late 1980s, the notion of moving away from the traditional economic system to a zero-waste economy gained traction. Among the pioneers of the CE is Walter Stahel[2], who has had a significant impact through his publications. His most comprehensive study offers insight into how a CE has developed since the publication of his first book. Michael Braungart[3] supports Stahel in the development of CE. Currently, CE is a stream with an extensive international and interdisciplinary community involving researchers, industry experts, policymakers, and practitioners (Pusz *et al.*, 2024). There are also area-specific initiatives, such as building and electronics.

The CE principles aim towards the minimization of waste via the redesign of resource life cycles. The core of CE is the concept of the "Closed Loop Cycle[4]", where resources are reused, repaired, and recycled for as long as possible. The principles of CE thus enable the implementation of an ecological economic model characterized by harmony between ecological sustainability and regenerative economic processes. In this context, the concept of CE requires changes in the behavior of not only the business sector but also consumers, which can be labeled as the entire society. An essential goal of the principles of CE is also the concept of value retention, products, components, and materials should maintain their value over time. Individual authors and organizations emphasize some principles of CE more than others (Skalli *et al.*, 2024) . In this chapter, we focus mainly on some of the key principles of CE in the manufacturing of durable products. When these principles are appropriately implemented, CE ensures the minimization of waste and the decrease of primary resources, fosters innovation, creates new jobs, and makes products and processing more resource- and environmentally efficient.

Historical Development

The concept of CE is neither new nor original but a derivative of earlier ecological and environmental movements. Representative authors of the CE point out the "zero emission" concept in the zero emissions systems[5] of the early 1980s. However, it is imperative to realize that the historical approach to the problem was a result of the then and current driving forces. The early 1980s were marked by the first demonstration of the physical superiority of systems not driven by fossil fuels, whereas the first decade of the 21st century was characterized by the growing urgency of coping with climate change and resource depletion (Shafik, 2024a). A history of CE provides a long-term and, therefore, indicative view of how the nascent era of resource abundance that saw waste as an asset slowly gave way to an economy that promoted present possessive acquisitions and resource monopolies. Neither globalization nor the dramatic reduction of consumption of agricultural commodities, facilitated by the increase in energy efficiency, indicated an imminent crisis of resource availability. European success stories from the 18th and 19th centuries did not involve trade in newly acquired technological, economic, and cultural monopolies with the rest of European countries. Instead, these countries adapted existing joint systems to the changing technological conditions of the time (Hahladakis *et al.*, 2024).

ECONOMIC IMPACT OF CIRCULAR ECONOMY

Communicating the economic and social implications of the CE is a powerful way forward for companies, policymakers, and governments to accept and embrace the CE model. The CE can lead to a reduction in the costs of extracting, transporting, and processing virgin resources, including energy, as well as those of waste management, in view of the extended life of products. Economic cost savings that can be made are mostly connected to the durability, reparability, recyclability, or refurbishment of products and are related to the maintenance of resource stocks. CE thus offers potential savings for businesses, as well as economic and welfare benefits for governments and households via more efficient use of public and private resources (Patra *et al.*, 2024). In fact, resource efficiency and the growth of environmental and low-carbon goods industries can lead to new sources of economic growth and improve the competitiveness of any economy. Such principles can also be incorporated into a CE package focusing on jobs and enterprise.

A CE can save costs in the public sector by reducing the costs of waste management and improving environmental quality. With a more "economically active" environmental sector offering significant employment and a high wage premium, the CE model could also provide new job opportunities to replace those lost in traditional or manual areas. There is thus a case for economic growth, as well as macroeconomic signals from circular practices. Innovation is seen as one of the main drivers of economic growth. The leveraging of higher value-added activities supporting continued economic growth through innovation is again a key part of the results of a CE. A specific point could be that the benefits of a CE are long-term. While the high costs of eco-innovation and regulation are the source of the environmental Kuznets curve, many of these benefits can only be demonstrated over the long term. Initial buyers are thus less likely to benefit from these environmental savings, and governments might be justified in supporting CE regulation. The evidence from eco-innovating businesses came from various sectors. However, businesses implementing eco-innovation have much broader sectors and locations. Europe is seen as leading on a policy level, although the benefits of eco-innovation go beyond the region (Gonella *et al.*, 2024). The macroeconomic perspective demonstrated that the overall net benefits of a CE could be significant. The economy and waste packages[6] are helping to create an environment in which a CE can flourish through the reduction of burdens on member states.

Resource Efficiency and Cost Savings

Given the scarcity of natural resources, resource efficiency is at the very core of the CE. Mere responsible consumption can no longer be relied upon to meet sustainability goals as the global population continues to rise and the middle class continues to grow. This demonstrates how natural raw materials can be used to effectively reduce waste at a time when the current industrial model engenders environmental and social degradation; the transition to a CE provides essential solutions to future sustainability. One crucial advantage of focusing on resource efficiency, cost savings, and potential long-term economic ramifications is the ease of integrating these exercises directly into the general management of a business, both on the operational and corporate sides. This places efficiency at the level of average management objectives as well as the overall company strategy, thus contributing directly to the competitiveness of an enterprise.

This concept of "asset optimization[7]" is based on minimizing waste and the use of any resource by adopting improved production and corporate-wide processes and machinery, changing the scale of the equipment utilized, or refining the management of such assets. Reducing material demand at this level frees up cash from its alternatives or costly fixed assets that are effectively tied up in resource wastage. Through the implementation of best practices and the mainstreaming of efficient operations, companies are able to redeem a higher selling price for decreased value, effectively gaining additional money from fewer products. A company-wide energy optimization program cut approximately 500,000 megawatt hours, resulting in significant financial savings after investing a fraction of that amount. Similarly, estimates suggest that, through implementing best practices, a small to medium-sized company could reduce energy demand by between 7% and 29%, with the added benefit of a 3.5-year payback period. In addition, companies involved in waste reduction programs have garnered cost savings of between twenty and fifty percent. With specific reference to material and machinery costs, an automotive glass manufacturer experienced an increase in raw material yield from 67% to 79% after adopting lean production manufacturing techniques, which saved the company a substantial amount (Tiwari *et al.*, 2024). A major initiative aimed at increasing the incorporation of efficient machinery and processes has generated a notable percentage of corporate revenue and exhibited a significant profit margin. From a more general stance, promoting efficiency is a form of a firm's investment, which can subsequently lead to cost savings by streamlining operations.

Job Creation and Economic Growth

Job creation is mainly expected in the utilization of waste not currently managed and in the implementation of waste treatment activities directed towards a more sustainable use of materials and resources. However, in order to reap the benefits of a more CE, there is a need for appropriate education and skills development for those working in emerging areas such as repair, manufacturing, and recycling. Economic growth[8] creates no waste because it uses only renewable energy, and recycled materials would flourish. As demand increases and the developed world shifts from a linear to a circular model, the number of new high-quality jobs will multiply. In many real cases, the funding for CE developments has been secured partly because of the potential for job creation. A way forward is to invest in training to support the transition to a CE, which will be key in realizing its employment and economic potential.

Peer learning between different organizations involved in training, sector-specific training needs identification, training offers and needs evaluation, competencies and skills listings, and qualifications setting activities is a potentially valuable process that would help trainers design new training programs aimed at accelerating progress towards a CE. The transition from linear to circular in resource use and economic activity could bring about new investments and projects that will create new jobs and additional training expectations. New occupational profiles could be created, but they could also render some older ones and some companies obsolete. Finally, the merger between current and future economic activities will also have an impact on the competencies and skills needed for workers and company directors. Frame approaches to deal with the current gaps in skills and competencies needed for the design and management of CE strategies (Kumar *et al.*, 2024). A CE of the scale that it becomes a major part of a wider transition can act as a buffer to disturbances.

Cost Savings and Efficiency

Not using resources in excessive or uneconomic ways keeps prices low and leads to more stable oscillations. Thus, the CE benefits the whole range of economic actors. Businesses can reduce their operational costs by using resources much more efficiently and effectively. Companies use about 30-50% of their resources for activities such as sales, marketing, branding, and more. This is not only a waste of resources, but it also reveals that their products are not competitive in terms of quality and innovation due to the mass marketing approach. Therefore, the adoption of a circular business model can significantly lower a company's costs and add value to it. In addition, it improves product quality, which is another critical issue for company competitiveness and business survival.

It is, therefore, essential to have an efficient way of using resources to facilitate competition between producers since the losses embedded in demand variations, in addition to cost variations, are related to the utilization of resources. Competition is between supply chains rather than individual companies. In doing so, the improvements of small gains can be seen as a giveaway. For example, producing less than what might be possible allows for the adjustment of the supply chain and the establishment of target performance indexes to evaluate operational efficiencies (Shafik, 2024b). Incremental innovations are crucial to achieving a resource-efficient and sustainable society, but they will not suffice on a grander scale.

New Business Opportunities

The expansion into CE business models opens new niches for business development. A fundamental piece for the success of new business opportunities is product and service innovation. The pursuit of sustainable growth is among the key drivers for new products and services in companies. An organization can offer a variety of services and products. To compete successfully, an organization mustn't only create new product options from the same raw material; there are possibilities within the life cycle and beyond a mono-business model. Currently, some of the most critical areas are leasing, renting, product-as-a-service, product life extension service and maintenance, service and long-term part provisioning, energy efficiency services, waste management, recycling, training, solutions, and other factor-input services for the customer.

Various companies are successful and profitable in their businesses related to CE. Product or service life-extension initiatives can be very attractive to keep track of the new and rapidly growing fashion clothing trends. Additionally, the fashion trends of accessories can complement each other as seasonal trends are relevant. Both online and street retailers are looking at two crucial market trends: consumers are increasingly shopping via the Internet and are more and more attracted to sustainable products. Then another trend occurs, namely that the trend of circular fashion emphasizes quality over quantity. Brands slow down their fashion cycles, which puts the attention back on quality (Shafik, 2024c). Throughout the entire life cycle of any chosen business model concept, some requirements must not be overlooked if an organization wants or needs to stay up to par, explore new markets, and mainstream its products and services in a short period.

SOCIAL IMPACTS OF CIRCULAR ECONOMY

The social impacts of the transition to a CE are becoming an increasingly important topic of research and projects. The social aspects of a CE are fundamental for explaining why and how communities engage and empower themselves to pursue environmentally and economically sustainable ways of living. In doing so, they are often able to foster community well-being and cohesion in ways that preserve the health of the environment. Many suggest that a move towards a CE is necessary for addressing key challenges around social equity and, in particular, in guiding communities towards more sustainable and less resource-intensive ways of living that provide a means of sustainable livelihoods and equity in the distribution of essential resources and opportunities. This, in turn, can contribute towards improved global conditions.

There is a long-standing tradition in sustainability education that relies on engaging individuals and communities in practical activities that promote systems literacy and develop the skills and sense of empowerment necessary for enacting change. In schools, communities, and workplaces, it is widely agreed that learning about a new practice is not enough. Sustainable communities on which we depend for resources and ecological systems are inherently amorphous in terms of the outcomes they value. Drawing on the idea of the "biography of work," that is, understanding how the change in work both reflects and drives social changes, one says that the transition to circular economies must be understood in terms of the social and technological shifts that are emerging in contemporary societies. Recent research with a wide range of communities in industrial and developing world settings shows that a transition to a CE would address a vast range of major social issues at the local and global levels (Herrador & Van, 2024). A CE would deliver health and well-being benefits. For example, recent reports highlight the health and agricultural benefits to surrounding communities of early-stage circular initiatives to reuse waste in cement production.

In the midst of initiatives to reintegrate informal waste economies into circular regional systems, researchers documented a diverse range of environmental and social co-benefits that low-income community entrepreneurs were delivering. These included employment benefits but extended to health and well-being benefits to themselves as business owners and employers, their workers, their families, customers, and the local communities where they operated. In all these places, the community health co-benefits arose primarily from the avoided environmental harm. This report does not focus on the avoided harm from climate change, pollution of air, water, or soil, or resource depletion in ecosystems. Instead, we explore the direct social benefits that have been found. We use case study analysis as a way to grasp the conceptual and practical shifts that are taking place. These case studies report solid social impacts, leading us towards the position we synthesize in the final section: that discussions on the jobs and social impacts of a CE are interconnected and cannot be disentangled (Mondello *et al.*, 2024).

Community Engagement and Empowerment

Community engagement is considered a key factor for implementing CE practices. Engaging local communities in decision-making processes regarding their desired future and local, sustainable development is the starting point of a CE approach. Being involved in the process of empowering oneself, businesses, and policymakers enables a larger sense of ownership and accountability for behavioral changes and responsible consumption and production. Therefore, this is a necessary step for integrating the CE into long-term community resilience building. Engaging individuals and organizations in transitions towards a CE also gives them the opportunity to present their ideas, products, or organizations, to network and learn from each other, and to prepare and launch innovative undertakings between supply chain actors. Practitioners can use stakeholder engagement approaches to facilitate either new CE venture brainstorming or existing local and business asset assessment (Shafik, 2024d).

The Resource to Action

A number of strategies have been used to engage communities in concentrating on sustainability, as circular initiatives imply. For example, in territorial cooperation workshops, participants had the opportunity to immerse themselves in the nested concept of the ecological cycle, the social cycle, and the local cycle, which represented businesses, natural resources in the region, and other components. They were also familiarized with the "4Rs" (reuse, renew, recycle, and redesign) as strategies to opt for or manage during the change. The resource to action, futures gardens, and value chains are other examples of processes where community engagement has led to the launch of successful social undertakings, business services, or relocalization projects (de Jesus Pacheco *et al.*, 2024). There have been increased approaches to CE models of 7Rs, though it has not been fully realized, such as replace, recycle, repurpose, recover, re-modify, reuse, and redesign. During the resource-to-action process, individuals in a local district came together to begin planning for a more locally resilient future. Collaboratively, they formulated the heart within the glove model. The heart stood for community spirit and neighborly support, and the glove represented local businesses, social entrepreneurs, and charities. The process kick-started community initiatives and has supported participants in forming food-growing associations and services. These projects changed perceptions of resource management and have helped relocalize the voice and actions of local people.

Health and Well-being

This subsection investigates the impacts of CE practices on public health and overall well-being. The reduction of waste and pollution associated with these practices also contributes to healthier living environments and collaborative communities. The connection between resource management, scarcity, pollution, and the quality of living environments is of critical importance when considering the long-term public health implications of these strategies. Sustainable resource management practices and access to clean resources are directly related to morbidity and mortality, as well as other prosocial health outcomes like education, gender equity, and economic development. Social and behavioral changes that enable positive environmental stewardship can further reduce morbidity and mortality, as well as improve psychological and emotional well-being. For example, community and school-based agriculture initiatives have been shown to improve access to sufficient, nutritious food directly. Ecosystem health and access to locally sourced food are derived benefits of this optimistic, community-based approach to policy and programmatic considerations. Systems that produce these benefits promote and foster the total nourishment of individual, community, and planetary health and well-being. Positive emotional and mental states and views on life are also linked to physical health benefits (Roberts *et al.*, 2024). More broadly, social cohesion and strong social networks in communities that share a common interest in improving the environment and living conditions demonstrate superior health-related characteristics compared to those that do not.

TECHNOLOGICAL INNOVATIONS IN CIRCULAR ECONOMY

In particular, technological innovations offer the potential to increase resource productivity by driving greater efficiency and innovation in relation to resource use, waste reduction, and material management. This can, in turn, have economic implications by reducing the costs of material procurement and management. This section also identifies the technological advances in recycling processes, such as separation technologies, which increase the rate of material recovery from waste at competitive costs.

Another innovation with the potential to have a significant and widespread impact is the increasing number of digital platforms that connect those with resources to spare with willing recipients. This sharing economy avoids the environmental footprint of new product creation and allows greater access to single-use items. This supports the expansion of digital and societal technology platforms that support sustainability, which ultimately can become an agent of change in the adoption of systemic changes. Circular initiatives have embraced a range of technologies in their attempts to manage resources better and support sustainable business operations (Pansera *et al.*, 2024). These include novel separation technologies, as well as automated sorting for recycling plants that sort food waste, produce compost, and bring the products to market. Other initiatives aim to reduce waste at source by encouraging consumers to reduce or change their consumption patterns by choosing more high-quality goods and products with a minimal environmental footprint.

Digitalization can also support the piloting, development, and evolution of new technologies with the potential to transform the industry towards a CE. Circularity Lab[9] connects engineers, researchers, start-ups, and firms to share insights on how best to develop and apply circular manufacturing assets. Advances in technologies, such as automation, advanced robotics, smart logistics, decentralized renewable energy, and other industry practices, are key technological trends that will support further development of the CE. For a circular transformation to happen, there must be uptake and adoption of these technologies. The future CE may have solutions that will be forged by strategic combinations of resources, including those that utilize AI for efficiency. There may be significant transition periods where there will be 'halfway' solutions that incorporate newer and older technologies. These strategic combinations will reflect the trade-offs that it takes to rationalize existing practices with the speed of transitioning to innovative alternatives (Pan *et al.*, 2024).

Recycling Technologies and Processes

This subsection considers the latest developments in recycling technologies and processes that support CE initiatives. Material recovery facilities increasingly use automated robotic technology for the more precise identification and sorting of a greater variety of materials. Crucial for closing the resource loop is the ability to include hard-to-recycle fractions currently considered waste, such as end-of-life plastics from post-consumer products. New technologies, including chemical recycling and bioprocessing, are receiving attention for their potential to recover value from these types of waste, but have also been criticized for having the potential to result in lower recycling rates at the expense of resource extraction pollution. Nevertheless, capturing these hard-to-recycle materials through more advanced recycling technologies allows for maximizing recovery rates due to reducing often high levels of waste contamination, alongside reducing the financial and environmental costs of landfill, export, or incineration.

State-of-the-art options and up-and-coming technologies to improve recycling rates continue to require more pilot-scale and full-scale deployment investment from both the government and the private sector. Recycling technology faces several challenges in processing the large volume of recyclate material and in rapid generations of recyclable products, including waste stream contamination through a heterogeneity of composition and shape. Chemical recycling and bioprocessing are growing research fields as they offer solutions for particularly problematic waste, such as multi-layered and composite materials. This subsection covers the technological benefits, loopholes, and challenges in more mineral processing, pyrolysis fast recycling, thermal and catalytic depolymerization, hydrogenation, ammonia process, solvolysis, and brominated flame-retardant recycling work, alongside several potential routes, yet challenges, associated with cellulose and bioprocessing (Mura *et al.*, 2024). Throughout the unit of analysis, current processes and separation techniques were also examined.

Digital Platforms and Sharing Economy

The emergence of digital platforms has introduced new aspirations for CE principles, giving people the ability to share resources more efficiently. The idea of sharing goods and assets on a peer-to-peer basis has become feasible partly as a result of the matching capabilities of global platforms, users, and the ability to manage the complex transactions of sharing. One of the central principles of resource efficiency and reduction of waste is sharing resources, and in particular durable assets, more effectively. The growth in this area can be an example of utility engagement in sustainable consumption. New digital media is essentially changing the grounds for the "eco-unfriendly levels" of increased consumption. A key focus of CE interventions has been on the production and consumption of new things rather than just disposing of what we already have. It asks questions about engaging users and communities in the process of designing and maintaining products and services beyond product conception. It speaks massively to a social ethics concept that has long existed in sharing valued, durable assets, and which might have resonance with the high levels of community engagement of the growing Better Together project. This approach has been given a new platform, indeed a virtual high street at the fingertips of local consumers, who can trade one of their very own things, from toys to tools. The attraction of digital channels is particularly marked in enabling a new and apparently more resilient and 'inherently sustainable' breed of businesses to develop around the sharing economy. Examples of this in broader markets include relatives or friends who have traditionally fulfilled this role. A number of other forms can typically be found as reuse or repair services, mainly clothes finders, charity shops, and furniture exchanges (Song *et al.*, 2024). Many local authorities see improving the market presence of the voluntary sector engaged in the repair and reuse of second-hand goods as a significant opportunity to offer a cost-effective form of waste management at the same time as reducing disadvantages and possibly helping citizens learn valuable new skills.

CHALLENGES AND BARRIERS TO CIRCULAR ECONOMY ADOPTION

The arguments for a CE are persuasive; however, there are more than a few hurdles in moving from a linear economic system to one of CE. Education is a high-level issue. All levels, from school children to adult education, of stakeholders, manufacturers, and consumers are at a low level. All stakeholders, and especially designers and manufacturers, need to embed design for disassembly and reuse. If businesses do not design for durability and obsolescence, society is unlikely to benefit from the potential savings that are claimed as rewards for this activity. Once an awareness program has been undertaken, there is still a great deal of mind-changing needed to affect deeper levels of society in terms of throwing away rather than repairing, and people deliberately opting for producers who embed CE values. Supply chain issues and the problem of getting waste recovered or recycled back to the manufacturer for further reuse exist, as current logistic models are based on traditional linear models (Oghazi *et al.*, 2024).

The sheer scale of the problem is a significant barrier. There is a lack of infrastructure available to support the move, and without the political will and massive investment, not enough recycling could be carried out to support the businesses engaged in the move to a one-way system. There is a degree of resistance to change by the financial community in moving away from the old economic model due to the potential risk in the early stages for businesses that are embracing the impact and developing strategies to reduce the risk of future volatility. Such a change in the financial system requires involvement from a number of other stakeholders. Pharmaceutical companies fear a change to a CE as a business model, as presently, medicine is based on a linear model of consumption. In Cape Town[10], there is interest from companies in adopting a CE in principle; however, changing current business models is a complex process given the pervasive nature of traditional business arrangements. Once change has occurred, confusion still reigns. The CE is reportedly a 'confusing term' brought about by policy touch paper. Policing the wrong burdens, such as setting wrong targets, and also enforcing non-value legislation, which includes energy and air quality legislation, is necessary (Gao *et al.*, 2024). To alleviate these and other obstacles, the report does put forward a number of strategies that could unlock CE potential. The strategies are varied but do emphasize the importance of policy and the need for significant educational input.

Lack of Awareness and Education

One of the leading factors that has contributed to challenges in adopting the CE is the lack of awareness and education. It is a general perception held by many that when you mention "recycling," it is interpreted as "CE." Besides, a circular approach, in general, is not undertaken because people are unaware of it or lack the knowledge of how to apply circular practices. One of the recommendations in the public roundtable was education. Community members, including business people and industrial sectors, agreed that changes were needed. They suggested that the system was beyond salvation and needed to be rebuilt on a circular model. Actions should be taken at various levels of education: from teaching young people and promoting this behavior at schools to parents, to including awareness and knowledge in community programs.

There have been some very successful campaigns carried out to fully inform all stakeholders of their terms and concepts, processes, *etc*., for recycling and developments in the fields of reuse, repurposing, refurbishing, and remarketing. Retailers have some of the most fundamental information that needs to get to the consumers, but with the need to demonstrate profitability, they are often not proactive; if asked, they inform the consumer but do not market their products from this perspective. There is also a recommendation for action in community education programs to consumers as well as industry stakeholders. It is imperative to include education in business curricula at varying levels. With specific reference to MRPs[11], if others are aware of the value and worth we ascribe to these materials, they may scuttle our efforts if something else is seen as more profitable, unless there is a change in business culture. Integration of concepts of the CE in human resource management development is also seen to be timely with corporations (Shafik, 2024e). A good idea is to engage public interest and financial support to begin initiatives, collecting enough toilet paper tubes to line them up and span the length of the country. It only takes a coordinator or intern and some gumption; what could it hurt to try?

Infrastructure and Logistics

These are identified as two key challenges to the successful implementation of CE practices. Insufficient infrastructure to manage and recycle waste, unwillingness to disclose resource recovery within existing systems, and lack of committed stakeholders have been predicted to form a barrier to the adoption of recycling and CE strategies. Recycling systems need to be in place for the industry to prepare for a circular transition. Circular supply chains rely on efficient and effective logistics processes and infrastructure. The complexities of reverse logistics and opportunistic actors within uncontrolled recycling networks are concerns that need to be addressed with suitable investments in technology and infrastructure to manage the deconstruction and material flows of dismantled products.

Investment in infrastructure to facilitate a circular transition is one of the barriers to the adoption of a CE. This category is assumed to exploit existing infrastructure and other resources to support their circular activities. As an example, it is clear that infrastructure is a requirement to undertake CE supply chain activities, including integration with decision-making systems and integration with technology used for resource recovery. Moreover, fragmented and low-transparency supply chains are considered to form a barrier to the adoption of CE activities as they may increase barriers to communication and knowledge sharing. Several identify that policies may provide interventions to address existing infrastructure and logistical gaps (Khan & Khurshid, 2024). Furthermore, resource supply and kit of parts requirements for circular transition activities may be undertaken in order to address a potential lack of appropriate infrastructure.

Technological Limitations

The key barrier to the transition to a CE and all the corresponding social and economic implications, which the various other individuals interviewed referred to, was technology. There are three subthemes under this grouping. The first technological limitation noted was inefficient extraction and a lack of advanced recycling and recovery technologies. Although the technologies for recycling and resource management are slowly becoming more efficient, the majority of interviewees noted that the process of extracting, processing, and refining resources is still very inefficient. For example, if 90% of the currently mined copper could be recycled, that would be "fantastic," a study participant who works on such technology in the automobile industry stated.

Circular production processes and end products require changing technological infrastructure, necessitating costly changes to production, development, and service systems. The current technological base is likely insufficient as it is not built to support circular flows or new features in products. Most machines that provide the first transformation, such as recycling and sorting machines, are old and do not perform at the same quality level as modern manufacturing devices. Similarly, vehicles and sorting infrastructure were designed for an entirely different supply chain model, which introduces difficulties in sorting products for recycling and likewise for extracting raw materials. Because of these technology barriers, businesses need to devote a part of their budgets to research and development to develop new business models, along with the advanced infrastructure needed to support these models (Schneikart *et al.*, 2024). Emerging technologies participate in the economic and social implications linked to establishing new instruments for resource management and coordination.

Technological Limitations

The key barrier to the transition to a CE and all the corresponding social and economic implications, which the various other individuals interviewed referred to, was technology. There are three subthemes under this grouping. The first technological limitation noted was inefficient extraction and a lack of advanced recycling and recovery technologies. Although the technologies for recycling and resource management are slowly becoming more efficient, the majority of interviewees noted that the process of extracting, processing, and refining resources is still very inefficient. For example, if 90% of the copper that is currently mined could be recycled, that would be "fantastic," a study participant who works on such technology in the automobile industry stated.

Circular production processes and final end products require changing technological infrastructure, necessitating costly changes to production, development, and service systems. The current technological base is likely insufficient as it is not built to support circular flows or new features in products. Most machines that provide the first transformation, such as recycling and sorting machines, are old and do not perform at the same quality level as modern manufacturing devices. Similarly, vehicles and sorting infrastructure were designed for an entirely different supply chain model, which introduces difficulties in sorting products for recycling and likewise for extracting raw materials. Because of these technological barriers, businesses need to devote a part of their budgets to research and development to develop new business models, along with the advanced infrastructure needed to support these models (Shafik, 2025). Emerging technologies participate in the economic and social implications linked to establishing new instruments for resource management and coordination.

The key barrier to the transition to a CE and all the corresponding social and economic implications, which the various other individuals interviewed referred to, was technology. There are three subthemes under this grouping. The first technological limitation noted was inefficient extraction and a lack of advanced recycling and recovery technologies. Although the technologies for recycling and resource management are slowly becoming more efficient, the majority of interviewees noted that the process of extracting, processing, and refining resources is still very inefficient. For example, if 90% of the copper that is currently mined could be recycled, that would be "fantastic," a study participant who works on such technology in the automobile industry stated.

Circular production processes and end products require changing technological infrastructure, necessitating costly changes to production, development, and service systems. The current technological base is likely insufficient as it is not built to support circular flows or new features in products. Most machines that provide the first transformation, such as recycling and sorting machines, are old and do not perform at the same quality level as modern manufacturing devices. Similarly, vehicles and sorting infrastructure were designed for an entirely different supply chain model, which introduces difficulties in sorting products for recycling and likewise for extracting raw materials. Because of these technology barriers, businesses need to devote a part of their budgets to research and development to develop new business models along with the advanced infrastructure needed to support these models (Park *et al.*, 2024). Emerging technologies participate in the economic and social implications linked to establishing new instruments for resource management and coordination.

Behavioral Change

Behavioral change is one of the main challenges that the concept of CE has to address at both the levels of organizations and whole communities. Resistance to change is an inherent feature of the paradigms that have run the economy and consumption for years. Therefore, the success of the CE depends on the extent to which stakeholders are aware of its benefits. Strategies for encouraging the acceptance of new rules, values, and norms should rely on both direct and indirect communication activities, which aim to generate and foster a new "culture of use" and "culture of making." The educational and cognitive dimension of behavioral change is one of the fundamental tools to inform stakeholders of a new idiom (Upadhayay *et al.*, 2024). Creating interdisciplinary and inter-institutional forums on the CE is one of the valuable actions that could lead to more widespread informal educational outcomes.

Internalization of the Circular Economy

Numerous studies indicate the key role of leadership in driving behavioral change in both public and private organizations, as well as across local communities or entire countries. Managers are indispensable in creating organizational learning competencies that facilitate learning from unwanted behavior. Moreover, commitment at the top management level can communicate a strong message to the rank-and-file that the organization provides not only "vision" but also "substance." Commitment at the top management level could speed up the organizational learning process and commitment by others. Nevertheless, those leaders who are willing to consider innovative measures hardly ever go further than the awareness level, and the challenge is to convert the initial awareness of the benefits into further engagement of those leaders in devising and deploying the circular strategies and required measures. Significant learning challenges are related to the internalization of the CE in the corporate culture (Hondroyiannis *et al.*, 2024). The process of unlearning and replacing current paradigms is essential; hence, the challenge lies in the need to replace the deeply ingrained established culture and habits.

Circular Economy Adoption

Much research has focused on investigating the motivations behind the implementation of the CE across different organizational levels. Small- and medium-sized organizations, in particular, are knowledgeable about the benefits of CE adoption. However, there are numerous challenges and barriers associated with the adoption of CE practices, highlighting the limited effectiveness of efforts in convincing companies of the need to transition towards a more sustainable and circular approach. One of the key challenges is the financial aspect. In almost all industries, organizations are focused on reducing costs to increase profits while maintaining or improving the quality of the products and services. Circularity generally involves engaging in the recycling, repair, and remanufacturing of products, often made from components and materials of unknown origin. There are efforts to prove the superior quality of reused or recycled elements; however, better quality connections with unknown inputs need further investigation.

Before they decide to transition to a CE, stakeholders are only aware of present values and are thus reluctant to accrue later returns. Another key challenge is that current business models usually operate on linear processes, with no active involvement of the organization throughout the full linear value chain. Convincing and enabling them to change their linear business model, with no guaranteed future benefits to them, is challenging. Transitioning entire supply chains towards sustainably sourced elements and materials is incredibly complex (Arsawan *et al.*, 2024). Additionally, no current market or policy incentives exist to encourage the long-term circular supply chain collaborations required. The financial and stakeholder issues are further exacerbated because circular practices and values must be rooted in company culture for full effectiveness.

Case Studies and Best Practices

This chapter compiles a series of case studies or best practices of CE from around the world. It is important to note that they draw from very diverse sectors, including an educational institution, territorial administration, wastewater and sludge management, solid waste management, a coffee shop chain, the Spanish railway company in its stores and locomotives, car rental, and a second-hand clothes shop. Some of these cases have been successful and are perfectly replicable or scalable, while others have had difficulties that make learning from them as interesting as knowing about their best practices. In some of the cases, the stakeholders that have made these initiatives possible have been cities or regions, territorial agglomerations, schools, collaborating government entities, companies, or entrepreneurs with visionary insight, and in others, they have been entire countries. Sometimes, the key players have been the businesses themselves, but always and without exception, local citizens or consumers have been relevant. The scope of the concept of circularity in each case allows us to understand that the CE is not a "one size fits all" phenomenon. What can be done and how to go about it depends not only on the sector or scale of action but also on the geographical context of the initiatives, both with regard to the area in which they have taken place and the potential for transference or adaptation to other areas, regions, or places in the world (Ferrante *et al*., 2024).

SUCCESSFUL CIRCULAR ECONOMY INITIATIVES

These present innovation and examples where other businesses can successfully work with and participate to become more resourceful and sustainable. All the case studies present positive outcomes on waste reduction, economic benefits, and opportunities, and can represent a strong case for where there are other examples in the UK. Key to replicating the success of these initiatives is genuine, committed collaboration of all stakeholders; engagement from businesses working together from the supply chain who are not just driven by core compliance but looking to improve their practices; inspiration, ambition, and attitude on the same level. The people involved are absolutely key; they are driven not by money or core compliance, but they have humanity, purpose, identity, dignity, and willingness to work with others who can critique and help them with the CE.

These initiatives have also faced barriers, and all initiatives are on journeys. Though leaders will continue to lead where others will follow, some are treading carefully while embracing uncertainty. These initiatives are also heavy on monitoring and evaluation. Measures must be in place on day one to count what a circular approach is saving and making a business, while also embracing a crowbar approach to open up other business models for competitive advantage. Monitoring of initiatives and success must remain open and transparent over several years if they are also to remain a leading example of what the CE can do. Also, initiatives might wholly or partly relate to other small amalgamated case studies (Mousavi *et al*., 2024). These amalgamated case studies also offer an international view of where the CE is working in the sectors of manufacturing, marine management, medical, chemical, plastic prevention, agriculture, bitumen, packaging, technology, sustainability, fashion, construction, reuse, waste management, philanthropy, and social and creative engagements. They include the Frugal Innovation Forum[12], Greener UK Supplier Relational Road Trip[13], Halcyon Art International[14], Kessler[15], Lancashire Becoming a Global Economic Influencer in all Things Circular[16], Pozzoni[17], Renaissance Public Relations Europe[18], Resonvate Diplomas[19], UK Tétris[20], and The Brew Coffee Company[21].

Lessons Learned and Recommendations

This chapter has featured a thematic series on CE offered to the scientific and professional communities, including CE and enabling conditions and impacts on innovation, business, employment, and society.

1. Context adaptation is necessary for every circular initiative. Adaptation processes must be supported by solid evidence concerning the depth of the challenges and the impact of corresponding changes.
2. Cross-level stakeholder engagement is critical. The application necessitates an ongoing cofactor role within governance where local-level plan execution can be tailored to local contexts, and the local level can build the bridge to initiatives.
3. "Try, learn, and adapt" with stakeholder and policy support is a critical program principle. The circular approaches in place that promise the best chance of success should be chosen and scaled on a trial basis.
4. Continuously gather data beyond the broader conversation. This would involve analyzing the data in real-time, every week and every month, to determine what is working and which other tactics also need to be developed.
5. Every business that wants to experiment should collaborate to support this platform. The impact of circular strategies in any specified area would strengthen mobile service industries and further foster small-to-medium companies.

CONCLUDING REMARKS

There has been a significant increase in the number of calls and references to CE practices among global corporations over the last few years. Therefore, looking at what is being cited in company reports and is likely to be on the horizon for future CE activities is paramount. Early circular businesses rolled out with the commercialization and conversion of secondary materials, and it is anticipated that this will continue. This suggests that the development of urban mining and associated industries will increase the practice of CE. Municipal waste categories are prioritized and could be a launch pad for these early businesses, especially e-waste, which appears in most plans. Supply chains are where these industries drive value. In the immediate future, collaborations and supplier network capacity should, therefore, be priorities. Global partnerships can also significantly affect the price of parts, particularly critical resources. Insourcing and cost-saving from waste management are expected to boost future interest, yet waste management remains a low priority in the plans. With urban mining and supplier networks in mind, it might be anticipated that organizational behavior management[22] as a service model will be pushed over the coming years. Collaborative networks will be significant in future circular economies as new businesses proliferate. With ongoing technological innovation, these could stretch farther than collaborative links between specific companies and even connect multiple industries in what is called circularity clusters, each with its own circular supply chain. Despite this, the number of calls that directly mention this gigatrend remains lower. Evolving consumer preferences will be a motivator in the practice of CE, but it will not quite mandate the practice. Businesses may attempt to build products that cater to the changing views of public opinion, as the political landscape has changed regarding which companies consumers purchase from. It is likely that industry will set the agenda and that regulation can further motivate the development of the CE. There is a viable prospect in the operation of a CE, though it does not provide any inconsistency between the two. Whether companies believe in a significant convergence, both of these statements do not counteract the winding path that businesses can take, driven by profit. Transitioning to stability now is inevitable for the future of sustainable development.

NOTES

[1] https://www.epa.gov/circulareconomy/what-circular-economy

[2] https://en.wikipedia.org/wiki/Walter_R._Stahel

[3] https://c2ccertified.org/speakers/michael-braungart

[4] https://www.greenwillowhomestead.com/blog/what-is-a-closed-loop-cycle

[5] https://www.agora-energiewende.org/topics/zero-emissions-power-system

[6] https://eurocities.eu/resources/packaging-and-packaging-waste-waste-as-a-valuable-resource/

[7] https://www.aspentech.com/en/cp/asset-optimization

[8] https://www.investopedia.com/terms/e/economicgrowth.asp

[9] https://gxn.3xn.com/project/circularity-lab

[10] https://en.wikipedia.org/wiki/Cape_Town

[11] https://tdmr-europe.com/what-are-tdrs-and-mrps/

[12] https://innovation.brac.net/fif2022/

[13] https://cat.org.uk/info-resources/free-information-service/green-living/transport-and-travel/

[14] https://www.prnewswire.com/news-releases/halcyons-by-the-people-festival-features-art-and-dialogue-june-15-23-300864500.html

[15] https://www.kesslersdiamonds.com/

[16] https://www.investprestoncity.com/article/3202/Preston-and-Lancashire-investment -and-development-projects-strategies-and-plans

[17] https://www.pozzoni.co.uk/

[18] https://renaissancepr.co.uk/

[19] https://resonvate.com/

[20] https://www.tetris-db.com/en/about-us/where-to-find-us/united-kingdom/

[21] https://brew-company.com/

[22] https://apmg-international.com/article/benefits-organizational-behavior-management-obm

REFERENCES

Arsawan, I.W., Koval, V., Suhartanto, D., Hariyanti, N.K., Polishchuk, N., Bondar, V. (2024). Circular economy practices in SMEs: Aligning models of green economic incentives and environmental commitment. *Int. J. Prod. Perform. Manag., 73*(3), 775-793.
[http://dx.doi.org/10.1108/IJPPM-03-2022-0144]

de Jesus Pacheco, D.A., Rampasso, I.S., Michels, G.S., Ali, S.M., Hunt, J.D. (2024). From linear to circular economy: The role of BS 8001:2017 for green transition in small businesses in developing economies. *J. Clean. Prod., 439*140787
[http://dx.doi.org/10.1016/j.jclepro.2024.140787]

Ferrante, M., Vitti, M., Facchini, F., Sassanelli, C. (2024). Mapping the relations between the circular economy rebound effects dimensions: A systematic literature review. *J. Clean. Prod., 142399*
[http://dx.doi.org/10.1016/j.jclepro.2024.142399]

Gonella, J.D., Godinho Filho, M., Ganga, G.M.D., Latan, H., Jabbour, C.J.C. (2024). A behavioral perspective on circular economy awareness: The moderating role of social influence and psychological barriers. *J. Clean. Prod., 441*141062
[http://dx.doi.org/10.1016/j.jclepro.2024.141062]

Gao, J.Q., Li, D., Qiao, G.H., Jia, Q.R., Li, S.R., Gao, H.L. (2024). Circular economy strategies in supply chains: Enhancing resource efficiency and sustainable development goals. *Environ. Sci. Pollut. Res. Int., 31*(6), 8751-8767.
[http://dx.doi.org/10.1007/s11356-023-31551-z]

Hondroyiannis, G., Sardianou, E., Nikou, V., Evangelinos, K., Nikolaou, I. (2024). Circular economy and macroeconomic performance: Evidence across 28 European countries. *Ecol. Econ., 215*108002
[http://dx.doi.org/10.1016/j.ecolecon.2023.108002]

Hahladakis, J.N., Iacovidou, E., Gerassimidou, S. (2024). Plastic waste in a circular economy. *Environmental materials and waste.* Elsevier.

Herrador, M., Van, M.L. (2024). Circular economy strategies in the ASEAN region: A comparative study. *Sci. Total Environ., 908*168280
[http://dx.doi.org/10.1016/j.scitotenv.2023.168280]

Khan, K., Khurshid, A. (2024). Are technology innovation and circular economy remedies for emissions? Evidence from the Netherlands. *Environ. Dev. Sustain., 26*(1), 1435-1449.
[http://dx.doi.org/10.1007/s10668-022-02766-w]

Kandpal, V., Jaswal, A., Santibanez Gonzalez, E.D.R., Agarwal, N. (2024). Circular economy principles: Shifting towards sustainable prosperity. *Sustainable energy transition.* (Circular Economy and Sustainability). Springer.

Kumar, B., Kumar, L., Kumar, A., Kumari, R., Tagar, U., Sassanelli, C. (2024). Green finance in circular economy: A literature review. *Environ. Dev. Sustain., 26*(7), 16419-16459.
[http://dx.doi.org/10.1007/s10668-023-03361-3]

Mondello, A., Salomone, R., Mondello, G. (2024). Exploring circular economy in the cosmetic industry: Insights from a literature review. *Environ. Impact Assess. Rev., 105*107443
[http://dx.doi.org/10.1016/j.eiar.2024.107443]

Mura, R., Vicentini, F., Botti, L.M., Chiriacò, M.V. (2024). Achieving the circular economy through environmental policies: Packaging strategies for more sustainable business models in the wine industry. *Bus. Strategy Environ., 33*(2), 1497-1514.
[http://dx.doi.org/10.1002/bse.3556]

Mousavi, M., Kowsari, E., Gheibi, M., Cheshmeh, Z.A., Teymoorian, T., Ramakrishna, S. (2024). Assessing bioplastics' economic, commercial, political, and energy potential with circular economy modeling: A sustainable solution to plastic waste management. *Materials Circular Economy, 6*(1), 6.
[http://dx.doi.org/10.1007/s42824-023-00098-2]

Oghazi, P., Mostaghel, R., Hultman, M. (2024). International industrial manufacturers: Mastering the era of digital innovation and circular economy. *Technol. Forecast. Soc. Change, 201*123160 [http://dx.doi.org/10.1016/j.techfore.2023.123160]

Park, H., Kim, K., Yu, M., Yun, Z., Lee, S. (2024). Economic analysis of the circular economy based on waste plastic pyrolysis oil: A case of the university campus. *Environ. Dev. Sustain., 26*(3), 6293-6313. [http://dx.doi.org/10.1007/s10668-023-02963-1]

Pusz, M., Jonas, A.E., Deutz, P. (2024). Knitting circular ties: Empowering networks for the social enterprise-led local development of an integrative circular economy. *Circular Economy and Sustainability, 4*(1), 201-232.
[http://dx.doi.org/10.1007/s43615-023-00271-4]

Patra, S.P., Wankhede, V.A., Agrawal, R. (2024). Circular economy practices in supply chain finance: A state-of-the-art review. *Benchmarking (Bradf.), 31*(7), 2197-2216.
[http://dx.doi.org/10.1108/BIJ-10-2022-0627]

Pansera, M., Barca, S., Martínez-Alvarez, B., Leonardi, E., D'Alisa, G., Meira, T., Guillibert, P. (2024). Toward a just circular economy: Conceptualizing environmental labor and gender justice in circularity studies. *Sustainability: Science. Practice and Policy, 20*(1)2338592
[http://dx.doi.org/10.1080/15487733.2024.2338592]

Pan, H., Sun, Y., Wang, M., Dong, Z., Wang, Z., Zhang, Y., Zhang, X. (2024). Rising from the ashes: Transitioning towards carbon neutrality through the pathways of circular economy agglomeration. *Ecol. Econ., 219*108146
[http://dx.doi.org/10.1016/j.ecolecon.2024.108146]

Roberts, H., Zhang, J., Bariach, B., Cowls, J., Gilburt, B., Juneja, P., Tsamados, A., Ziosi, M., Taddeo, M., Floridi, L. (2024). Artificial intelligence in support of the circular economy: Ethical considerations and a path forward. *AI Soc., 39*(3), 1451-1464.
[http://dx.doi.org/10.1007/s00146-022-01596-8]

Skalli, D., Charkaoui, A., Cherrafi, A., Garza-Reyes, J.A., Antony, J., Shokri, A. (2024). Analyzing the integrated effect of circular economy, Lean Six Sigma, and Industry 4.0 on sustainable manufacturing performance from a practice-based view perspective. *Bus. Strategy Environ., 33*(2), 1208-1226.
[http://dx.doi.org/10.1002/bse.3546]

Shafik, W. (2024). Environmental conservation and sustainable development. *Developing digital inclusion through globalization and digitalization.* IGI Global.

Shafik, W. (2024). Exploring the potential of Internet of Things (IoT) and challenges in enabling circular economy practices in smart cities. *Smart cities and circular economy.* Emerald Publishing.

Shafik, W. Community and artificial intelligence-enabled disaster management and preparedness. In G. Meraj, S. Hashimoto, & P. Kumar (Eds.), *Navigating natural hazards in mountainous topographies* (Disaster Risk Reduction). Springer.

Shafik, W. (2024). Industry 4.0 technologies' opportunities and challenges for realising net-zero economy. *Net zero economy, corporate social responsibility and sustainable value creation* Springer.

Song, A., Dan, Z., Zheng, S., Zhou, Y. (2024). An electricity-driven mobility circular economy with lifecycle carbon footprints for climate-adaptive carbon neutrality transformation. *Nat. Commun., 15*(1), 5905.
[http://dx.doi.org/10.1038/s41467-024-49868-9]

Shafik, W. Generative AI for social good and sustainable development. In K. Raza, N. Ahmad, & D. Singh (Eds.), *Generative AI: Current trends and applications* (Studies in Computational Intelligence, Vol. 1177). Springer.

Schneikart, G., Mayrhofer, W., Löffler, C., Frysak, J. (2024). A roadmap towards circular economies in pharma logistics based on returnable transport items enhanced with Industry 4.0 technologies. *Resour. Conserv. Recycling, 206*107615

[http://dx.doi.org/10.1016/j.resconrec.2024.107615]

Shafik, W. (2025). Pathways to climate neutrality: Understanding ice cap reduction, glacial melt, and sea level change and adoption. In: Singh, R., Filho, W.L., (Eds.), *Climate neutrality through smart eco-innovation and environmental sustainability.* Springer.

Serrano-Arévalo, T.I., Díaz-Alvarado, F.A., Tovar-Facio, J., Ponce-Ortega, J.M. (2024). The impact of circular economy indicators in the optimal planning of energy systems. *Sustainable Production and Consumption, 44*, 234-249.
[http://dx.doi.org/10.1016/j.spc.2023.12.018]

Tiwari, S., Mohammed, K.S., Mentel, G., Majewski, S., Shahzadi, I. (2024). Role of circular economy, energy transition, environmental policy stringency, and supply chain pressure on CO_2 emissions in emerging economies. *Geoscience Frontiers, 15*(3)101682
[http://dx.doi.org/10.1016/j.gsf.2023.101682]

Upadhayay, S., Alqassimi, O., Khashadourian, E., Sherm, A., Prajapati, D. (2024). Development in the circular economy concept: Systematic review in context of an umbrella framework. *Sustainability, 16*(4), 1500.
[http://dx.doi.org/10.3390/su16041500]

CHAPTER 8

Reinventing Employee Skills for Building Circular Economies

P. Bhanumathi[1,*] and **Hemavathi G.P.**[2]

[1] *M S Ramaiah Institute of Management, Bangalore, Karnataka, India*

[2] *R N S Institute of Technology, Bangalore, Karnataka, India*

Abstract: In today's era, a circular economy calls for a great transition towards sustainable development, and these circular economic models or frameworks are crucial in combating resource depletion and environmental degradation. This chapter explores the strategies and practices for developing talent to thrive in circular economies. This chapter outlines the reinvention of employee skills and capabilities to support the transition from a linear to a circular economy. It explores the competencies and knowledge required for employees to succeed in circular economies, including thought processes, innovative problem-solving, and proficiency in sustainable practices and technologies. The chapter also highlights practical strategies for upskilling and reskilling the workforce. The chapter concludes by discussing the challenges and opportunities associated with workforce transformation in circular economies, emphasizing the need for collaborative efforts among stakeholders to achieve a sustainable and resilient economic future.

Keywords: Circular economy, Competencies, Reinventing skills, Sustainable goals.

INTRODUCTION

The focus on the circular economy has intensified in today's businesses, governments, and communities, as they strive to adopt more sustainable economic models. Transforming a traditional linear economy into a circular one requires technological expertise, skill, and a mindset shift. Employees must have the necessary knowledge and skills to initiate this transformation. Initiating this process can be challenging, so the organization must focus on developing the required skills.

* **Corresponding author Bhanumathi P.:** M S Ramaiah Institute of Management, Bangalore, Karnataka, India; E-mail: bhanumathi@msrim.org

The organization focuses on understanding the principles of the circular economy and innovation that can adapt and utilize digital technologies to develop sustainable practices (Rodríguez-Espíndola *et al.*, 2022). Formulating and implementing various strategies and approaches will help the organization continually learn and encourage innovation, emphasizing circular principles. This method can implement a new economic paradigm.

INTRODUCTION TO CIRCULAR ECONOMIES

A circular economy emphasizes the importance of a resource-efficient model that promotes waste reduction through recycling and innovative practices. This method will promote sustainable development and lead to economic growth. The transformation process will not only lead to a reduction in waste but also a shift in the skills and proficiencies of the personnel. The essential resource required for the skill shift is a diverse group of people with various skills. Hence, the organization must equip its employees with the necessary competencies through regular analysis and training methods.

The circular economy involves changing the product or design and transforming the personnel's skills and capabilities (López, 2021). The organization must invest in developing new skills and encourage a culture of innovation and collaboration that creates sustainable transformation. Circular economies benefit society and the environment, leading to the organization's success and global sustainability.

Circular economies create numerous job opportunities in various sectors, including refurbishment and remanufacturing. Economic resilience is achieved by fostering local manufacturers and reducing product imports. The environmental benefits of the circular economy include reducing pollution and waste in landfills, as well as promoting the materials that can be reused, repaired, and recycled. This approach enables resources to be used more efficiently and sustainably (Ogunmakinde *et al.*, 2022). The circular principles reduce the extraction and processing of raw materials, resulting in lower greenhouse gas emissions and helping to mitigate climate change. Organizations can save costs through more efficient resource use, minimizing waste disposal, and potentially lessening the cost associated with materials. The shift towards circular business can enhance a company's reputation, create demand for sustainable products, and drive higher creativity in product design, manufacturing, and the way the company is approached.

Circular economies aid in many UN SDGs, including consumption patterns and production, climate actions, *etc.* (Ogunmakinde *et al.*, 2022). By keeping materials in use for an extended period, circular economies help preserve resources, reduce environmental degradation, and foster international collaboration, which is essential for addressing global environmental challenges.

Principles of Circular Economies

Reducing waste and maximizing resource efficiency are paramount, essential principles of a circular economy. Certain principles are established to transition the traditional linear economy model to a regenerative approach. Some principles are discussed below (Velenturf & Purnell, 2021).

1. **Eliminate waste and pollution:** Products must be designed to curtail waste and pollution. Non-toxic, recyclable, and biodegradable materials should be preferred to remove waste and reduce pollution generation.
2. **Maintain products and materials in use:** The material should be selected and planned to be durable and upgradable for long-term product usage. Maintain the standard to allow the product to be reused, repaired, and recycled.
3. **Regenerate Natural System:** The organization can use renewable energy and resources to maintain a sustainable system and take necessary steps to maintain the ecosystem. It can also protect the soil and biodiversity by using farming practices.
4. **Foster Systemic Thinking:** Develop innovative methods to adapt to the changing environment through network connectivity across various businesses to exchange ideas and materials, and foster better development
5. **Transparency and Traceability:** Transparency in the supply chain will facilitate the tracing and improvement of resource management and accountability. Through digital mechanisms, sharing and storing relevant information is easy and fast.

Comparison between Linear and Circular Economies

A "Take-make-dispose" framework characterizes the linear economy model. In this system, raw materials are extracted and transformed into finished products, which are subsequently marketed to consumers. Once these products have fulfilled their intended purpose, they are discarded, often resulting in waste. This model reflects a one-directional flow of resources, lacking considerations for sustainability or the recycling of materials.

The circular economy aims at sustainable development through the cycle mentioned above. It operates by minimizing the use of materials, implementing proper planning, and designing a waste management mechanism that incorporates reuse and recycling processes. Circular economies create sustainable practices that, in turn, build economic growth (Rashid & Malik, 2023).

Introduction to Reinventing Skills

The circular economy necessitates a reinvention of the workforce skills to develop expertise for innovation and the practical implementation of circular practices. Employees must understand the requirements and design of eco-design principles to create eco-friendly products, so they must reinvent their skills. The reinvention of employees' skills involves utilizing technology, manufacturing techniques, tracking, optimizing resources, and monitoring (Pla-Julián & Guevara, 2019). Business leaders must develop the skills to understand the requirements of a circular economy, develop effective business models, frame policies and regulations, enhance management skills, and create a continuous learning and development environment.

Importance of Reinventing Skills

Reinventing skills is critical for every organization to remain competitive in a changing environment. Some of the aspects to be considered are as follows:

- Recognizing future skills: Organizations must identify the essential skills required to meet industry needs and trends, enabling better growth and staying current. This process involves assessing the existing employee skill sets and identifying the expected skills to determine the gaps that need to be addressed through upskilling and reskilling employees.
- Continuous Learning: Organizations must encourage employees to continually update their skills by creating an environment that supports diverse learning opportunities through online courses, training workshops, and other learning platforms, thereby maintaining a competitive advantage.
- Personalized Learning: Organizations support employees in planning their self-directed goals and learning through tailor-made learning. Also, mentors and coaches offer guidance.
- Leveraging Technology: Organizations support and provide opportunities for employees to learn through e-learning platforms, allowing them to access learning materials at any time based on their availability and convenience. Organizations utilize AI and Analytics to provide personalized learning experiences for employees, enabling them to track and monitor their progress.
- Collaboration and Knowledge Sharing: Organizations encourage employees to collaborate across departments to develop diverse skill sets (Shahriar *et al.*, 2023).
- Agile Learning: Organizations emphasize and adapt training to meet emerging needs by implementing short, iterative learning cycles followed by feedback.
- Measuring the outcome and its impact: Organizations must identify key performance indicators to measure the efficacy of skills developed, using

feedback as a loop to improve their learning process (Annosi *et al.*, 2020).
- Job Security: Upskilling will enhance employability and offer career progression opportunities for every employee, making them feel more secure (Burger *et al.*, 2019; Borms, 2024).

Challenges for Reinventing Skills

Reinventing skills is a multifaceted challenge for an organization. It is complex and requires overcoming many obstacles, as discussed below.

- Resistance to learning: Many employees resist learning new skills or changing to new working methods because they are comfortable with their current mode of operation.
- Identification of Skills: Identifying the skills required is a significant challenge due to the rapid pace of technological changes and shifting market dynamics.
- Time constraint: Managing routine tasks within the organization and finding time to acquire new skills will be challenging.
- Training Programs: Identifying and designing relevant training for current and future job requirements, while engaging employees, is a challenging task.
- Technological Integration: Upskilling and reskilling often require the use of new tools and technologies, which must be integrated with existing systems.

Addressing the challenges mentioned earlier requires a strategic approach that involves commitment, collaboration, continuous learning, and a willingness to adapt and evolve in the dynamic business environment (Piila *et al.*, 2022).

Challenges for Reinventing Skills in a Circular Economy

Reinventing skills for a circular economy in an organizational setup face unique challenges and are discussed below (Feyer, 2024):

- Lack of Awareness: Employees and leaders are not aware of the principles of the circular economy and their benefits. Moving from linear to circular economy practices can be challenging for employees as it requires a shift in their mindset.
- Training Gaps: Employees must be experts in various areas, including sustainability, processes, product life cycles, and other relevant fields. Traditional training programs may not adequately cover concepts related to the circular economy. Circular economy principles often require skills in multiple disciplines, including environmental science, business, and engineering (Summerton *et al.*, 2019).
- Resistance to adapting changes: Organizational Culture may resist adopting circular practices. Redesigning the process and navigating regulatory policies

becomes challenging at the organizational level.

- Metrics: Developing and using metrics to measure the efficacy of circular economy practices is challenging.

Addressing the aforementioned pain points requires a well-thought-out approach that emphasizes creating awareness, providing education, offering training, and fostering interdisciplinary collaboration based on principles of the circular economy.

Strategies for Upskilling and Reskilling for the Circular Economy

Organizations aiming for a circular economy implement various strategies to upskill and reskill employees, emphasizing creativity, innovation, sustainability, and resource efficiency. Some of the strategies adopted are as follows (Li, 2022; Feyer, 2024):

- Workshops: Conduct workshops on circular economy initiatives, sustainability, and resource efficiency methods for employees.
- Certifications in Circular Economy: Support and encourage employees to take certification courses related to circular economy principles and practices
- Research collaboration with universities: Organizations establish collaborations with academic institutions to engage in research projects to develop new methodologies and technologies for the circular economy. Additionally, employees should be encouraged to participate in real-world projects that implement circular economy practices within the organization.
- Simulation Tools: Use simulation and virtual reality tools to offer immersive learning experiences for the circular economy and its principles.
- Mentorship and Coaching: Offering guidance for leaders to help them drive circular economy initiatives and foster a culture of sustainability.
- Hackathons and Innovation Challenges: The organization conducts internal hackathons, challenges, and idea incubation programs for its employees, emphasizing the development of innovative solutions for a circular economy.
- Introducing incentives and rewards: Organizations introduce incentive schemes and rewards for employees who enthusiastically participate in upskilling and reskilling initiatives connected to the circular economy.
- Knowledge-Sharing Platforms and Communities of Practice: Develop internal platforms and communities to discuss and share knowledge, as well as best approaches and methods used in the circular economy.

Competencies for the Circular Economy

The movement from a linear to a circular economy is crucial for addressing various global issues, including resource depletion, climate change, and environmental degradation. So, individuals and organizations must upskill and reskill to successfully transition to the circular economy (Drakulevski & Boskov, 2019). Specific competencies must be harnessed among employees to contribute to a circular economic system (Chowdhury *et al.*, 2022). HR competencies enable organizations to adopt sustainable practices effectively and efficiently.

Reasons for HR professionals to have competencies are as follows (Ramlall, 2006; Janssens *et al.*, 2021):

- HR professionals must develop specific competencies and take up strategic roles that help create sustainable practices across the organization.
- A circular economy needs specific skill sets; HR must specify such requirements in the job description and equip employees by offering T&D (Kumar *et al.*, 2020).
- A leadership role will ensure the transformation to a circular economy by influencing organizational initiatives and driving change.
- An HR professional can support active employee engagement by linking it with sustainable goals and providing employees with opportunities to contribute to the organization.
- A circular economy thrives on collaboration across different sectors and disciplines. HR can facilitate proper collaboration by encouraging teams within and with stakeholders to accomplish sustainability goals.
- HR professionals must ensure the workforce is adaptable and resilient through transitions.
- HR can support and develop a culture that promotes an innovative mindset and skills, thinking creatively about reuse and recycling, that focuses on organizational sustainability (Ajor & Alikor, 2020).
- HR must ensure ethical and inclusive organizational practices and support diversity and equity across the organization (Bhanumathi *et al.*, 2024).
- HR professionals must develop competencies to contribute significantly to the circular economy practices, driving both environmental sustainability and business resilience.

Benefits of Competencies for a Circular Economy

The various benefits of competencies for a circular economy are as follows.

- HR professionals with diverse competencies drive initiatives that minimize waste and optimize the utilization of available resources, resulting in more sustainable procurement, production, and organizational consumption patterns (Chams & García-Blandón, 2019).
- Prioritizing sustainability and circular economy principles attracts and retains competent employees worthy of environmental responsibility. HR competencies would help create programs and policies that enhance employee engagement and job satisfaction.
- HR professionals who know about circular economy-related regulations can ensure environmental laws are followed, reducing the threat of legal action and augmenting the company's status (Brears, 2018).
- Applying circular economy principles and practices leads to reduced costs by minimizing waste, improving resource efficiency, and reducing associated costs through enhanced HR competencies (Klein *et al.*, 2020).
- Companies committed to sustainability and the circular economy often enjoy a better brand reputation. HR can play a critical part in building and maintaining this reputation through effective communication and employee involvement in sustainability initiatives (Adegoke *et al.*, 2024).
- HR can align talent management strategies with the goals of the circular economy by identifying and developing skills crucial for sustainability. This includes hiring practices, performance management, and leadership development, all of which are focused on achieving long-term environmental and economic benefits.
- HR competencies can facilitate collaboration across departments and external partners to support circular economy goals. By fostering a collaborative culture, HR can help break down silos and encourage a systems-thinking approach to problem-solving.
- HR can implement continuous learning programs to keep the workforce updated on the latest trends and technologies related to the circular economy (Bag *et al.*, 2021). This adaptability is crucial for staying competitive in a rapidly changing business environment.
- HR competencies in circular economy practices can enhance the company's CSR initiatives, making them more impactful and aligned with global sustainability goals (Stahl *et al.*, 2020). These competencies strengthen the company's social license to operate and build goodwill in the communities it serves.
- By integrating HR competencies with circular economy principles, organizations can improve their sustainability performance and realize noteworthy merits, including cost savings, heightened reputation, and a more engaged and innovative workforce.

The competencies to effectively implement and sustain a circular economy are discussed below (Sillaman & de Colle, 2024):

- Technical and Production Competencies: Abilities related to the identification and comprehension of materials and their applications, emphasizing sustainability, recyclability, and biodegradability. Competencies in product design should enhance longevity and facilitate repair, recycling, and the reuse of materials. Technical expertise encompasses the use of 3D technology and other methods to minimize waste and optimize the efficiency of raw material utilization.
    - Business and Economic Competencies: Rising innovative business models such as product-as-a-service, sharing platforms, and creating a supply chain that minimizes waste and optimizes resources and efficiency. Ability to attract investments for circular initiatives by knowing the economic implications of circular practices.
    - Digital and Data Competencies: Involve utilizing advanced data management systems to monitor and trace all materials and products throughout their entire lifecycle. This capability allows organizations to enhance resource efficiency and significantly reduce waste. Companies can continuously track and analyze resource consumption and product movement in real-time by integrating smart technologies, such as Internet of Things (IoT) devices and cloud-based platforms. For instance, implementing blockchain technology provides a secure and immutable framework that guarantees transparency and traceability within supply chains, allowing stakeholders to verify the sustainable practices associated with each product (Veleva & Bodkin, 2018).
    - Regulatory and Policy Competencies: Knowledge of and adherence to environmental regulations prioritizing recycling, waste minimization, and sustainability. Skills to formulate policies that promote circular economy practices. Ability to establish standards for sustainable production methods.
        - Social and Cultural Competencies: Competencies to create awareness, educate consumers on the circular economy and practices, and promote sustainable consumption patterns. Building network communities that believe in and support circular practices helps lead and manage sustainability within and across the organization.
    - Interdisciplinary and Collaborative Competencies: Working across different sectors and industries to create synergies and shared value, and developing new ideas and approaches to overcome challenges and leverage opportunities within the circular economy.
    - Lifecycle and Impact Assessment Competencies: Evaluate the environmental impact of products throughout their entire lifecycle, from cradle to grave. Develop and use metrics to measure the circularity of processes and products. Analyze and minimize the ecological footprint of production and consumption activities.

- Leadership and Strategic Vision: Inspiring and guiding organizations towards a sustainable and circular future. Developing long-term strategies that align with various principles of the circular economy. Engaging with multiple stakeholders, including governments, NGOs, businesses, and consumers, to drive circular economy initiatives (Veleva & Bodkin, 2018).
  - Systems thinking skills: These are increasingly recognized as essential competencies in the transition toward a circular economy. This thinking approach enables individuals and organizations to comprehend and navigate the intricate interdependencies within economic, environmental, and social systems. At its core, systems thinking involves recognizing that the components of a system are interconnected and that changes in one element can have significant effects on other elements. In the context of a circular economy, which enables the minimization of waste and promotes the continual use of resources, systems thinking encourages a holistic understanding of how products are designed, produced, used, and disposed of.
    - Understand holistically and recognize the interconnections and dependencies between the various components of any system. It illustrates how one part of a supply chain influences other parts and how economic activities affect the environment and social systems.
    - Integrating knowledge and perspectives from various disciplines to solve complex problems. Combining insights from economics, environmental science, engineering, and social sciences to develop sustainable solutions.
    - Identify and understand feedback loops that reinforce or counteract changes, leading to resource savings that further reduce waste and create a positive feedback loop.
    - Understand how systems change over time, anticipating the long-term impacts of products and materials, and predicting how resource availability may change.
    - Identifying cause-and-effect relationships in a system and understanding how production processes contribute to pollution, as well as how alternative practices can mitigate these effects.
    - Design supply chains that are resilient to resource shortages and can quickly adapt to new regulations or market demands (Molderez & Ceulemans, 2018).

Strategies to develop systems thinking skills include education and training, engaging in interdisciplinary activities, conducting workshops and seminars, and knowing and studying real-life examples.

- Design thinking skills: Design thinking is a user-centered methodology for innovation that synthesizes user needs, technological capabilities, and business objectives to achieve organizational success. Competencies in design thinking are crucial for fostering a circular economy, enabling the development and delivery of diverse, sustainable, efficient, and regenerative products, services, and systems (Pillai *et al.*, 2020).
  - Empathize with users' and other stakeholders' needs, behaviors, and emotions to design user-friendly and environmentally sustainable activities across the organization.
  - Defining the problem in the context of sustainability and circularity, which focuses on waste reduction, optimal utilization of resources, and increased product longevity,
  - Generating ideas by brainstorming for various products and services that embrace circular principles, *i.e.*, reuse, recycle, and resource efficiency.
  - Prototyping serves as a critical phase in the product development process, where ideas transition from conceptualization to tangible forms. In the context of circular economy principles, this process assumes added significance, as it focuses on sustainability, resource efficiency, and lifecycle impact. The prototyping of products designed with circular principles involves several key steps. Initially, idea generation must align with the core tenets of the circular economy, which advocate for minimizing waste, extending product life, and promoting resource recovery. This entails considering materials that can be recycled or repurposed and designing for disassembly, thus facilitating future reuse or recycling.
  - Testing prototypes to ensure circular economy goals are achieved.
  - Design solutions that consider the entire lifecycle of products, from raw material extraction to end-of-life, and their impact on the environment and society.
  - Engage designers, engineers, marketers, and sustainability experts in co-creating solutions that integrate circular economy principles. Design thinking enables a flexible approach, allowing solutions to be developed based on feedback and trends, ensuring they remain relevant (Poleac, 2022).

The shift towards a circular economy necessitates various competencies, including technical, economic, regulatory, social, digital, interdisciplinary, and leadership skills. Cultivating and enhancing these competencies enables the promotion of sustainable development and addresses the environmental challenges that organizations, governments, and societies face.

HR competencies for supporting and driving a circular economy encompass various skills, knowledge, and attitudes, and are discussed below:

1. Strategic HR Leadership Competencies: Ability to develop and implement HR strategies aligning with the circular economy principles and practices.
2. Talent Management and Development: Attracting and recruiting individuals with expertise in circular economy principles and practices. Identifying and developing the skill sets essential for circular economy roles, namely, eco-design of products and services, resource management, and sustainable engineering (Vacchi *et al.*, 2021). Encouraging continuous learning to ensure employees stay updated on sustainability practices and their supporting technologies.
3. Employee Engagement and Motivation: Engaging employees in sustainability initiatives and making them advocates for circular economy practices, fostering a sense of purpose by aligning individual and organizational goals with sustainability objectives (Viterouli *et al.*, 2023).
4. Organizational Development: Creating a culture that encourages innovation and creative thinking around sustainability and resource efficiency. Moreover, it supports cross-functional teamwork to leverage diverse expertise in implementing circular economy solutions (Attah *et al.*, 2024).
5. Diversity and Inclusion: Ensuring that sustainability efforts are inclusive and equitable, addressing diverse perspectives and needs, and understanding and managing cultural differences in global organizations to implement circular economy practices (Burlacu *et al.*, 2023) effectively.
6. Performance Management: Developing and implementing performance metrics that include sustainability and circular economy objectives and designing reward systems that recognize and incentivize employees who follow sustainable practices and achieve (Awan *et al.*, 2019).
7. Communication and Advocacy: Communicating the importance and benefits of the circular economy to all stakeholders, including employees, management, and external partners, using storytelling to highlight successes and challenges in the organization's circular economy journey (Salvioni & Almici, 2020).
8. Health, Safety, and Well-being: Promoting sustainable practices that boost employee well-being and help contribute to the organization effectively and efficiently.
9. Technology and Digital Competence: Leveraging digital tools and platforms to support circular economy initiatives, such as data analytics for resource tracking and IoT for waste management, as well as utilizing HR technology to enhance sustainability practices, including virtual training programs on circular economy principles.

HR competencies in the circular economy are integral to nurturing an organizational culture that supports sustainability and resource efficiency.HR professionals can drive the successful implementation and sustainability of circular economy practices across organizations.

Use Cases

Housing circular economies include creating a system where resources are reused, recycled, and remanufactured to minimize waste and promote sustainability. Reinventing employee skills is crucial for organizations to adapt and succeed in today's evolving economies.

Common strategies for the reinvention of skills across various industries, with a technical emphasis, include (Raimi, 2021; Chandiok & Kukreja, 2025):

- Implementing data analytics frameworks to systematically track and optimize resource utilization and waste management processes, facilitating the transition to a circular economy model.
- Deploying digital twin technology and advanced simulation tools to create precise models that enable the evaluation and enhancement of circular economy practices.
- Conducting specialized training programs focused on sustainable sourcing methodologies and circular manufacturing techniques to ensure employees are well-versed in best practices.
- Prioritizing employee upskilling initiatives towards reverse logistics, emphasizing effective product returns management, refurbishment processes, and recycling protocols.
- Designing and executing comprehensive incentive schemes that motivate and support employees in achieving sustainability targets and actively participating in circular economy initiatives (van Langen *et al*., 2021).
- Fostering the development of innovative service models and product designs that align with circular economy principles, thereby enhancing customer engagement and participation.
- Establishing Key Performance Indicators (KPIs) focusing on quantifying employee contributions and their direct impact on circular economy projects, facilitating continuous improvement.
- Training organizational leaders in advanced change management techniques to effectively guide the adoption and implementation of circular economy practices across all levels of the organization (Gonella *et al*., 2024).
- Implementing “Best Practice Sharing” sessions across departments, leveraging collaborative technologies to ensure knowledge transfer and continuous learning among teams.

As the global economy faces increasing environmental challenges, numerous companies are responding by embracing circular economy principles in their business models. Leaders such as IKEA, Godrej, TCS, Renault, Philips, and others are pioneering innovative initiatives that reduce waste and promote sustainable resource management and product lifecycle optimization. These organizations are redefining their operational frameworks to facilitate the reuse, recycling, and remanufacturing of materials, thereby creating a more sustainable future.

These companies are making significant strides in transforming traditional linear models into circular practices through strategic investments in employee training and upskilling, collaboration with stakeholders, and integration of advanced technologies. Their commitment to sustainability aligns with the global movement towards environmental stewardship and positions them as frontrunners in the transition to a more resilient and resource-efficient economy.

1. **IKEA**
   Reinventing Skills: IKEA implements a multifaceted training framework designed to equip employees with a foundational understanding of the circular economy, emphasizing strategies for waste minimization, enhancing product lifecycle, and creating sustainable offerings tailored to diverse customer segments. The organization conducts interdisciplinary workshops on implementing circular economy initiatives, fostering cross-functional collaboration, and innovative thinking. Additionally, IKEA has established circular innovation clubs and design thinking laboratories that amplify employee creativity and facilitate innovative problem-solving processes pertinent to sustainable practices. Through these initiatives, IKEA educates its workforce on the principles of sustainable product development and the intricacies of circular supply chain management, reinforcing its commitment to sustainability at all operational levels.
   Instance: IKEA employees undergo training on furniture design optimized for ease of repair, reuse, and recycling. This training aims to enhance product longevity while minimizing the demand for new raw materials, aligning with sustainability principles and the objectives of the circular economy. (https://www.ikea.com/global/en/our-business/people-planet)

2. **Godrej**
   Reinventing Skills: Godrej, a leading conglomerate with diverse interests, including construction and manufacturing, recognizes the critical importance of sustainable practices in today's industrial landscape. The company's commitment to training its workforce in eco-friendly construction techniques

and sustainable production processes is a proactive step towards minimizing environmental impact while promoting economic growth.

Godrej's training programs teach employees about sustainable materials, energy-efficient building practices, waste reduction strategies, and sustainable sourcing. By educating the workforce on eco-friendly techniques, Godrej enhances its employees' skill sets and fosters a culture of environmental stewardship within the organization.

Eco-friendly construction techniques often involve using sustainable materials, such as recycled or locally sourced items, and technologies that reduce the carbon footprint, including energy-efficient systems and renewable energy sources. For instance, implementing green building certifications, such as LEED (Leadership in Energy and Environmental Design), emphasizes the importance of sustainable practices in the construction industry. In this context, training is crucial in ensuring that workers understand these standards and can apply them effectively in their projects.

Instance: Godrej is at the forefront of green building initiatives and sustainable manufacturing practices. The workforce undergoes training in environmentally responsible construction methods, energy-efficient technologies, and the use of recycled materials to facilitate the development of sustainable infrastructure and products (https://www.godrej.com/).

3. **Tata Motors**

   Reinventing Skills: Tata Motors implements comprehensive training programs for its employees focused on the remanufacturing and recycling of automotive components. These initiatives focus on integrating sustainable practices within the automotive industry, enhancing resource efficiency, and minimizing environmental impact. By equipping employees with the necessary skills and knowledge, Tata Motors promotes a circular economy approach, encouraging the responsible use of materials and minimizing waste in the production processes.

   Instance: Tata Motors has initiated remanufacturing engines and other vital components, extending their lifecycle. Employee training was focused more on reverse engineering, remanufacturing processes, and sustainable disposal practices to help reduce waste and raw material consumption (https://www.tatamotors.com/).

4. **Dabur**

   Reinventing Skills: Dabur implements comprehensive training programs to enhance employee knowledge and understanding of sustainable sourcing methodologies and the importance of eco-friendly packaging solutions. These educational initiatives are designed to inform employees about sustainability principles, including the ethical and responsible procurement of raw materials.

Furthermore, the programs emphasize the environmental impacts of packaging choices and promote practices that minimize waste and reduce the carbon footprint of products. By equipping employees with this knowledge, Dabur aims to foster a culture of sustainability within the organization, ensuring that its operations align with contemporary environmental standards and contribute positively to the ecosystem.

Instance: Employees are trained in agricultural practices that emphasize sustainability, the optimal utilization of available natural resources, and the development of biodegradable packaging, which supports a circular economy (https://www.dabur.com/).

5. **ITC**

Reinventing Skills: ITC conducts extensive training programs to equip employees with the skills and knowledge necessary for effective waste management practices. This initiative is part of ITC's broader sustainability strategy, underscoring the importance of minimizing waste across all operational areas. The training focuses on various aspects of waste management, including waste segregation, recycling, and reducing waste at the source. Moreover, ITC strongly emphasizes sustainable packaging as a critical component of its environmental responsibility. Employees are educated on eco-friendly packaging design principles, which include utilizing biodegradable materials, minimizing excess packaging, and ensuring that packaging solutions are both functional and environmentally sustainable.

Instance: ITC's sustainability initiatives focus on achieving zero waste in landfills and developing sustainable packaging. Employees are skilled in segregating waste, recycling processes, developing eco-friendly packaging, reducing environmental impact, and supporting circular economy principles (https://www.itcportal.com/sustainability/skilling-vocational-traini-g-programme.aspx).

6. **Wipro**

Reinventing Skills: Wipro has implemented comprehensive training programs focused on e-waste management, recognizing the growing concern over electronic waste in today's digital age. These training sessions are designed to educate employees about the environmental impacts of e-waste and the importance of responsible disposal and recycling practices. By fostering a culture of awareness, Wipro aims to equip its workforce with the knowledge to handle electronic devices and components in an eco-friendly manner.

Instance: Wipro initiatives are focused on e-waste recycling programs and promoting sustainable IT practices. Employees are trained on the various e-waste disposal, recycling techniques, and energy-efficient activities that reduce environmental impact and support a circular economy (https://www.wipro.com).

7. **Tata Consultancy Services (TCS)**
   Reinventing Skills: Tata Consultancy Services places a significant emphasis on sustainability within its operations, particularly in IT services and green technologies. The company recognizes the importance of environmental responsibility and actively trains its employees to ensure they are well-equipped to implement sustainable practices. The training programs at TCS focus on various topics related to sustainable IT services. Employees learn about the principles of green IT, which include optimizing energy consumption in data centers, utilizing virtualization technologies to reduce hardware needs, and adopting energy-efficient software solutions. They are also educated about the environmental impact of e-waste and the significance of proper disposal and recycling methods to minimize harm to the planet.
   Instance: Employees receive training in sustainable IT practices, the integration of renewable energy, and eco-friendly technologies, with a focus on reducing the carbon footprint and supporting a circular economy (https://www.tcs.com/).

8. **Philips**
   Reinventing Skills: Philips trains employees on the reverse logistics process, its challenges, remanufacturing processes, and cutting-edge recycling techniques.
   Instance: Philips has adopted a circular economy approach to design and develop products that focus on longevity, ease of disassembly, and recycling. Employees are trained to disassemble used products and recover valued components for reuse, reducing waste and material costs (https://www.philips.com/).

9. **Renault**
   Reinventing Skills: Renault trains employees in remanufacturing and refurbishing automotive parts. The company's ECO^2 program focuses on reducing the environmental impact of its vehicles throughout their entire product lifecycle and encourages cross-functional teams to collaborate on sustainability initiatives.
   Instance: Renault uses a remanufacturing facility to refurbish car parts to a new condition. Employees are equipped with the necessary skill sets to identify problem areas, diagnose, disassemble, clean, and reassemble parts, emphasizing the reuse of raw materials and reducing the need for new ones (https://www.renaultgroup.com/en/innovation-2/openinnovation/).

FUTURE RESEARCH DIRECTIONS

Integrating employee skills in building circular economies presents numerous technical research opportunities. Some of them are listed below;

1. Creating Innovative Frameworks for Competency Mapping: Current competency mapping frameworks do not adequately incorporate the principles of a circular economy. There is an opportunity for research aimed at developing comprehensive frameworks that include key elements such as systems thinking, circular design principles, collaborative resource consumption, the integration of sustainable practices, the establishment of Key Performance Indicators (KPIs) aligned with circular economy objectives, and the promotion of an organizational culture that supports a circular economy, among other factors.
2. Creating Innovative Models for Skills Gap Analysis: The scope of this research is to utilize advanced statistical models to perform a skills gap analysis, highlighting the gaps and weaknesses in current workforce capabilities. The aim is to facilitate organizational changes that support the implementation of circular economy practices. To accomplish this, the research will utilize various contemporary tools for gap analysis, including benchmarking tools, gap analysis templates, data analytics, and 360-degree feedback.
3. Building Partnership Models for Cross-Disciplinary Collaboration in the Circular Economy: The circular economy necessitates a holistic approach to innovation that transcends traditional disciplinary boundaries. Researchers are encouraged to investigate various collaborative methodologies to foster partnerships between organizations that span inter-disciplinary and cross-disciplinary domains. Such alliances may encompass a diverse range of stakeholders, including private sector entities, governmental agencies, academic institutions, and industries specializing in skill development. By leveraging the unique strengths and insights of each partner, these collaborative frameworks have the potential to enhance the efficacy of initiatives aimed at promoting sustainable practices and driving systemic change within the circular economy.
4. Behavioral Dynamics and Change Management Tool to Implement Circular Economy Practices: With employees at the center of our study, we need to develop effective techniques to understand employee behaviors and identify adoption constraints related to the new change. Research is necessary to develop straightforward and effective processes that attract new-age employees to adopt a circular economy. This can involve developing educational programs and incentive schemes, launching campaigns, leadership programs, and community development initiatives, among others.

5. Bringing transformation through digitization: As technology advances, adopting new-age technologies such as Artificial Intelligence, Data Science, Virtual Reality, and Augmented Reality in employee training and assessment has become increasingly crucial. Research is needed to develop technical solutions based on these technologies and implement them where necessary. This integration would pique the interest of employees by enhancing their decision-making capabilities and optimizing processes.

CONCLUDING REMARKS

The shift from a traditional to a circular economy calls for a broad range of competencies, namely cultural, technical, leadership, and economic skills. Employees must upskill and reskill in sustainable design, resource efficiency, waste management, and lifecycle assessment to meet the evolving needs of the industry. In conclusion, reinventing employee skills is not merely a means to develop circular economies, but also an essential step. The organization's success depends on developing a creative, innovative, skilled, and resilient workforce. By fostering a culture of continuous improvement, the organization strives for sustainable growth and makes significant contributions to circularity.

REFERENCES

Annosi, M.C., Martini, A., Brunetta, F., Marchegiani, L. (2020). Learning in an agile setting: A multilevel research study on the evolution of organizational routines. *J. Bus. Res., 110*, 554-566.

Ajor, L., Alikor, L.O. (2020). Innovative mindset and organizational sustainability of small and medium enterprises in Rivers State, Nigeria. *British Journal of Management and Marketing Studies, 3*(1), 20-36.

Adegoke, A.A., Oyindamola, K.A., Offonabo, N. (2024). The Role of HR in Sustainability Initiatives: A Strategic Review. International Journal of Research in Engineering. *Science and Management, 7*(5), 31-37.

Attah, R U, Garba, B M P, Gil-Ozoudeh, I, Iwuanyanwu, O (2024). Cross-functional team dynamics in technology management: a comprehensive review of efficiency and innovation enhancement.

Awan, U., Sroufe, R., Kraslawski, A. (2019). Creativity enables sustainable development: Supplier engagement as a boundary condition for the positive effect on green innovation. *J. Clean. Prod., 226*, 172-185.

BURLACU. (2023). Socio-cultural Sustainability for Resilience in Public Services: Strategies for Achieving Inclusive and Equitable Service Delivery. *Eur. J. Sustain. Dev., 12*(3), 29-29.

Burger, M., Stavropoulos, S., Ramkumar, S., Dufourmont, J., van Oort, F. (2019). The heterogeneous skill base of circular economy employment. *Res. Policy, 48*(1), 248-261.

Borms, L. (2024). *Out with jobs and in with skills: measuring current circular jobs and analyzing future necessary skills.*

Bhanumathi, P, Jeevitha, R, Naidu, MA (2024). Effective human resources management in the multigenerational workplace. *Diversity, Equity, and Inclusion* Business Science Reference.

Brears, R.C. (2018). *Natural resource management and the circular economy.*. Springer.

Bag, S., Yadav, G., Dhamija, P., Kataria, K.K. (2021). Key resources for industry 4.0 adoption and its effect on sustainable production and circular economy: An empirical study. *J. Clean. Prod., 281*, 125233.

Chams, N., García-Blandón, J. (2019). On the importance of sustainable human resource management for adopting sustainable development goals. *Resour. Conserv. Recycling, 141*, 109-122.

Chandiok, S, Kukreja, J (2025). Reinventing Learning: Educational Innovations for Tomorrow's Skills. *Innovative Educational Frameworks for Future Skills and Competencies* IGI Global Scientific Publishing.

Chowdhury, S., Dey, P.K., Rodríguez-Espíndola, O., Parkes, G., Tuyet, N.T.A., Long, D.D., Ha, T.P. (2022). Impact of organizational factors on the circular economy practices and sustainable performance of small and medium-sized enterprises in vietnam. *J. Bus. Res., 147*, 362-378.

Drakulevski, L., Boskov, T. (2019). Circular economy: Potential and challenges. IJIBM International Journal of Information. *Business and Management, 11*(2), 45-52.

Feyer, C. (2024). Reinventing Skills–Changing Paradigms and the EU Response. *Inter Econ., 59*(3), 132-135.

Gonella, J.D.S.L., Godinho Filho, M., Campos, L.M.D.S., Ganga, G.M.D. (2024). People's awareness and behaviours of circular economy around the world: literature review and research agenda. Sustainability Accounting. *Management and Policy Journal, 15*(5), 1118-1154.

Janssens, L., Kuppens, T., Van Schoubroeck, S. (2021). Competences of the professional of the future in the circular economy: Evidence from the case of Limburg, Belgium. *J. Clean. Prod., 281*, 125365.

Kumar, A., Garza-Reyes, J.A., Khan, S.A.R. (2020). *Circular Economy for the Management of Operations..* CRC Press.

Klein, N., Ramos, T.B., Deutz, P. (2020). Circular economy practices and strategies in public sector organizations: An integrative review. *Sustainability, 12*(10), 4181.

López, JV (2021). Design of professional skills in higher education within the framework of a circular economy. *EDULEARN21 Proceedings,* 310-317.

Li, L. (2022). Reskilling and upskilling the future-ready workforce for Industry 4.0 and beyond. *Inf. Syst. Front.,* 1-16.

Molderez, I., Ceulemans, K. (2018). The power of art to foster systems thinking is one of the key competencies of education for sustainable development. *J. Clean. Prod., 186*, 758-770.

Ogunmakinde, O.E., Egbelakin, T., Sher, W. (2022). Contributions of the circular economy to the UN Sustainable Development Goals through sustainable construction. *Resour. Conserv. Recycling, 178*, 106023.

Pla-Julián, I., Guevara, S. (2019). Is the circular economy the key to transitioning towards sustainable development? Challenges from a Care Ethics Perspective. *Futures, 105*, 67-77.

Piila, N., Sarja, M., Onkila, T., Mäkelä, M. (2022). Organizational drivers and challenges in circular economy implementation: An issue life cycle approach. *Organ. Environ., 35*(4), 523-550.

Pillai, S.V., Vipin, H., Abhilash, V.S. (2020). Design Thinking: Transforming Strategic Thinking towards Human-Centric Innovations. *Review of Professional Management, 18*(2)

Poleac, D. (2022). Responsive design thinking: Transitioning from human-centered to a planetary-centric approach to innovation. *Principles and Perspectives. In International Conference on Modern Trends in Business Hospitality and Tourism,* 1-13.Cham: Springer International Publishing.

Raimi, L (2021). Human Capital Development through Reinventing, Retooling, and Reskilling Strategies. *Conference Towards ASEAN Chairmanship 2023 (TAC 23 2021),* Atlantis Press.Dec;22-29.

Rodríguez-Espíndola, O., Cuevas-Romo, A., Chowdhury, S., Díaz-Acevedo, N., Albores, P., Despoudi, S. (2022). The role of circular economy principles and sustainable-oriented innovation to enhance social, economic, and environmental performance: Evidence from Mexican SMEs. *Int. J. Prod. Econ., 248*, 108495.

Rashid, S., Malik, S.H. (2023). Transition from a Linear to a Circular Economy. *Renewable Energy in Circular Economy.* (pp. 1-20). Cham: Springer International Publishing.

Ramlall, S.J. (2006). Identifying and understanding HR competencies and their relationship to organizational practices. *Appl. H.R.M. Res., 11*(1), 27.

Stahl, G.K., Brewster, C.J., Collings, D.G., Hajro, A. (2020). Enhancing the role of human resource management in corporate sustainability and social responsibility: A multi-stakeholder, multidimensional approach to HRM. *Hum. Resour. Manage. Rev., 30*(3), 100708.

Sillaman, N.K., de Colle, S. (2024). Four core competencies toward the circular economy: Insights from a born-sustainable firm. *Journal of Business Venturing Insights, 22*, e00475.

Salvioni, D.M., Almici, A. (2020). Transitioning toward a circular economy: The impact of stakeholder engagement on sustainability culture. *Sustainability, 12*(20), 8641.

Shahriar, S.H.B., Arafat, S., Islam, I., Nur, J.E.H., Rahman, S., Khan, S.I., Alam, M.S. (2023). The emergence of e-learning and online-based training during the COVID-19 crisis: an exploratory investigation from Bangladesh. *Management Matters, 20*(1), 1-15.

Summerton, L., Clark, J.H., Hurst, G.A., Ball, P.D., Rylott, E.L., Carslaw, N. (2019). Industry-informed workshops to develop graduate skill sets in the circular economy using systems thinking. *J. Chem. Educ., 96*(12), 2959-2967.

Veleva, V., Bodkin, G. (2018). Corporate-entrepreneur collaborations to advance a circular economy. *J. Clean. Prod., 188*, 20-37.

Vacchi, M., Siligardi, C., Cedillo-González, E.I., Ferrari, A.M., Settembre-Blundo, D. (2021). Industry 4.0 and smart data as enablers of the circular economy in manufacturing: Product re-engineering with circular eco-design. *Sustainability, 13*(18), 10366.

Viterouli, M, Belias, D, Koustelios, A, Tsigilis, N, Bakogiannis, D (2023). Fostering Sustainability Through the Integration of Green Human Resource Management and Change Management: Nurturing Eco-Conscious Organizational Practices *Managing Successful and Ethical Organizational Change* IGI Global.

van Langen, S.K., Vassillo, C., Ghisellini, P., Restaino, D., Passaro, R., Ulgiati, S. (2021). Promoting circular economy transition: A study about perceptions and awareness by different stakeholders groups. *J. Clean. Prod., 316*, 128166.

Velenturf, A P, Purnell, P (2021). Principles for a sustainable circular economy. *Sustainable Production and Consumption, 27*, 1437-1457.

CHAPTER 9

Greening the Footwear Industry: Sustainable Approach to Reduce the Carbon Footprint

Mona Mahecha[1], **Swati Beniwal**[1], **Sushila Choudhary**[1,*] and **Mohammed Majeed**[2]

[1] *Faculty of Law, Manipal University, Jaipur, Rajasthan, India*

[2] *Department of Marketing, Tamale Technical University, Tamale, Ghana*

Abstract: Shoes are a widely used commodity universally owned by individuals worldwide. However, excessive quantities of shoe waste are detrimental since the shoe industry has numerous environmental consequences that cannot be disregarded. The increasing awareness of health and fitness among individuals is driving the expansion of the footwear market. In 2022, the worldwide footwear market was valued at USD 389.23 billion. By 2031, the projected value is expected to reach USD 568.54 billion, with a Compound Annual Growth Rate (CAGR) of 4.31% throughout the projection period from 2023 to 2031. Significant quantities of carbon dioxide are emitted throughout the production process. It accounts for 1.4% of global Greenhouse Gas (GHG) emissions. Over 300 million pairs of shoes are discarded annually in the United States, with 95% ending up in landfills. The emission of chemicals into the soil and groundwater results in environmental contamination. Dyes emit toxic heavy metals, whilst soles undergo decomposition to become compounds such as polyurethane. The manufacturing process of shoes is also harmful to the environment. Manufacturers utilize fossil fuels or coal as the primary energy source for their facilities. Carbon dioxide and several other greenhouse gas emissions are produced by combusting these fuels. Greenwashing in the footwear industry is also a serious concern. As defined by the United Nations, sustainable development entails meeting the present generation's demands while safeguarding the future's requirements. This necessitates the application of systems thinking, which involves comprehending the interconnectedness and interdependence of Environmental, Social, and Governance (ESG) factors. The research methodology employed in this study is normative legal research with a conceptual approach. It involves the analysis of diverse reports and policies concerning the footwear industry and its environmental and social impacts. This method aims to critically examine and interpret the normative frameworks and regulations associated with fast fashion and its environmental and societal consequences. The study's objective is to explore the effect of greenwashing within the footwear industry and examine the repercussions of unsustainable manufacturing processes on the environment and society, including the international and national efforts for a sustainable footwear industry.

* **Corresponding Author Sushila Choudhary:** Faculty of Law, Manipal University, Jaipur, Rajasthan, India; E-mail: sushila.choudhary@jaipur.manipal.edu

Theodore Tarnanidis, Vijaya Kittu Manda, Vivek Gupta (Eds.)

Keywords: Carbon footprints, Climate policies, Environment, Environmental contamination, ESG, Footwear industry, Footwear market, Fossil fuel emission, Green Washing, Greenhouse gas mitigation, Sustainability, Unsustainable manufacturing process.

INTRODUCTION

The shoe business is undoubtedly quite profitable. Demand for socially and environmentally sustainable footwear is rising along with it. According to recent Certilogo research, over 70% of consumers are worried about the sustainability of their fashion purchases, and 1 in 3 people are prepared to spend an extra 25% on average for sustainable products (Certilogo-commerce, 2022). Regrettably, numerous footwear companies have been sluggish in embracing sustainable methods. Footwear is an essential requirement for life. However, the number of discarded shoes continues to increase every year. The issue of shoe waste on a global scale has reached a critical juncture that demands our immediate attention. According to experts, the worldwide footwear industry is projected to reach a value of USD 568.54 billion by the year 2031. Advertisers persuade consumers to purchase more products, augmenting the demand for production. In 2019, the footwear industry in Bangladesh witnessed a significant production of 378 million pairs of shoes. Notably, a substantial portion of these shoes, ranging from 200 to 250 million pairs, were purchased by local consumers. The demand for local and international footwear is experiencing a steady and upward trend (Kumar *et al.*, 2019). Annually, almost 20 billion shoes are produced (DiNapoli, 2024a).

Furthermore, the footwear industry has significantly contributed to foreign exchange (Moktadir *et al.*, 2019). The observed trend of footwear exports to foreign countries is on the rise, suggesting its significance in relation to the developmental rates of various nations. Based on data derived from the financial years 2018-2019, it has been observed that the revenue generated by leather-based footwear items amounted to 607.88 million USD. Therefore, it can be inferred that the footwear industry is experiencing growth, as evidenced by the upward trajectory of its foreign currency earnings. In addition to its notable impact on foreign currency earnings, the industry is currently encountering challenges in benchmarking its practices to enhance its overall performance (Moktadir *et al.*, 2021).

As per the data available in The World Footwear Yearbook 2023, China is the leading consumer of footwear and shares 17.9% of the world's consumption. The United States and India hold 2nd (12.2% share) and 3rd (11.5%) rank, respectively. Other countries under the top 10 are Brazil, Indonesia, Japan, Pakistan, Germany, the United Kingdom, and France. These top 10 consumer countries collectively represent 59% of worldwide footwear consumption. Footwear Distributors and Retailers of America (FDRA) defines shoe sustainability as "shoe design, development, manufacturing, distribution, and selling processes that minimize negative environmental impacts, conserve energy and natural resources, are safe for employees, communities and consumers, and are economically sound" (Shoe Sustainability, 2025). Shoes are integral to the fast-fashion industry, known for their affordability and fashionable appeal. Occasional purchasing transformed into regular purchasing. The affordability of shoes comes with a cost for both the workers who create them (exploitative labor) and the environment (chemical and waste pollution).

FOOTWEAR INDUSTRY AND UNSUSTAINABILITY

Akin to the textile industry, the footwear business exerts a substantial environmental impact. According to a study, a standard pair of running shoes made of synthetic materials emits approximately 14 ± 2.7 kg of CO_2 throughout its lifespan. The shoe composition consists of a total of 65 distinct components, necessitating a total of 360 processing steps for the assembly process (Cheah *et al.*, 2012). All the stages in the production of shoes pattern creation, cutting, sewing, lasting, and finishing are linked to various kinds of health risks (Mahmud *et al.*, 2020). However, the most harmful substances are the noxious organic solvents, which are especially found in the adhesives, as well as in the hardeners, cleaning solutions, and degreasers utilized during the shoemaking procedure (Gangopadhyay *et al.*, 2011).

A large amount of carbon dioxide is released into the atmosphere during the production process. It is responsible for 1.4% of the total emissions of greenhouse gases (GHG) worldwide. A pair of sneakers generates 30 pounds of carbon dioxide (CO_2) emissions, which is equivalent to the amount of energy that would be consumed by a light bulb with a power output of one hundred watts if it were left on for a week (DiNapoli, 2024b). The manufacturing of trainers is highly carbon-intensive, accounting for 1.4% of total global greenhouse gas emissions (Fashion, 2022).

The escalating growth of footwear factories has been observed to exert adverse impacts on both the environment and human health. The manufacturing stage of a shoe's life cycle is widely recognized as one of the most significant contributors to its environmental impact. During the manufacturing stage, the production of shoes necessitates the utilization of a substantial quantity of machinery and chemicals. In order to operate these machines, a substantial quantity of fossil fuels is required, which, upon combustion, emit greenhouse gases. Coal, as a prominent energy source, is frequently employed in the operation of factories due to its cost-effectiveness in comparison to alternative energy sources such as oil. The combustion of coal results in the release of carbon dioxide into the atmosphere, thereby exacerbating the greenhouse effect (Van Rensburg *et al.*, 2020). The Footwear Industry represents 1.4% of global climate impacts (700 million metric tons CO_2eq), out of which the manufacturing of shoes contributes 43% (700 million metric tons CO_2eq). The per capita emissions associated with the estimated global consumption amount to 94 kg of CO_2 equivalent. This is comparable to a 900 km continental flight or a 2,350 km journey in a passenger vehicle (Kibbey *et al.*, 2018). The Manufacturing and Raw Material Extraction phases are the primary contributors to environmental impact.

In addition, shoes are composed of synthetic materials that require several years to undergo biodegradation. The immediate effects of their impact on the environment may not be visible to us. Throughout their entire lifecycle, from production to disposal, they have a detrimental impact on the environment. Footwear emits hazardous substances that have detrimental effects on our well-being. Furthermore, they have detrimental effects on both the environment and the well-being of wildlife. Disposal of shoes into landfill sites is the most prevalent end-of-life method (Van Rensburg *et al.*, 2020a). The footwear industry is confronted with a major environmental challenge, which is the substantial amount of post-consumer waste produced during the end-of-life phase. The issue is further intensified due to the fact that the majority of shoes that are discarded in landfills result in significant environmental contamination of rivers and groundwater reservoirs. This contamination primarily arises from the presence of landfill leachate (Staikos & Rahimifard, 2007). It contaminates the environment through the discharge of pollutants into the soil and groundwater. Dyes release harmful heavy metals when they decompose, while soles emit substances like polyurethane.

Burning footwear is not a sustainable solution, either. It releases a greater quantity of chemicals into the environment, thereby exacerbating air pollution. These substances pose undeniable health risks that permeate our systems. Pollution poses significant health risks, notably contributing to the onset of cancer.

The materials commonly utilized for constructing the upper part of a shoe are typically nylon, polyester, and polyurethane. Nylon and polyester are petrochemical-based synthetic materials that are not capable of being broken down by natural processes, making them non-biodegradable. In addition, the production of nylon generates nitrous oxide, a greenhouse gas that is believed to be 310 times more powerful than carbon dioxide, according to certain calculations. In addition, it should be noted that the vibrant colors commonly found on contemporary running shoes, which are attained through the employment of textile dyes, require the utilization of hazardous chemicals. These chemicals are frequently disposed of by being poured into water sources and ditches, resulting in the contamination of local communities. The outsole of running shoes accounts for 13% of the emissions in a pair of running shoes. The outsoles of these shoes are mostly comprised of tough carbon rubber, which is the same material used in tires. Additionally, they may also contain blown rubber, a lighter and less durable type of rubber commonly found at the front part of the shoe. After being disposed of, these artificial rubbers contribute to the accumulation of minuscule plastic polymers that contaminate seas, lakes, and waterways. Moreover, the production process of these artificial rubbers leads to the emission of trash that contains many questionable organic compounds, some of which are believed to be cancer-causing agents (Staikos & Rahimifard, 2007). The processing of footwear involves exposure to various hazardous compounds, including volatile organic compounds, toxic organic solvents, hydrocarbons, adhesives, shoe polishes, and other similar substances (Deb *et al.*, 2018).

Carbon Footprint of One Pair of Shoes

The aggregate energy footprint amounts to 18.004826 MJ, the cumulative water footprint is 8.37167 litres, and the combined carbon footprint is 9.174979 kg CO_2 eq. The manufacture of paper has the greatest impact on the energy footprint, with a consumption of 12.13 MJ. This energy is allocated to the production of both the box and the paper packing (Mahmud *et al.*, 2020).

Greenwashing in the Footwear Industry

A global review, conducted by the CMA (Competitions & Markets Authority), of randomly chosen websites has discovered that 40% of environmentally friendly assertions made online may potentially deceive consumers. Members noticed that these websites were employing strategies that could be deemed deceptive and, hence, could violate consumer laws. These comprised (Competition and Markets Authority, 2021):

a. Unclear and imprecise statements that use terminology like ‘eco’ or ‘sustainable’ or mention ‘natural products’ without proper clarification or supporting evidence.
b. Unaccredited organization logos and labels for own-brand eco products.
c. Using deception to portray products as environmentally friendly by concealing details like pollution levels.

INTERNATIONAL EFFORTS FOR SUSTAINABILITY IN THE FOOTWEAR INDUSTRY

Although most of the **Sustainable Development Goals (SDGs)** can be used to some degree at various stages of the footwear supply chain, the goals that are particularly important for most businesses' sustainability or Environmental, Social, and Governance (ESG) initiatives are as follows:

"**SDG 8 – Decent Work and Economic Growth** - 8.2 Achieve higher levels of economic productivity through diversification, technological upgrading, and innovation.

8.4 Improve progressively global resource efficiency in consumption and production.

8.5 Achieve full and productive employment and decent work for all women and men, including young people and persons with disabilities.

SDG 9 – Industry, Innovation and Infrastructure - 9.2 Promote inclusive and sustainable industrialization.

9.4 Upgrade infrastructure and retrofit industries to make them sustainable.

9.5 Enhance scientific research, upgrade the technological capabilities of industrial sectors.

SDG 12 - Responsible Consumption and Production - 12.2 Achieve the sustainable management and efficient use of natural resources.

12.4 Achieve the environmentally sound management of chemicals and all wastes throughout their life cycle.

12.5 Substantially reduce waste generation through prevention, reduction, recycling, and reuse.

SDG 13 – Climate Action - 13.2 Integrate climate change measures.

13.3 Improve education and awareness-raising on climate change mitigation."

UN Guiding Principles on Business and Human Rights 2011 mandate to the companies the need to uphold human rights. Considering this obligation, companies have a responsibility to prevent damaging the environment since it violates human rights (Mahecha & Punia, 2023). Under the Guiding principles, it is the duty of the State also to enforce such laws which might range from nondiscrimination and labour laws to environmental, property, privacy, and anti-bribery laws (United Nations, 2011).

The Green Claims Code, implemented on September 20, 2021, intends to address greenwashing in the UK. Greenwashing refers to the deceptive tactic employed by businesses to make false claims about the eco-friendliness of their products. The purpose of the Code is to assist businesses in comprehending and adhering to their current responsibilities under consumer protection law when asserting sustainability assertions (Green Claims Code, 2024).

The Sustainable Fashion Communication Playbook was launched on June 28, 2023, by the United Nations Environment Programme (UNEP) and the UN Climate-Change-convened Fashion Charter. This guide is designed for communicators in the global fashion industry who interact with consumers, providing them with a framework to align their efforts with sustainability targets. The playbook incorporates both environmental and social factors (UNEP, 2023a).

During 2018, fashion stakeholders collaborated under the guidance of UN Climate Change to explore strategies for the textile, garment, and fashion industry to collectively commit to addressing climate change in a comprehensive manner. The Fashion Charter was established with the objective of compelling the fashion sector to achieve net-zero greenhouse gas emissions by 2050, in accordance with the goal of limiting global warming to below 1.5 degrees. The Fashion Charter was introduced during the COP24 conference in December 2018 and subsequently reaffirmed during the COP26 conference in November 2021 (UNEP, 2023b). Adidas, Nike, and Puma are the signatories of the Charter.

The United Nations Alliance for Sustainable Fashion is a collaborative effort between United Nations agencies and affiliated groups aimed at promoting the achievement of the Sustainable Development Goals by taking coordinated action within the fashion industry (UN Alliance for Sustainable Fashion, 2024).

A SHIFT TOWARDS SUSTAINABLE FOOTWEAR

The achievement of sustainability necessitates the implementation of strategic and sustainable business practices (Lai *et al.*, 2020). From a pragmatic standpoint, sustainability is centered on the reduction of the negative impact that a company has on the environment, the improvement of positive social relationships, and the enhancement of the economic benefits that the company enjoys all at the same time (Hendiani *et al.*, 2020).

The issue of overflowing landfills and the subsequent environmental burdens has prompted the implementation of various measures aimed at mitigating the volume of post-consumer waste that ultimately finds its way into landfills. The Waste Management Law 2011 of the Bangladesh government mandates that landfills are exclusively permitted to receive biodegradable waste that has undergone thermal, biological, or mechanical treatment (Mia *et al.*, 2016).

Several shoe manufacturers are adopting new strategies to address the issue of shoe waste. They are aware that discovering unconventional ways to decrease emissions can have a positive impact on the environment. Additionally, it can lead to an enhanced brand reputation. Their goal is to establish sustainable methods and improve working conditions. Companies are also concerned with the ethical sourcing of materials and improving trash disposal methods. Major players such as Adidas and Nike, along with certain smaller brands like Allbirds and Veja, are actively seeking to decrease their carbon emissions through various means, including improvements in manufacturing techniques and advancements in materials.

Nike has a target to implement 100% renewable energy (Derrick, 2024), but without any regulations, checks and balances, and reporting, it is difficult to ensure that promises made by companies are fulfilled or not. Nike's main objective is "Double business while halving environmental impact" (McLoughlin, 2024a). If the company's target is to double the business, then there is no point in such practices because such extra pairs of shoes will end up in landfills.

The process of recycling shoes involves the systematic collection, sorting, deconstruction, and reprocessing of materials to transform them into new and usable products (Van Rensburg *et al.*, 2020). Nike has also launched a Reuse--Shoe program designed to reduce the impact of sneakers at the end-of-life stage. Under which consumers can give Nike their unwanted shoes, which will be ground up and used to make gym floors, basketball courts, and running tracks. But most of the consumers are not aware of the programme. Sustainability is not related to the manufacturing part only, but sustainability in disposing of the shoes is also very important (McLoughlin, 2024b).

In the year 2022, Nike's utilization of freshwater in the process of dyeing and finishing textiles was less than 77 liters per kilogram. This represents a marginal decrease compared to the previous year, declining from around 78.68 liters per kilogram. Indeed, Nike's utilization of freshwater has consistently declined annually since FY 2016 (Statista, 2024).

Adidas, a prominent player in the sportswear industry, has undertaken a sustainable initiative involving the utilization of recycled plastic materials in the manufacturing process of its sports footwear. In addition, the organization has made a commitment to eradicate the utilization of all virgin plastics by the year

2024 (Rogers, 2018). Adidas has a target to achieve 100% sustainable cotton (Adidas Group, 2025). But the production of one kilogram of cotton, which is approximately the same as a t-shirt and a pair of jeans, requires almost 20,000 gallons of water. Cotton cultivation requires a significant amount of land. Consequently, there is a rise in the rate of deforestation. Cotton is the most pesticide and insecticide-intensive crop globally (Newell, 2016).

Allbirds declared in February 2023 the introduction of their new eucalyptus tree fiber-based Tree Runners. With their reduced environmental effect over conventional shoes, the Tree Runners are the company's most sustainable shoe to date. In March 2023, Veja introduced its latest product, the V-10 B-Mesh sneakers, crafted using recycled materials. The V-10 B-Mesh sneakers are engineered to possess greater sustainability compared to Veja's prior models, utilizing a blend of recycled polyester, recycled rubber, and organic cotton (Sky Questt, 2024).

In March 2023, Toms, a sustainable footwear business, declared its intention to introduce a fresh collection of shoes crafted from recycled materials. Additionally, the company intends to contribute a pair of shoes to an underprivileged child for each pair of shoes that is purchased (Straits Research, 2023). Likewise, Puma, a prominent footwear manufacturer, made a public statement in April 2023, declaring its intention to invest a sum of USD 100 million towards sustainable efforts within the next five years. The company intends to utilize the funds to advance the development of more environmentally friendly products, diminish its ecological footprint, and enhance its working conditions (Straits Research, 2023).

Rothy's introduced its Spring 2023 collection in April 2023, showcasing a diverse range of environmentally-friendly footwear crafted from upcycled materials. The Spring 2023 collection features footwear such as sneakers, flats, and sandals that are crafted from repurposed materials such as recycled plastic bottles, water bottles, and fishing nets (Straits Research, 2023).

Other companies that are top players in the sustainable footwear industry are Reebok, Ecco Sko A/S, Timberland, Patagonia, Vivobarefoot, Nisolo, Ahimsa, Beyond Skin, *etc*.

CONCLUDING REMARKS

Engaging in sustainable practices is widely recognized as a paramount imperative for companies operating within the contemporary industrial landscape. There are numerous companies that manufacture footwear all around the world. The manufacturing of footwear is one of the most widespread types of industrial activities. In order to achieve a more favorable outcome, it is imperative that the supply chain responsible for the footwear sector implements sustainable practices. The administration of the sector will become less difficult if the supply chain is developed to be more environmentally friendly.

The main challenge for sustainable fashion is that several sustainable resources, such as organic cotton and recycled polyester fibers, may be costlier and more difficult to obtain compared to conventional materials. In addition, implementing sustainable production practices, such as utilizing non-toxic dyes and minimizing water consumption, can result in higher expenses. The fashion brands generate a substantial quantity of garbage, and conventional means of disposal, such as landfilling or burning, are not environmentally sustainable. The footwear industry should actively seek methods to minimize waste and encourage the recycling and reusing of footwear.

In order to achieve a significant reduction in emissions across the footwear industry, the most effective approach is for industries to prioritize the use of renewable energy and improve energy efficiency throughout their supply chains. This should particularly focus on the stages of the production process that have the greatest impact on emissions, such as Dyeing and Finishing, Fiber Production, Yarn Preparation, Fabric Preparation, and Assembly. By doing so, the industry can move towards a future with lower carbon emissions.

Some companies like Adidas, Brooks Adrenaline, Nike, *etc*., introduced Eco-sneakers. An average pair of eco-sneakers is responsible for emitting around 12.77 kg of carbon. By purchasing eco-sneakers, individuals can reduce their annual carbon emissions from 42 kg to 38.31 kg. This is a decrease of 8.8%. Nevertheless, acquiring eco-friendly footwear is not the most efficient method to reduce one's ecological impact. One of the most effective things a customer can do is reduce the number of pairs of sneakers they purchase annually, which will result in a reduction in their carbon footprint by one-third. Also, the eco sneakers are more expensive than conventional sneakers. It means environmentally conscious consumers are being charged more for the elimination of carbon emissions. If businesses were truly committed to environmental conservation, they would enhance the durability of their products, reduce the number of product variations, and actively promote a shift in consumer behavior from excessive consumption to practicality.

We should adopt a circular economy. A circular economy is characterized by a mindset that involves the processes of making, using, recycling/repairing, and reusing, while also addressing unsustainable consumption patterns. To do this, we must reconsider the number of diverse materials and colors we desire for our shoes. As we increase the use of diverse and multi-component materials, the negative impact on the environment will also increase. The government should also establish a place like "shoe-banks" for the collection of waste footwear, recycling, or its disposal.

Footwear brands face significant problems in terms of consumer attitude and demand. This is due to the fact that a significant number of consumers may be unaware of the detrimental effects that rapid fashion has on the environment and the advantages of sustainable fashion. For the purpose of addressing this challenge, fashion brands need to strive towards educating customers and collaborating with legislators, marketers, and retailers in order to promote sustainable fashion and lessen the impact that fast fashion has on society and the environment. Customers also hesitate to purchase sustainable footwear as much because they think it will cost more, and because the materials aren't easy to find. This is because the Indian market for sustainable footwear is still pretty new. When buying eco-friendly shoes, quality is another question that comes up. People don't know how long they will last since it's a new area.

Sustainability Reporting should be mandatory for all types of businesses, whether small, medium, or Large. Sustainability reporting refers to the act of disclosing a company's Environmental, Social, and Governance (ESG) goals.

REFERENCES

Authority, C. a. M. (2021). Global sweep finds 40% of firms' green claims could be misleading. *GOV.UK.* Available from: https://www.gov.uk/government/news/global-sweep-finds-40-of-firms-green-claims-could-be-misleading

Certilogo-commerce. (2022). *Sustainability in the footwear industry.* Available from: https://discover.certilogo.com/ blogs/insights/sustainability-in-footwear-industry

Cheah, L., Ciceri, N.D., Olivetti, E., Matsumura, S., Forterre, D., Roth, R., Kirchain, R. (2012). Manufacturing-focused emissions reductions in footwear production. *J. Clean. Prod., 44*, 18-29. [http://dx.doi.org/10.1016/j.jclepro.2012.11.037]

DiNapoli, T. (2024). *Global Shoe Waste: The Environmental Impact of Footwear.* Available from: https://www. unsustainablemagazine.com/global-shoe-waste/

Deb, A.K., Chowdhury, M., Bin Azam, F.A., Hossain, Md. (2018). I., & Institute of Leather Engineering and Technology, University of Dhaka, Dhaka-1209, Bangladesh. (2018). Workers' Health and Workplace Condition Evaluation (WCE) Of the Footwear Industries in Bangladesh. In A. K. Deb. *IOSR Journal of Environmental Science, Toxicology and Food Technology (IOSR-JESTFT), 12*(8), 7-13. Available from: https://www.iosrjournals.org/iosr-jestft/papers/Vol12-%20Issue%208/Version-1/B1208010713.pdf

Derrick, M. (2024). *How Nike is Increasing Reliability on Renewable Energy.*Energy Digital. Available from: https://energydigital.com/articles/how-nike-is-increasing-reliability-on-renewable-energy

DiNapoli, T. (2024). *Global Shoe Waste: The Environmental Impact of Footwear.* Available from: https://www.unsustainablemagazine.com/global-shoe-waste/

Fashion, E. (2022). *How Sustainable Are Sneakers? The Environmental Impact of Sneaker Production Make Fashion Better. Make Fashion Better* . Available from: https://www.makefashionbetter.com/blog/ environmental-impact-of-sneaker-production

Green claims code. (2024). Green Claims Code. https://greenclaims.campaign.gov.uk/.

Gangopadhyay, S., Ara, T., Dev, S., Ghoshal, G., Das, T. (2011). An Occupational Health Study of the Footwear Manufacturing Workers of Kolkata, India. *Stud. Ethno-Med.,* *5*(1), 11-15. [http://dx.doi.org/10.1080/09735070.2011.11886386]

Hanson, M., Hanson, M. (2023). *Running Shoes are Part of an Environmental Crisis. Is Change Coming?*Trail Runner Magazine. Available from: https://www.trailrunnermag.com/people/culture-people/running-shoes-are-part-of-an-environmental-crisis-is-change-coming/?scope=anon

Hendiani, S., Liao, H., Bagherpour, M., Tvaronavičienė, M., Banaitis, A., Antucheviciene, J. (2020). Analyzing the status of sustainable development in the manufacturing sector using multi-expert multi-criteria fuzzy decision-making and integrated triple bottom lines. *Int. J. Environ. Res. Public Health,* *17*(11), 3800. [http://dx.doi.org/10.3390/ijerph17113800]

Kumar, A., Moktadir, A., Liman, Z.R., Gunasekaran, A., Hegemann, K., Khan, S.R. (2019). Evaluating sustainable drivers for social responsibility in the context of ready-made garments supply chain. *J. Clean. Prod.,* *248*119231 [http://dx.doi.org/10.1016/j.jclepro.2019.119231]

Kibbey, J., Johnson, D., McGill, M., Pepper, L.R. (2018). Sustainable Apparel Coalition, Brooklyn Fashion + Design Accelerator, Pratt Center for Sustainable Design Strategies, Textile Exchange, World Apparel & Footwear Life Cycle Assessment Database (WALDB), Hugo Boss, Legero, Swiss Federal Office of the Environment, LVMH, Texaid, Ikea, Cotton, Inc., Chrobot, P., Faist, M., Gustavus, L., Martin, A., & Stamm, A. (2018). Measuring Fashion. *Environmental Impact of the Global Apparel and Footwear Industries Study.* Available from: https://quantis.com/wp-content/uploads/2018/03/measuringfashion_globalimpactstudy_ful--report_quantis_cwf_2018a.pdf?trk=article-ssr-frontend-pulse_little-text-block

Lai, H., Liao, H., Šaparauskas, J., Banaitis, A., Ferreira, F.F., Al-Barakati, A. (2020). Sustainable cloud service provider development by a z-number-based dnma method with gini-coefficient-based weight determination. *Sustainability,* *12*(8), 3410. [http://dx.doi.org/10.3390/su12083410]

Moktadir, M.A., Rahman, T., Ali, S.M., Nahar, N., Paul, S.K. (2019). Examining barriers to reverse logistics practices in the leather footwear industry. *Ann. Oper. Res.,* *293*(2), 715-746. [http://dx.doi.org/10.1007/s10479-019-03449-y]

Moktadir, M.A., Mahmud, Y., Banaitis, A., Sarder, T., Khan, M.R. (2021). Key performance indicators for adopting sustainability practices in footwear supply chains. *E+M Ekon. Manag.,* *24*(1), 197-213. [http://dx.doi.org/10.15240/tul/001/2021-1-013]

Mahmud, Y., Rashed-Ul-Islam, M., Islam, M.O., Moin, T.S., Rahman, K.T. (2020). Assessment of the carbon footprint and vocs emissions caused by the manufacturing process of the footwear industry in bangladesh. *Textile & Leather Review,* *4*(1), 23-29. [http://dx.doi.org/10.31881/tlr.2020.19]

Mahecha, M., Punia, M. (2023). Climate change and business development: a critical analysis of ways to achieve sustainable development. *Revista Brasileira De Políticas Públicas,* *13*(1) [http://dx.doi.org/10.5102/rbpp.v13i1.8805]

Mia, Md. (2016). Waste management & quality assessment of footwear manufacturing industry in bangladesh: an innovative approach. *International Journal of Engineering and Management Research,* *7*(4), 402-407. Available from: https://www.researchgate.net/publication/319873669_Waste_Management_Quality_Assessment_of_Footwear_Manufacturing_Industry_in_Bangladesh_An_Innovative_Approach

McLoughlin, D. (2024). *All Eco Sneakers Do Is Kill The Planet a Little Bit Slower [Study].*RunRepeat - Athletic Shoe Reviews. Available from: https://runrepeat.com/eco-sneakers-research

McLoughlin, D. (2024). *All Eco Sneakers Do Is Kill The Planet a Little Bit Slower [Study].*RunRepeat - Athletic Shoe Reviews. Available from: https://runrepeat.com/eco-sneakers-research

Newell, A. (2016). *Quenching Cotton's Thirst: Reducing the Use of Water in the Cotton Lifecycle.*Triple Pundit. Available from: https://www.triplepundit.com/story/2016/quenching-cottons-thirst-reducing-use-water-cotton-lifecycle/57196

*Our Targets - adidas Group.*Adidas. Available from: https://www.adidas-group.com/en/sustainability/focu--on-sustainability/our-targets

Rogers, S. (2024). Adidas to Only Use Recycled Materials in Products by *Interesting Engineering.* Available from: https://interestingengineering.com/science/adidas-to-only-use-recycled-materials-in-products-by-2024

Staikos, T., Rahimifard, S. (2007). Post-Consumer Waste Management Issues in the Footwear Industry. *Proc. Inst. Mech. Eng., B J. Eng. Manuf., 221*(2), 363-368.
[http://dx.doi.org/10.1243/09544054jem732sc]

*Shoe Sustainability*Shoe Sustainability. Available from: https://www.shoesustainability.com/

Straits Research. (2023). Market Research Report. *Straits Research (No. SRCP54823DR).* Available from: https://straitsresearch.com/report/sustainable-footwear-market

Sky Questt. (2024). Global Sustainable Footwear Market. *Skyquestt (SQMIG25L2011).* Available from: https://www.skyquestt.com/report/sustainable-footwear-market

Statista. (2024, July 11). Nike's freshwater use intensity in textile dyeing and finishing 2016-2023. https://www.statista.com/statistics/861772/volume-of-freshwater-use-by-nike/.

The UN Alliance for Sustainable Fashion. (2024). *Home - The UN Alliance for Sustainable Fashion.* Available from: https://unfashionalliance.org/

UNEP. (2023). *UNEP and UN Climate Change provide fashion communicators with practical guide to contribute to sustainable change.* Available from: https://www.unep.org/news-and-stories/pre-s-release/unep-and-un-climate-change-provide-fashion-communicators-practical

UNEP. (2023). *UNEP and UN Climate Change provide fashion communicators with practical guide to contribute to sustainable change.* Available from: https://www.unep.org/news-and-stories/pre-s-release/unep-and-un-climate-change-provide-fashion-communicators-practical

United Nations. (2011). Guiding Principles on Business and Human Rights: Implementing the United Nations "Protect, Respect and Remedy" Framework. *Guiding Principles on Business and Human Rights: Implementing the United Nations "Protect, Respect and Remedy" Framework.* . Available from: https://www.ohchr.org/sites/default/files/documents/publications/guidingprinciplesbusinesshr_en.pdf

Van Rensburg, M.L., Nkomo, S.L., Mkhize, N.M. (2020). Life cycle and End-of-Life management options in the footwear industry: A review. *Waste Management & Research the Journal for a Sustainable Circular Economy, 38*(6), 599-613.
[http://dx.doi.org/10.1177/0734242x20908938]

CHAPTER 10

Financing and Investment for the Circular Economy

Oksana Polyakova[1], **Kartikey Singh**[2] and **Surabhi Sangal**[2,*]

[1] *Department of Regional Geology and Mineral Resources, Kazan Federal University, Kazan, Russian Federation*

[2] *School of Business and Management, Christ University, Banglore, Karnataka, India*

Abstract: The transition from a linear to a circular economy is imperative to ensure sustainable resource utilization and environmental preservation. This paper delves into the critical role of financing and investment in advancing circular economy initiatives. It explores the challenges of aligning traditional financial systems with circular economic principles, emphasizing the need for innovative financial tools, public-private partnerships, and regulatory frameworks. The study highlights the benefits of circular economy practices, such as resource efficiency, waste reduction, and socio-economic advantages, while addressing barriers like high investment risks and limited financial accessibility. Through a comprehensive analysis of financing instruments, investment strategies, and case studies, the paper provides actionable insights into fostering a circular economy. It underscores the importance of integrating circular economy principles in financial training and education, advocating for global cooperation to overcome structural and regulatory hurdles. The findings aim to guide policymakers, investors, and businesses in adopting sustainable financial practices to facilitate the global shift toward a circular economic model.

Keywords: Circular economy, Environmental sustainability, Investment strategies, Public-private partnerships, Resource efficiency, Sustainable financing.

INTRODUCTION TO CIRCULAR ECONOMY

Industrialization has been the driving force of the modern revolution, making possible the improvement of the quality of life. The advance is commonly achieved by producing as much as possible. The maximization of production, however, places the planet at risk of resource exhaustion and environmental destruction. Although economic benefits are important considerations, the considerations of resource exploitation and environmental destruction, if not the

* **Corresponding author Oksana Polyakova:** School of Business and Management, Christ University, Banglore, Karnataka, India; E-mail: surabhi.sangal@christuniversity.in

Theodore Tarnanidis, Vijaya Kittu Manda, Vivek Gupta (Eds.)

most important, are equally significant. There is a need to manage economic activities to achieve a balance between the pursuit of economic value and resource preservation and environmental protection. To create such a balance, the concept of circular economy has been proposed (Velasco-Muñoz *et al.*, 2021).

In the circular economy, economic activities are managed to create circular loops in the utilization of resources. Products are produced to have minimal environmental impact. When no longer in use, products are disposed of in a manner that can minimize the impact on the environment. Resource utilization is optimized, aiming to extract the full economic value of the resources. In the utilization, the value of products is preserved. The management of economic activities calls for changes to current corporate finance practices. Businesses, if they aspire to improve overall sustainability, may face trade-offs between financial and non-financial performance. In this chapter, the financing and investment practices that can facilitate the advancement of the circular economy are discussed (Vernimmen *et al.*, 2017).

Definition and Principles

The principle of circular economy is reducing production losses and benefiting the value of each product at the highest level. This involves viewing existing materials as resources and minimizing waste as much as possible. The phenomenon, which is called dumping scrap, refers to the production residues and losses that are disposed of because they are not potentially valuable. Increasing raw material costs necessitate a transformation from a linear production-consumption-waste chain to a cyclic economy. The raw material to be used in order to obtain the desired value from the product to be produced is defined as the net material. In general, the productivity of the product value that is produced by the total material during its life cycle is inevitably associated with social, environmental, and economic factors. You can formulate the equation that provides a direct model with net materials. The equation is as follows, and the values are expressed in kilograms (Roy *et al.*, 2022).

Through this equation, value generation through a product that is more efficient both in terms of minimum wastage and outstanding resource planning over the entire life cycle of the product is aimed at. The circular economy concept, which covers waste prevention, reuse, recycling, potential recovery, and energy recovery, evaluates the planning of a broad category of departments together. The production activities that are included within the scope of the circular economy aim to plan the products and production processes in such a way as to minimize loss as much as possible. Circular economy practices allow companies and consumers to benefit from available resources. The basic model is to reduce raw material consumption, recycle supplies that have lost their use, and continue the cycle of resources. Thus, the main purpose is to implement the continuous value-added model. In this respect, the recycling process alone is not enough. Establishing a network in which all the elements of waste, minimum preparation, and recycling are taken into consideration in a series of diagrams in the context of the resources of the economic model is essential. The characteristics of circular systems are being further analyzed in their social and economic aspects. The weighted system of the circle may require less labor and material use than linear structures, but it may change the use of all production resources in such a way that it is necessary to change production methods. Reuse, preventing waste, and promoting consumer awareness are important benefits of the industry (Kowalski *et al.*, 2022).

Importance and Benefits

Financing and investment in the circular economy are crucial, as the topic for the implementation of circular economy projects is complex, and the missing resources are one of the most common barriers to the circular economy. Circular economy projects are often associated with a higher level of risk, longer payback periods, and lower returns. These characteristics make it difficult to attract private investment, even though circular economy projects offer numerous long-term benefits for the economy and its citizens. Benefits of the circular economy include the reduction in materials, water consumption, and pollution, creation of jobs, cost and energy savings, and a competitive advantage. The circular economy is also recognized as an important sector for reducing security risks and preventing socio-economic problems. In addition to the EU-wide policy measures, national and European measures can be implemented to improve access to financing, especially for small and medium-sized enterprises. The EU's regional funds, development banks, guarantee and risk-sharing mechanisms, venture capital, green bonds, tax incentives, and green public procurement are some of the measures that can be used (Salmenperä *et al.*, 2021).

In the context of this study, the work aims to highlight the drivers and the associated actions for the circular economy to be more effectively and adequately financed. This is especially important when circular business models are more capital and knowledge-intensive and have a dynamic relationship with the economic, social, and environmental impacts of the sector. In order to achieve the present work, several methodologies were used, such as the development of a business model based on a set of 24 drivers and 53 actions associated with monetary and socio-environmental impact structures. These drivers and associated actions take into account market competitiveness, environmental compliance, and bonds. This will contribute to better monitoring and evaluation of monetary indicators with the described model. The importance of the results that emerged from this study is essential for companies in selecting a business model that most closely meets an enterprise's circular economy goals (Audretsch & Fiedler, 2024).

KEY CONCEPTS IN FINANCING AND INVESTMENT

Rethinking financing and investment from the circular economy perspective is quite new. Basic concepts in financing and investment defined in economic textbooks have been designed for the linear economy model, or a 'take-mak--dispose' model. This model maintains the tax structure for business opportunities to take environmental costs and social costs without limitations. It also presupposes that natural, human, and social capital will continue to generate unlimited resources and human life and capability without thresholds. Circular economy and its application require different, integrated, and new thinking, including the parallel accounting perspective of the external economic and environmental impacts of all business operations and products. A fundamental aspect of the circular economy reconsiders the relation between the financial systems and the natural, human, and social capital structure. The money and banking systems underlying these structural relations make the contribution of natural, human, or social value less visible or less important than the financial and real capital underlying the principles of economics of demand and supply, and risk and return. The existing financial and capital allocation system, including stocks, securities, financial markets, and accounting systems, is basically favorable to linear short-term profit maximization and capable of externalizing environmental, social, and governance burdens. Locating profit at the core of business and capital allocation is not the specific responsibility of corporate shareholders. Such responsibility should be more aligned with sustainable benefits for all companies' stakeholders. The capital allocation system for driving the circular economy requires different goals and incentives. The capital structure of the circular economy or resource management includes both financial and real capital, and also environmental, natural, and social capital, with value linked to synthetic currencies of greenness and well-being (Basu *et al.*, 2022).

Types of Financing Instruments

There is no uniform definition or categorization of financing instruments. A distinction can be made between demand-driven and supply-driven instruments, and between policy-driven instruments that are available without specific issues, and instruments that are intended specifically to provide financing solutions to companies with a certain specificity. Broadly, five types of financing instruments can be defined for the financing of measures that are typically associated with the circular economy. These are, in order of growing intensity: 1) General forms of finance commonly available, 2) Export credit and concessional finance for general projects and investment, 3) Subsidized financing and grants for measures that foster better resource efficiency and lower environmental impacts, 4) Financing and guarantees that target specific circular instruments, such as green growth guarantees, green bonds for closed-loop projects, and financial institutions that specialize in financing these measures, and 5) Public financial instruments and guarantees that provide support towards contracts that explore circular solutions within a public-private partnership from the public sector, and 6) Dedicated auxiliary financial instruments and venture capital (Rizos & Bryhn, 2022; Mishra *et al.*, 2022)

General forms of finance, such as commercial bank loans or working capital loans from businesses and department stores, financial paper messages, leasing, financing with equity, guarantees, and significant commercial leasing, are all traditional financial products and services used by both the private and public sectors nowadays. Most banks have sustainable finance products to meet the increased interest of both their commercial and social customers, in meaningful banking and in meaningful investments. The proportion of these products that are specifically designed for tasks linked to the circular economy is nonetheless very limited. Loans for purchasing high-quality second-hand equipment or machinery might be challenging to obtain. The regular renewal of range and product lines that are aligned with the circular model might be less suited to financing from regular banks (Sharma *et al.*, 2021).

Investment Strategies for Circular Economy Projects

The transition to the circular economy is triggered by investment flows generated by and in various sectors and industries. This calls for new ways to assess circularity in business strategy development and investment decisions. An assessment of such a new paradigm is the term "circularity invested," referring to strategies that harness and amplify the transformative power of the circular economy. With a focus on how value is created, delivered, and extracted throughout the economic life cycle, rather than on how resources are depleted and how negative externalities are created, invested circularity is a model of economic thought that stands in stark contrast to traditional GDP-centric analyses and policy tools that focus almost exclusively on boosting the rate of resource extraction, raw material imports, the intensity of partial utilization of these raw materials, and the creation of negative externalities, which are mislabeled as "value additions." If circular business models are, at their core, revenue-generating circular economy projects, investors are and will be stakeholders, and their capital funds should flow towards circular projects. However, traditional financial evaluation of business models is not yet able to fully embrace the long-term sustainability features of circularity. Consequently, some of the priorities and development needs that have to be addressed with regard to circular economy projects deserve particular attention from investors. First, there is a need for a standardized identification of circular economy business models and their main critical aspects. Second, governments and international financial institutions should develop appropriate hinge instruments to leverage the rate of return for private circular economy investors. Third, there should be accelerated support for risk-taking and learning through pilot projects and by early-stage circular economy entrepreneurs themselves (Chizaryfard *et al.*, 2021).

CHALLENGES AND OPPORTUNITIES IN FINANCING THE CIRCULAR ECONOMY

As governments around the world unleash fiscal policies of unprecedented scale to boost their economies amidst the crisis, there is a new urgency for investments aligned with the transition to a circular economy. At the same time, investment in the circular economy remains relatively nascent and risks being constrained by challenges associated with regulatory ambiguity, business model uncertainty, and profound technological, social, and material shifts taking place alongside the transformation to a circular economy. This calls for a clearer view of what investment in the circular economy means; particular attention to the challenges related to financing circular economy business models, sectors, and companies; and a deeper appreciation of the opportunities arising from the circular transition, the levers that businesses and policymakers need to consider, and the means to scale investment (Cezarino *et al.*, 2021).

This chapter begins by defining the circular economy, its importance, and the significance of increasingly aligning economies with the principles of a circular model. It then analyzes the shifts that are taking place within the circular economy, such as changes in business models, supply chain processes, and consumer demands, as well as some of the investment opportunities emerging from these transition dynamics. The chapter goes on to discuss what investing in the circular economy means and the significant barriers to this transition. These challenges often mean that the financing that the circular economy attracts is currently not sufficiently aligned with the principles of a circular economy. The chapter then articulates the consequences of a misalignment of the forces underpinning the financial system and the circular economy. To extract the potential of finance during the transition to the circular economy, the chapter discusses the vital role of public policymaking in making the circular economy more investment-friendly (Asgari & Asgari, 2021; Rodríguez-Espíndola *et al.*, 2022).

Barriers to Financing Circular Economy Projects

One of the major challenges that CE start-ups, small and medium enterprises face is attracting finance for their innovative ideas. It is widely accepted that 'funding gaps' exist for yet underdeveloped but commercially viable circular economy business models. Indeed, the current market situation cannot significantly support the transition towards the circular economy, mainly because market failures prevent the effective supply of finance for circular models. The insufficiency of available finance to remodel the existing linear business models towards CE is associated with less traditional, successful, and widely adopted methods for which access to funds is achievable. The three key difficulties that may constrain the move to circularity are: (a) the need to invest in a physical or digital platform that is shared among all agents involved in a closed-loop model, and by providing incentives to all agents to participate in the transition to CE, (b) the CE shift requires that production processes evolve as the structure of the entities invested in, making them sellers of goods since they are the producers of the inputs, and (c) the difficulty of attracting the needed investment finance in innovative CE projects (Saarinen & Aarikka-Stenroos, 2023).

Some scholars point out other barriers and constraints concerning circularity investments, which are related but distinct. Specifically, they suggest that one barrier is investing in designs and organizing business models that are novel and thus perceived as high-growth risky. Moreover, discussing the financing obstacles to CE, we have to recognize the existing credibility gap among pioneering and impact-oriented solution investors, as well as the differences in the long-term values generated by CE models compared to traditional solutions. These are not always linear and measurable, and considering the limited and preliminary nature of CE approaches, they may further accumulate well-known uncertainties. In conclusion, both classic and innovative finance need to extend the classic set of strategic investments aimed at scaling a given model and organizing enabler investments that remove or neutralize the obstacles and additional constraints that can lock in the old model (Zhao *et al.*, 2021).

Innovative Financing Solutions

Circular economy is, by nature, innovative and may require time to become efficient. However, the circular economy also has the potential for high returns, and new businesses may be created. Innovative financing should be developed to provide adequate opportunities for circular economy start-ups to mature. Traditional ways of financing may, for the moment, not fit well with circular business models. Innovations in traditional financing are foreseen, but the circular economy also calls for new financial tools that may provide certainty and long-term cost advantages (Mehrotra & Jaladi, 2022).

Due to the inherent uncertainty and long lead time associated with financing many circular economy projects, lower-cost funding would be important. It would support such technologies and projects until they mature and can compete in the mainstream financial markets. Long-term strategies to support financing for the circular economy are necessary and may need to be designed for the long term. These strategies would support the development of new or improved circular economy business models; incentives to foster innovation, allowing more circular solutions for resource-intensive sectors; incentives to develop, demonstrate, and deploy circular economy projects; and the development of supporting financial buffers to increase the share of circular economy in overall investment and financing (Giorgi *et al.*, 2022).

ROLE OF GOVERNMENTS AND POLICIES

The shift towards a circular economy will not only create opportunities for companies to profit from new, innovative business models, but also impose challenges unique in their political and societal dimensions. Solutions may depend on governments and governmental organizations around the world. Governments will play a central role in determining the success of a circular economy. They can support innovation, particularly in the early stages of the new business models and technologies, foster the development and stability of markets, and remove or mitigate the obstacles and market failures. As facilitators of the circular economy, governments can themselves become increasingly circular. Similar actions can also be undertaken at the level of supranational and regional agencies. Policies that are consistent with the principles of the circular economy place the reduction, reuse, and recycling of materials at their core. Impacts on employment and society need to receive similar policy attention. Stronger product standards for performance and durability stimulate eco-innovation and circular business models, and strengthen incentives for producers to raise their competitive performance in an era of new business challenges built on process innovation and service provision models instead of volume. Promoting product design for reuse methods that support longer-lasting and/or easily upgradeable urban infrastructures also involves the reduction of materials related to whiteness—materials that have a high environmental impact when changing their characteristic color to meet ocular preferences—or that are large generators of waste, like the fast fashion industry (Salmenperä *et al.*, 2021).

Regulatory Frameworks and Incentives

The move to a low-carbon, resource-efficient economy will require a range of measures. These might include regulatory changes, taxes, and incentives, such as tax breaks, to try to shift activity in the right direction. There has been considerable work looking at the incentives, as well as disincentives, that can play a role in encouraging circular economy development. Market failures, externalities, information, and transparency are key drivers of policy action, inviting government policies to favor circular economic activities (Khan *et al.*, 2022).

Tax incentives in this domain can take many forms. They often try to nudge activities in a certain direction, for example, the tax breaks given to those firms that invest in pollution-reducing technologies such as energy-efficient office buildings. There is an increasing body of evidence that suggests that subsidies and many direct environmental policies aimed at reducing or preventing pollution have little effect on innovation. On the other hand, market-wide price signals, such as those offered by environmental taxes or emissions permit trading programs, have been found to be effective. The market, if it is efficient and free from externalities, should allocate the right resources to the right activities (Carmichael *et al.*, 2021).

Public-private Partnerships

Governments can work together with businesses and investors to co-finance investments and build trust by creating transparent and effective regulatory environments. The private sector has a key role to play in financing the circular economy. Business-led initiatives are quickly emerging that will displace the traditional models of consumption with new growth strategies built on the premise of using fewer resources and maintaining those resources in the cycle for as long as possible. However, all these initiatives depend on the engagement of the public sector, particularly through research support and through creating the policy, institutional, and market conditions necessary to complement corporate efforts. Structural policies contribute to promoting the shift toward a circular economy. They provide powerful incentives for efficient resource use and its facilitation in the context of sustainable development. To strengthen policy action and redirect economic incentives, many governments are developing policies and legal frameworks based on dialogue and public-private consultation. Some governments are far ahead in establishing partnerships with the business community to promote the restructuring of economies and stimulate investment, taking into account the concept of the circular economy. With ambitious sustainable development strategies, they are creating favorable conditions for business (Kazancoglu *et al.*, 2021).

FINANCIAL MECHANISMS FOR THE CIRCULAR ECONOMY

Shifting towards the circular business model is a capital-intensive venture, involving the development and upgrading of production factors and integrated processes, which is beyond the financial capacity of single companies. Moreover, the model is not conducive to traditional performance standards, such as profit maximization, due to the extended life cycle of resources and assets. Thus, it is important to establish a circular economy financial support and investment system, with long-term stakeholders and shareholders for alignment of corporate interests and broadening of funding sources. Over the last few years, new forms of financing that serve the common good, and specifically the environment, have blossomed all over the world. We shall merely mention collective loans, other than classic factoring, franchising, and equity crowdfunding (Saarinen & Aarikka-Stenroos, 2023).

A defining feature of the modern economy is financial globalization and regionalization. While circular economic activities occur on a regional level, a great deal of funds can be raised in the global financial market. Financial engineering also provides opportunities for local governments and firms to mobilize private savings to promote the realization of circular economy benefits in the short term. Cross-regional and cross-border financing has provided new ways of promoting regional circular economy development. Central and local governments should take the lead to promote social and economic transformation and provide investment funds and support policies for circular economy constructs. The expected cash flows caused by the realization of listed companies' social values can be used as OPB of green funds under the principle of expected benefits. Funds created according to corporate value and investment in companies based on realizing their social value alignment will form long-term interests, which will promote corporate growth and sustainable development (Yang & Ma, 2023).

Green Bonds and Sustainable Finance

Green bonds for circular projects can benefit from a dedicated support scheme, such as guarantees, or from participation in "circular economy"-labelled investment funds or securitization vehicles. These should foster a process whereby massive amounts of capital continue to be directed to the circular economy. A range of specific solutions is available for various economic sectors offered by institutional investors, corporate bond issuers, and regulators. Developing circular-labelled equity products and solutions for listed companies should become an important objective in order to enable capital market investors to engage in the sustainable financing of circular businesses and to diversify their portfolios. Players at a very early stage should also be defined as potential beneficiaries of support. Equity and equity-like solutions have substantially lower leverage than debt, are able to offer smaller companies the patient capital needed in fast-paced, early-stage disruptive environments, and create value through timely liquidity events at a later point in time. Such solutions inject capital during the developing phase, mentor, and monitor the companies' impact both on the environment and results (de Assis *et al.*, 2022).

Impact Investing

Impact investing is an area that has already been mentioned previously in the book. As we know, it is a worldwide movement allowing people to invest in companies and funds that are beneficial to society and the environment, and promote the circular model and sustainability. Quite importantly, this is also gaining significant strength as investing in organizations that operate with clear positive criteria, driving impact. If an investor determines, for example, that their priority goal is to invest in organizations creating jobs for disadvantaged people or in a specific city, then it is possible for their portfolio to be directed to those companies that are working in these areas. Some are protected by law, requiring multinational corporations to recognize their responsibility for the broader health of society, prompting some to invest in positive projects that contribute to, among other positive areas, employment in the more disadvantaged regions (Alkaraan *et al.*, 2023).

The truth is that impact investors have the responsibility to contribute to the resolution of economically and socially significant issues. As part of the impact investors' conference, there was an initiative called the US SIF, which has the synergistic purpose of growing the impact investing industry by doubling the amount of assets. The Circular Economy presents an important opportunity for impact investors, given the potential number of projects across multiple investable countries that could deliver both financial returns and benefits for the globe as a whole. However, such impact investment opportunities have so far been unexploited at the scale required due to four typical barriers that currently constrain investment into a typical project (Ibn-Mohammed *et al.*, 2021).

CASE STUDIES AND BEST PRACTICES

The development of the circular economy brings both new financing opportunities and the need to adapt, especially corporate access to investment, for the benefits of the circular economy principles to become effective. The case studies and best practices presented here consider regulatory compliance, a professional view on the business, social and environmental gains, financing strategies, and the upfront planning in corporate design. Socio-economy and finance will benefit from wider commitments, more accurate risk quantification, and better risk management. However, not all developing projects may be able to manage high capital costs, potentially experiencing a lock-in effect. Regulatory Compliance, Boosting Corporate Governance. In several countries, environmental aspects play an increasing role in the checks of corporate governance. Recent changes by the Italian legislature introduced the obligation for the board of directors of large enterprises to express and document their opinion on the interaction between strategic business plans and social interest, environmental matters, and the treatment of human resources. They must decide, when generating positive externalities, which part of profits may be assigned to increasing capital and which to other capital. The rules governing the collaboration with the company branches in forming the so-called strategic business plan are aligned with these changes, under penalty of administrative liability for the administrators. All this follows the enforced discipline of reports on how the undertaken activities conform to the principles of sustainability, of the so-called non-financial statements, now enriched with more consistent and complete guidelines (Stefanakis *et al.*, 2021; Dagilienė *et al.*, 2021).

Successful Financing Models in Circular Economy Projects

As specified in Section 2 above, circular economy projects are an emerging and groundbreaking field of interest for the financial community worldwide. Their profile is typically different from conventional businesses as they consume fewer materials, energy, and water and produce less waste. Their risky profile is different from that of conventional businesses. The circular profile is less available in terms of quantitative descriptors, and impacts are delayed over time, meaning that while being highly impactful over a long horizon, circular businesses are typically modest concerning short-term performance. Moreover, circular economy business models are most of the time based on highly innovative circular solutions tackling high complexity business challenges (Sánchez-García *et al.*, 2024).

These models are directed to multiply value creation opportunities since they link many more services, solutions, and ecosystem relationships than their linear counterparts. When a circular economy investment proposal is accompanied by a reliable and accurate trigger enabling sufficient levels of trust on a more equal footing of fairness, investment decision-making becomes easier and more sound. Circular economy businesses cannot be served by standard financial schemes. These characteristics and challenges call for innovative financing solutions capable of working with new business challenges and the CEOs. Prioritizing impact capital among the stakeholders' economic objectives, familiar solutions such as mezzanine-structured financing, phased revenue-sharing, or hybrid financial packages are the suggestions to be further analyzed (Rizos & Bryhn, 2022).

Lessons Learned from Failed Initiatives

A typical circular economy project faces two types of barriers. The first barriers are related to the transformational character and the multidisciplinary repair work needed to overcome path dependencies. The circular pathway deviates from long-standing linear lock-ins and, therefore, may lead to several obstacles, such as non-market resistance in existing linear product chains or consumer bargaining power falling outside institutional agent control. Firms fixing market problems, particularly new market-making ventures, are likely to be vulnerable. Second, several circular start-ups suffer from market failure, including in the financing market. Thus, the solution to the circular economy is to make a series of fragmented local policies, including economic, fiscal, or financial tools specifically designed to make the market work well for circular-minded businesses (von Kolpinski *et al.*, 2023).

The main conclusions drawn in line with the review of the company cases are that the real barrier to circular economy companies is firm size, which affects their credibility; the focus on only half of the circle, primarily geared to processes; the pertinent rigid institutional framework; and the financing-related business model. First, learner business models need to overstate the beneficial potential. Small firms are not taken seriously; only first-generation CE pioneers with a limited number of CE initiatives in their early stages, striving to show that they are genuinely serious with full diversity for fast improvers, received financing facilities. One policy intervention would be to change the current mix of policy tools that are geared toward large innovative high-standard target companies and to promote the growth potential to boost the credibility of enabling design and local repair startups. Large firms could leverage these startups by bundling fragmented circular potential that works on the other half of the circular pathway: the individual recovery policies to the local cluster. The place-based policy design could create synergies by expanding the use of international resources and bridging CE diffusion gaps. To accommodate the different financing needs of the entrant versus the later-stage CE pioneer, place-based private credit support instruments need to remain adjustable based on the ambition of startups' scope and scale (Al-Awlaqi & Aamer, 2022).

MEASURING AND REPORTING IMPACT

Continued development of standardized methodologies and reporting standards for the circular economy across the financing and investment spectrum will enhance decision reliability, comparability, and robustness. This will lead to an improved ability to assess where efforts and investments can have the greatest impact and also reduce the risk of misallocation of funding. A key challenge to creating a framework for the circular economy relates to the broad scale and extensive range of areas of circular activity that all ultimately fall under the same umbrella label. A robust measurement framework that is durable, dynamic, and reliable can help to identify the benefits and possibilities and create a clear and robust vocabulary for describing business activities and impacts. This will help businesses, consumers, interest groups, and governments to enhance their understanding and help capital market participants to channel resources where they are most needed and to the most effect. Measurement, reporting, and valuation are fundamental to advancing the circular economy and will be important drivers in helping to achieve a circular, sustainable, and inclusive economy. The question that arises is how to ensure that the growth today is on a more sustainable trajectory that provides for the needs and welfare of everyone tomorrow. The circular economy offers a vision for the economy based around three principles: designing out waste and pollution; keeping products and materials in use; and regenerating natural systems. It creates business models that rethink the design patterns inherent in the linear economy, such as the take, make, and waste characteristics of our economy, and that prioritize the use of renewable resources (Gonçalves *et al.*, 2022).

Key Performance Indicators for Circular Economy Investments

Key performance indicators for circular economy investments perform two tasks: 1) they can be used as a decision-making tool to assess and prioritize prospective projects; KPIs help in identifying and prioritizing circular economy project financing opportunities by comparing the circular economy project investment demand against the availability of risk capital. 2) They serve as metrics for portfolio management, performance measurement, and investment steering. The qualified circular economy project investment KPIs address the objectives of the circular economy investment strategy, which includes environmental externalities and societal impacts, and aligns closely with the six principles of the circular economy initiative. High-quality, robust data is essential for decision-making, reporting, regulation, and policy. The KPIs cover environmental risks, environmental impact, the real economy role, ethical considerations, and societal impact. There is a stated ambition to generate circular economic impact that is quantifiable, and there is a desire to drive circular economy thinking, project development, and technical studies (Torgautov *et al*., 2022).

Sustainability Reporting Standards

There is an ongoing debate as to whether sustainability information should be standardized at all. Proponents of standardization argue that it can facilitate more comparable, reliable, and verifiable information. It is against this background that institutions have created (or are in the process of creating) voluntary sustainability reporting standards. These standards are only voluntary; in contrast to more traditional financial accounting standards, the only actor capable of making these mandatory is political authority, and society has not yet given the latter the mandate to do so (Opferkuch *et al*., 2021).

Notwithstanding, the trend is for ever more standardization. In the past, sustainability reporting followed six main 'camps': financial reporting standards, standards for reporting on eco-efficient projects, voluntary sustainability reporting standards, quasi-legal standards, illegal standards, and soft law standards. The trend now is for these 'camps' to undergo institutional integration as part of overall sustainability reporting standards. The EU has been at the forefront of sustainability reporting standards. However, standardization has hitherto been exclusively financial, and only in recent decades has it taken into consideration certain environmental aspects (Sisaye, 2021).

TECHNOLOGICAL INNOVATIONS IN FINANCING

One of the core aims of the business model driven by the circular economy is to keep resources in use for as long as possible and to derive the greatest value from these resources. Nowadays, there are many innovations in technological and infrastructure systems that could both enable better understanding and identification of the security and traceability of the materials. A technologically enabled business model is really the first step that a company could take in a circular direction, but innovations that bring value to stakeholders and the financial market can be further explored, too. Financially self-sustaining solutions to address the base costs of recycling are really useful as an aid for municipalities and other stakeholders active in waste recycling management. A B2B circular platform could support sustainable management with competitive and economically viable supply chains, which is an innovative and alternative financial model with private companies assuming the role previously provided by local and city authorities (Franzò & Urbinati, 2023).

Open software platforms for open innovation provide advanced services on data and intelligence through analysis of the supply chain of materials and their profitability. To achieve this, advanced models based on best practices and enhanced decision-making systems are included that can optimize production processes and extensively monitor the relevance of solutions. Small and medium-sized enterprises benefit jointly from shared knowledge, as market trends, data, and information, in real time, enable more effective resources directed to their business; they can focus on their core business rather than collecting data and best practices concerning the circular economy, and enhance recycling efficiency according to shared solutions. Platforms could also enable the use of innovative financial instruments to leverage new investments. Data-enabled solutions that monitor and optimize flow are supported by a chain of financial services, including leasing management, pay-per-use models, insurance programs, and financial support for recycling infrastructure (Croxson *et al.*, 2023).

Blockchain and Smart Contracts in Financing Circular Economy Projects

The circular economy is one of the most promising concepts of sustainable development, offering a radical rethink of production processes and the design of today's products. It is based on linking economic ecosystems to achieve maximum efficiency in all spheres of economic activity. The scientific novelty of this work lies in the need to use the latest legal and financial mechanisms to stimulate the implementation of business models based on the principles of the circular economy. The role of blockchain technology and smart contracts in financing circular economy projects is discussed. The key projects of the circular economy are analyzed using blockchain technology and smart contracts, which are of interest to investors. Since the practice of using smart contracts in financing the principles of the circular economy is not very developed at the moment, the study is based on the method of analyzing this legal and financial mechanism in the disclosed projects (Shojaei *et al.*, 2021).

Fintech Solutions for Sustainable Investments

With the web evolution, financial technologies – also called fintech – have been expanding year by year, allowing the development of innovative digital financial services, resulting in safer, low-cost, and high-quality financial services that satisfy society's diversified restructuring pain points. Blockchain, social networks, big data technologies, and other emerging technologies are bringing revolution to investment and financing tools and methods. Now, investment transactions can be done 24 hours a day, freeing financial activities from physical office stations. Mobile payment technologies enable payments through a fingerprint passcode or a facial recognition system, with such transaction tools transferring data at a speed of 220 terabytes per second. From a risk perspective, governments and enterprises can use the KYC, KYE, and real-name account mechanisms to carry out identity and data management on investors and borrowers, enabling closed credit services for credit uncertainty, credit risk, credit cost, and other problems in the past (Bhat *et al.*, 2023).

New financial technologies also have the advantage of being more convenient and efficient, such as digital payment, peer-to-peer lending, crowdfunding, robo-advisers, virtual banks, online insurance, and other innovative financial services. One-third of the world's financial market takes the form of a digital financial service. As a green financial technology, green investment and financing are mainly represented by green credit cards, carbon asset management, green bonds, carbon finance, and green funds, which offer convenient, efficient, and transparent information services to the public for individual investors. By mining innovative and flexible information requests, they solve inefficiencies between information suppliers and users in traditional mainstream financial markets and cost problems in information transmission. With the rise of a circular economy, fintech has an important role to play in the field of sustainable investments. First, public awareness of a responsible and sustainable economy is growing, and clients are increasingly asking for transparency, traceability, verification, and impact. Such requests may be easily met by fintech, which uses new communication and blockchain technologies to capture strong sustainability web connections. These technologies help financiers to capture the full importance of sustainability both in terms of corporate responsibilities and industrial performance. Second, while understanding the importance of sustainability, it is also necessary to remember that the whole industrial system needs to be developed in a way that minimizes the potential adverse effects of growth. This second necessity can be more easily reached by a synergistic integration of physical and financial components of the overall organizational system by checking, developing, and verifying performance. Once more, fintech has a key role because it represents a main conduit for valorizing industrial innovations based on circular economy principles. Third, the growing visibility of the United Nations for Sustainable Development Goals tells us that the world commercial system is in transition and, of course, that technology must progress to manage and measure value driven by the implementation of environmental and social policies: it is logical to manage industrial growth aimed at human well-being from both social and economic points of view. Indeed, fintech is the concept engaged today in knowledge management and, tomorrow, with a focus on the value of industrial activities inspired by the principles of a circular economy (Chueca Vergara & Ferruz Agudo, 2021).

CAPACITY BUILDING AND EDUCATION

The transition process towards a circular economy affects, in principle, the whole of society. It is indeed a health and social educational process aimed at raising awareness and stimulating different patterns of behavior and consumption from how they have developed so far at the individual, community, and business levels. On the other hand, from the didactic and training point of view, the circular economy represents an integrated economic and environmental concept that calls into question all the activities of a company and all the economic and social factors of a country, up to the individual choices in the everyday life of the citizens. It is necessary to demystify the theme of the circular economy, as a topic only for technicians and workers of specific sectors, who have specific expertise in the case study (Mies & Gold, 2021).

Universities, through foundations linked to them, support, through strategic planning lines, different training actions to reach a target defined in terms of the number of alumni and, in this case, companies, to be involved, with specific terms of reference. The same type of approach can also be used by specialized and industry associations, with memoranda of agreement with universities, dealing with themes and problems particular to their sectors of belonging. This is aimed, as in the case of an industrial association, at economic-social training and the environment. In general, the new economic paradigms can no longer only refer to the traditional courses in economic science or to the social sciences, although these courses, in many cases, could represent the optimal "container to be filled" to better prepare graduates, with economic-social and technical-scientific skills, useful for the economy, with particular reference to the business system involved in the sustainability process. The future could indeed lead to the elimination of traditional courses of civic, economic, and financial education as distinct subjects in the educational curricula of studies and courses, with a single course of circular economy par excellence. The examples illustrated above, concerning the role of the university and associations in training-attracting, represent a variation of the same concept. Access to energy production is vital for economic development (Khan *et al.*, 2022).

Training Programs for Financial Professionals in Circular Economy Finance

Getting a suite of financial products and services adequately designed for the circular economy and offered at an affordable price by a diverse range of financial institutions is essential to building up financial and business ecosystems that can support the growth of circular economy startups and enable the transition to a circular economy by the industry at large. A starting point is the training of financial professionals in the principles and best practices of these financial products and services. A wide array of financial products and services is designed specifically to address the peculiar operating model of circular economy businesses. Circular economy entrepreneurs must be able to identify and properly exploit these financial resources. So, financial professionals need to become well-versed with circular economy business models, the peculiar operating dynamics of circular economy businesses, the peculiar features of their balance sheets and their income statements, and the specific financial risks that these peculiarities expose circular economy businesses to. Innovative financial products are designed to address these specific financial needs (Pieroni *et al.*, 2021).

A number of existing financial competencies and products are now upgraded to respond to the specific needs of the circular economy businesses. Financial risk management in the circular economy business moves centrally on the ground of specific risk exposures caused by supply chain uncertainty and volatility, by changes in customer demand patterns, and by the reversibility or irreversibility of the value retention contents of the circular economy business model. More specific financial products enhance the financial capacity of circular economy businesses to carry such exposures over time. A large number of financial instruments are proposed to pass through and securitize the cash flows that underlie the value retention services for non-hazardous and hazardous circular economy businesses. Circularity indicators contribute to pricing such financial products over time. An overview is provided for the different ways of remunerating the financial services that cater to such risks. Risk capital attempting to meet the growth needs of circular economy businesses is becoming increasingly available at the right terms. What is missing is the know-how of the professionals in the financial sector. Econometric finance models can be developed to price risk as assessed from the ground up on the basis of the specific risk characteristics of the circular economy business model, while the expected cash flow yields are passed through and risk capital incentivized to grow responsibly towards the expected financial capabilities of the circular economy business. Ecosystem finance is the next frontier. A large systemic risk is still related to the incumbents providing financial services for the linear economy for residual assets that are at risk in a circular economy. The training of a new generation of financial professionals is the key to unlocking this risk (Haddad & Hornuf, 2023).

Integration of Circular Economy Principles in Business Schools

Incorporating new economic thinking in the business administration programs in linear-dominated educational institutions is a substantial challenge. Many actions can be taken to help the inclusion of circular economy principles in business schools, such as incorporating green areas on campuses, fostering collaboration between faculty members and entrepreneurs working with circular business models, including public and private players in discussions and practical cases, developing innovative master's degree programs focusing on products and services that follow circular economy criteria, and defining specific areas where future research may evolve in an atmosphere of intellectual freedom. Encouraging students to participate in and create entrepreneurial initiatives that are more sustainable, ethical, and have knowledge that augments the growth of business value in a circular economy should be the ultimate aim of educational institutions (Akhimien *et al.*, 2021).

Graduates should understand that the economic cycle is always part of the biosphere, and for the creation of value in an organization, business leaders should be able to fit new paradigms into business models. Business schools have a prominent place in the current globalized business environment, and it is their role to be the cradle of multilevel and multiparadigm thinking. With an open mind and a proactive role, business schools can play a critical role in the future success of the economy, playing a key role in the transformation of linear to more circular value chains. Circular business models can create value in an economy by reducing waste, adding resilience, and promoting a more sustainable use of natural resources in the economic cycle. These models intend to look at economic activities with another logic, not waste resources, nor consume so much energy and other inputs, nor produce waste. A business school is expected to provide development, research, and teaching of a model of behavior that companies, communities, and the economy can take to optimize the use of current natural and human resources. With vision and leadership, the long-lasting learning of circular economy business principles will make the difference, and even with the current deceleration in higher education, due to the challenges it faces, there is a demand for people and organizations to be mobilized for the challenge that the circular economy imposes on current learning (Salvador *et al.*, 2021).

COLLABORATION AND NETWORKING

Ensuring that cross-sector and international collaboration and networking operational plans contribute to the successful development of regional and thematic hubs and provide points of entry and contacts for business, clusters, and other potential stakeholders within the regions and cross-regional networks; interacting with suppliers, customers, R&D and testing labs, education and training facilities, and social innovators; developing new markets and business opportunities; reconnecting value chains; and identifying investment opportunities, including those benefiting from public procurers and considering the role of the first customer in bringing circular business models to market. Cross-border circular value chains require an efficient customs framework, notably for goods with zero value after repairing. National and international collaboration and networking are needed to synchronize the introduction of financial, tax, legal, accounting, and reporting instruments to promote the circular economy; improve asset maintenance and sharing and transnational movement of collections, promoting collaboration and networking across the public and private sectors to adapt the governance and use of collection systems. Europe is aiming for multinational demonstration projects with a high social science input, capitalizing on the opportunity for member states and their regions to participate to tap the new cluster for innovative training networks in the research program. Proactive interactions with member states in relation to shaping the national reform programs will be important for maintaining a circular economy vision in the cohesion policy and other funds. Japan has announced its target to target specific activities of the consortia around cities of the future for short-term outcomes, and the U.S. will benefit from the lessons learned for boosting eco-innovations in line with the design and mobilization of funding. New and existing financial investments should align with the circular economy model and generate experiences before the broader market policy is put in place. Meeting the market access guidelines for reuse, repurpose, and refurbishment markets opens additional investment opportunities beyond investing in advanced, eco-innovative materials and advanced eco-innovative solutions (Scarpellini *et al.*, 2021).

Platforms for Connecting Investors with Circular Economy Projects

Like any domain, connecting circular economy projects with finance is key to their implementation. Linking investors to those wanting to implement circular economy projects will support the development of a circular economy. Facilitating this process, a variety of platforms have been emerging that aim to connect sustainable or circular investments with projects. These platforms specifically target the identification and funding of projects, companies, or funds that facilitate the implementation of the circular economy. They are built for different stages of the project development cycle and project scale, for projects located in different parts of the world, and/or for different business models. They are all trying to contribute to mainstreaming circular investment with investors through crowdfunding for smaller projects, making finance-ready projects known to larger investors, or creating partnerships between technology developers and major corporations (Salmenperä *et al.*, 2021).

Existing platforms selected are aiming to facilitate the financing of circular economy projects or companies that adopt circular business models. They contribute to higher cross-sector cooperation by matching projects with investors in various stages of the project development cycle. Implemented circular economy business models can be characterized as designing waste out of companies, delaying disposal, and lasting infrastructure, reallocating waste through sharing, platforms providing marketplaces and asset sharing, and utilizing the embedded value in waste (Awan & Sroufe, 2022).

International Cooperation in Financing Sustainable Initiatives

International cooperation among institutions, aligned with the Action Plan for the Circular Economy, is required to tackle the barriers that prevent innovative circular economy initiatives from accessing financing due to their novelty, size, location, and other characteristics. The existing global and national traditional and innovative financial instruments, such as grants, concessional credit, equity, debt, guarantees, and public-private partnerships, need to be further refined, complemented, and coordinated with different stakeholders and funding sources. International organizations should play an important facilitating role in international coordination, in consultation with Circular Economy projects and under the principles of country ownership, continuity, and consistency (Dagilienė *et al.*, 2021).

Development finance also includes advisory services and technical intelligence that can build a bankable project pipeline, manage risks, secure environmental and social sustainability, and establish off-taker relationships. Smaller projects from Circular Economy companies can be bundled together with less risky infrastructure and energy efficiency projects in order to raise the minimum and optimal size for direct, institutional, and green bond finance. It can also result in cost and time savings in undertaking due diligence, credit underwriting, receipt of insurance policies, as well as tracking, reporting, and oversight by financial institutions. The indirect impact of Circular Economy projects on achieving sustainable development can be considerably larger than the direct investment required, leading to a multiplier effect for a variety of Sustainable Development Goals (Takacs *et al.*, 2022).

FUTURE TRENDS AND EMERGING ISSUES

Emerging Trends. Conclusion: The Emerging Issues in Circular Economy. Acknowledging Emerging Issues. Final Remarks. Business opportunities to capture the value of the circular economy. Trends for the Future. Emerging Business Models. The policy agenda for the after-sales and repair services market. Digitalized optimization of performance management in the shift toward the circular economy. The Performance Management Process is discussed in a study (Guerra *et al.*, 2021).

To this end, the future performance management process has to be replaced with a new apt process that reflects circular economy ideology. Under the new term, performance-oriented circular economy management, the result of an explorative case study research on a German textile company creates an integrated circular performance measurement model as well as a web-based application prototype for measuring circular performance by providing the management dashboard to increase the decision-making utility of companies. The prototype might provide practical insights, since respective management was involved again and came equipped with a practical approach and criteria that are applied and deployed directly into companies, solving the given pain points. Providing an adequate decision basis for actors within companies (Cagno *et al.*, 2023).

These decades are termed the fourth industrial revolution. The circular economy offers comprehensive solutions and can be considered a way for improved sustainable development, and can support the global sustainability goals of society. In contrast to linear thinking, the circular economy introduces a cycle rather than a line, rethinking progress starting from the design of products with minimal environmental impact and long-lasting life, and subsequently recovering, reusing, and repairing the components and materials through a cycle of 'remaking' mechanisms, *etc*. As such, the relationship between capital and the environment, in combination with the economic cycle, has become circular in essence (Dantas *et al.*, 2021).

Circular Economy in the Post-pandemic World

In the face of the COVID-19 pandemic, the private sector has stepped up to keep global supply chains functioning. But there is still much more that can be done, both to contain the spread of the virus, reduce the impact of the pandemic on the economy, and indeed to help businesses recover. This help should be built on the circular economy business model, which can provide both short- and long-term advantages to manufacturers. The pandemic has disrupted global trade and revealed just how vulnerable our current linear and waste-generating economic model is. Indeed, it is the inflexibility of supply chains and the linear business model that have resulted in the emergence of funding support packages to support businesses and workers and prop up economies (Ibn-Mohammed *et al.*, 2021).

The circular economy, based on the principles of 'zero waste' and closed-loop systems, can indeed help the economy, as argued by advocates in recent years with increasing vigor. Over the past decade, forward-thinking companies have started to integrate circular economy approaches with the help of advanced technologies, seeking to profit from the increased efficiency, robustness, and resilience potential the circular economy offers. It is to these forward-thinking companies that governments should be looking in order to enhance and ultimately transform the economy. These companies have already begun the journey to 'future-proofing' operations and entire supply chains. They provide valuable insights into best practices and technical barriers, as well as into the innovative solutions that were previously just theory. The response to the recent pandemic has offered a potent opportunity to evaluate government incentives in order to support system transitions while guaranteeing a change in the operations of companies previously showing limited commitment to sustainability (Sgroi, 2022).

Inclusive Finance for Marginalized Communities in the Circular Economy

India's long-standing philosophy of "antodaya" or reaching out to the "last person" has driven the country's pro-poor inclusive economy. Yet, the Indian population often has garnered the dubious distinction of simultaneously comprising the world's greatest number of poor people. Expanding access to sustainable finance for India's poor communities is a key challenge of the circular economy that will continue to be debated in upcoming policy forums. This chapter elaborates upon the theme of "inclusive finance and marginalized communities in a circular economy". Financial inclusion of marginalized communities should become an integral part of government policy. Micro-enterprise, social, and impact investment in circular economy-based SMEs will result in strong growth. Innovative, local, people-centered, community-led, and community-based financial mechanisms are critical to understanding poor people's associations with rural values and to creating systems that enable marginalized communities' access to the global knowledge-based economy. Small innovations: unleashing the potential of community-based finance and enterprise. Building partnerships between donor agencies, the private financial sector, and communities that are organized around cooperatives, self-help groups, and micro-credit institutions is key to advancing the financial inclusion process for marginalized communities. Establishing a facility that would help small businesses adopt more climate-friendly or environmentally sustainable practices is essential. The need for alternative models of inclusive financial products or social finance that are targeted specifically toward the poor, squatters, and slum settlements was a critical point of interest in our intervention. Inclusive finance for marginalized communities in the Indian context could be found in micro-finance models implemented by NGOs with financial resources from donor agencies, and their transformation into a more inclusive model of development finance. The Indian scenario revealed that the government in rural and urban areas was working to provide increased financial access and services, and noted that progress was slow but moving in the right direction. Government initiatives aimed at spreading the banking network and promoting formal and informal freedom of enterprise should further inclusive growth and development in nuclear-powered India. Addressing the entrepreneurial dimensions of low-income communities through an integrated focus on key areas, including the increase in financial resources earmarked for inclusive banking, is crucial. Measures to guide the banking sector toward less adverse selection in lending to the poor, low-cost finance options, banking sector reforms, selective credit control limiting, refinancing, regrouping, and social banking in order to better serve low-income clients could help democratize India's banking sector. Interventions to foster inclusive economic development, with an aim to create sustainable finance against type initiatives while leveraging public and donor resources to create favorable conditions for the provision of inclusive financial services that are focused on the needs and aspirations of poor entrepreneurs, were another key pathway for transformation into a more inclusive model of development finance. Finally, research should also focus on the crossroads of micro-finance and sustainable development.

CONCLUSION

In conclusion, this chapter has provided a thoughtful and comprehensive analysis of the key themes and important concepts explored throughout the entire text. We have thoroughly examined the various perspectives and arguments that have been presented, highlighting their relevance and far-reaching implications within the broader context. The insights that we have gained from this deep exploration not only enhance our understanding of the subject matter at hand but also pave the way for further inquiry and deeper investigation into these vital ideas. As we progress and move forward, it is crucial to take a moment to reflect on the interconnectedness of these diverse ideas and to consider their profound impact on future developments and discussions in the broader academic landscape. Overall, this chapter serves as a pivotal foundation for the subsequent discussions that will follow, reinforcing the critical importance of the topics that have been addressed and underscoring their significance in the ongoing dialogue within this dynamic and evolving field of study. The themes explored here are not merely academic exercises; they resonate deeply with the real-world challenges and intellectual currents we face today. By articulating and connecting these diverse strands of thought, we not only enrich our discourse but also empower ourselves to engage meaningfully with future questions and debates that will undoubtedly arise, ensuring that we remain relevant and responsive to the ever-changing demands of our intellectual pursuits.

REFERENCES

Audretsch, D.B., Fiedler, A. (2024). Bringing the knowledge spillover theory of entrepreneurship to circular economies: Knowledge and values in entrepreneurial ecosystems. *International Small Business Journal: Researching Entrepreneurship, 42*(4), 480-505. [http://dx.doi.org/10.1177/02662426231218357]

Asgari, A., Asgari, R. (2021). How circular economy transforms business models in a transition towards circular ecosystems: Barriers and incentives. *Sustainable Production and Consumption, 28*, 566-579.

[http://dx.doi.org/10.1016/j.spc.2021.06.020]

Alkaraan, F., Elmarzouky, M., Hussainey, K., Venkatesh, V.G. (2023). Sustainable strategic investment decision-making practices in UK companies: Governance mechanisms and synergy between Industry 4.0 and circular economy. *Technol. Forecast. Soc. Change, 187*, 122187.
[http://dx.doi.org/10.1016/j.techfore.2022.122187]

Al-Awlaqi, M.A., Aamer, A.M. (2022). Individual entrepreneurial factors affecting adoption of circular business models: Evidence from a resource-constrained economy. *J. Clean. Prod., 379*, 134736.
[http://dx.doi.org/10.1016/j.jclepro.2022.134736]

Akhimien, N.G., Latif, E., Hou, S.S. (2021). Application of circular economy principles in buildings: A systematic review. *J. Build. Eng., 38*, 102041.
[http://dx.doi.org/10.1016/j.jobe.2020.102041]

Awan, U., Sroufe, R. (2022). Sustainability in the circular economy: Insights and dynamics of designing circular business models. *Appl. Sci. (Basel), 12*(3), 1521.
[http://dx.doi.org/10.3390/app12031521]

Bhat, JR, AlQahtani, SA, Nekovee, M (2023). FinTech enablers, use cases, and the role of future internet of things. *J King Saud Univ Comput Inf Sci, 35*(1), 87-101.
[http://dx.doi.org/10.1016/j.jksuci.2022.08.033]

Basu, J.B., Dawn, S., Saha, P.K., Chakraborty, M.R., Ustun, T.S. (2022). A comparative study on system profit maximization of a renewable combined deregulated power system. *Electronics (Basel), 11*(18), 2857.
[http://dx.doi.org/10.3390/electronics11182857]

Chizaryfard, A., Trucco, P., Nuur, C. (2021). The transformation to a circular economy: Framing an evolutionary view. *J. Evol. Econ., 31*(2), 475-504.
[http://dx.doi.org/10.1007/s00191-020-00709-0]

Cezarino, L.O., Liboni, L.B., Stefanelli, N.O., Oliveira, B.G., Stocco, L.C. (2021). Diving into emerging economies bottleneck: Industry 4.0 and implications for circular economy. *Manage. Decis., 59*(8), 1841-1862.
[http://dx.doi.org/10.1108/MD-10-2018-1084]

Carmichael, R., Gross, R., Hanna, R., Rhodes, A., Green, T. (2021). The demand response technology cluster: Accelerating UK residential consumer engagement with time-of-use tariffs, electric vehicles and smart meters *via* digital comparison tools. *Renew. Sustain. Energy Rev., 139*, 110701.
[http://dx.doi.org/10.1016/j.rser.2020.110701]

Croxson, K., Frost, J., Gambacorta, L., Valletti, T. (2023). Platform-based business models and financial inclusion: Policy trade-offs and approaches. *J. Compet. Law Econ., 19*(1), 75-102.
[http://dx.doi.org/10.1093/joclec/nhac010]

Chueca Vergara, C., Ferruz Agudo, L. (2021). FinTech and sustainability: Do they affect each other? *Sustainability, 13*(13), 7012.
[http://dx.doi.org/10.3390/su13137012]

Cagno, E., Negri, M., Neri, A., Giambone, M. (2023). One framework to rule them all: An integrated, multilevel and scalable performance measurement framework of sustainability, circular economy and industrial symbiosis. *Sustainable Production and Consumption, 35*, 55-71.
[http://dx.doi.org/10.1016/j.spc.2022.10.016]

Dantas, T.E.T., De-Souza, E.D., Destro, I.R., Hammes, G., Rodriguez, C.M.T., Soares, S.R. (2021). How the combination of circular economy and Industry 4.0 can contribute towards achieving the Sustainable Development Goals. *Sustainable Production and Consumption, 26*, 213-227.
[http://dx.doi.org/10.1016/j.spc.2020.10.005]

de Assis, T.F., Monteiro, T.G.M., de Abreu, V.H.S., D'Agosto, M. de A., Santos, A.S. (2022). Enabling the green bonds market for sustainable transport projects based on monitoring, reporting and verification methods. *Environmental footprints and eco-design of products and processes.* Springer.

Dagilienė, L., Varaniūtė, V., Bruneckienė, J. (2021). Local governments' perspective on implementing the circular economy: A framework for future solutions. *J. Clean. Prod., 310*, 127340. [http://dx.doi.org/10.1016/j.jclepro.2021.127340]

Franzò, S., Urbinati, A. (2023). Managing resource loops in circular supply chains: A taxonomy of multi-sided platforms in the B2B setting. *Ind. Mark. Manage., 115*, 185-197. [http://dx.doi.org/10.1016/j.indmarman.2023.09.016]

Guerra, B.C., Leite, F., de Souza, D.M., Ramos, T.B. (2021). Circular economy applications in the construction industry: A global scan of trends and opportunities. *J. Clean. Prod., 324*, 129125. [http://dx.doi.org/10.1016/j.jclepro.2021.129125]

Giorgi, S., Lavagna, M., Wang, K., Osmani, M., Liu, G., Campioli, A. (2022). Drivers and barriers towards circular economy in the building sector: Stakeholder interviews and analysis of policies and practices in five European countries. *J. Clean. Prod., 336*, 130395. [http://dx.doi.org/10.1016/j.jclepro.2022.130395]

Gonçalves, B. de S. M (2022). Circular economy and financial aspects: A systematic review of the literature. *Sustainability, 14*(5), 3023. [http://dx.doi.org/10.3390/su14053023]

Haddad, C., Hornuf, L. (2023). How do fintech start-ups affect financial institutions' performance and default risk? *Eur. J. Finance, 29*(15), 1761-1792. [http://dx.doi.org/10.1080/1351847X.2022.2151371]

Ibn-Mohammed, T., Mustapha, K.B., Godsell, J., Adamu, Z., Babatunde, K.A., Akintade, D.D. (2021). A critical analysis of the impacts of COVID-19 on the global economy and ecosystems and opportunities for circular economy strategies. *Resour. Conserv. Recycling, 164*, 105169. [http://dx.doi.org/10.1016/j.resconrec.2020.105169]

Khan, S.A., Mubarik, M.S., Paul, S.K. (2022). Analyzing cause-and-effect relationships among drivers and barriers to circular economy implementation in an emerging economy. *J. Clean. Prod., 364*, 132618. [http://dx.doi.org/10.1016/j.jclepro.2022.132618]

Kowalski, Z., Kulczycka, J., Makara, A., Verhé, R., De Clercq, G. (2022). Assessment of energy recovery from municipal waste management systems using circular economy quality indicators. *Energies, 15*(22), 8625. [http://dx.doi.org/10.3390/en15228625]

Khan, I., Zakari, A., Dagar, V., Singh, S. (2022). World energy trilemma and transformative energy developments as determinants of economic growth amid environmental sustainability. *Energy Econ., 108*, 105884. [http://dx.doi.org/10.1016/j.eneco.2022.105884]

Kazancoglu, I., Sagnak, M., Mangla, S.K., Kazancoglu, Y. (2021). Circular economy and policy: A framework for improving corporate environmental management in supply chains. *Bus. Strategy Environ., 30*(1), 590-608. [http://dx.doi.org/10.1002/bse.2641]

Mies, A., Gold, S. (2021). Mapping the social dimension of the circular economy. *J. Clean. Prod., 321*, 128960. [http://dx.doi.org/10.1016/j.jclepro.2021.128960]

Mishra, R., Singh, R.K., Govindan, K. (2022). Barriers to the adoption of circular economy practices in micro, small and medium enterprises: Instrument development, measurement and validation. *J. Clean. Prod., 351*, 131389. [http://dx.doi.org/10.1016/j.jclepro.2022.131389]

Mehrotra, S., Jaladi, S.R. (2022). How start-ups in emerging economies embrace circular business models and contribute towards a circular economy. *Journal of Entrepreneurship in Emerging Economies, 14*(5), 727-753.

[http://dx.doi.org/10.1108/JEEE-10-2021-0410]

Opferkuch, K., Caeiro, S., Salomone, R., Ramos, T.B. (2021). Circular economy in corporate sustainability reporting: A review of organisational approaches. *Bus. Strategy Environ., 30*(8), 4015-4036. [http://dx.doi.org/10.1002/bse.2854]

Pieroni, M.P.P., McAloone, T.C., Pigosso, D.C.A. (2021). Circular economy business model innovation: Sectorial patterns within manufacturing companies. *J. Clean. Prod., 286*, 124921. [http://dx.doi.org/10.1016/j.jclepro.2020.124921]

Roy, T., Garza-Reyes, J.A., Kumar, V., Kumar, A., Agrawal, R. (2022). Redesigning traditional linear supply chains into circular supply chains: A study into its challenges. *Sustainable Production and Consumption, 31*, 113-126. [http://dx.doi.org/10.1016/j.spc.2022.02.004]

Rizos, V., Bryhn, J. (2022). Implementation of circular economy approaches in the electrical and electronic equipment sector: Barriers, enablers and policy insights. *J. Clean. Prod., 338*, 130617. [http://dx.doi.org/10.1016/j.jclepro.2022.130617]

Rodríguez-Espíndola, O., Cuevas-Romo, A., Chowdhury, S., Díaz-Acevedo, N., Albores, P., Despoudi, S., Dey, P. (2022). The role of circular economy principles and sustainable-oriented innovation to enhance social, economic and environmental performance: Evidence from Mexican SMEs. *Int. J. Prod. Econ., 248*, 108495. [http://dx.doi.org/10.1016/j.ijpe.2022.108495]

Salmenperä, H., Pitkänen, K., Kautto, P., Saikku, L. (2021). Critical factors for enhancing the circular economy in waste management. *J. Clean. Prod., 280*, 124339. [http://dx.doi.org/10.1016/j.jclepro.2020.124339]

Sharma, N.K., Govindan, K., Lai, K.K., Chen, W.K., Kumar, V. (2021). The transition from linear economy to circular economy for sustainability among SMEs: Prospects, impediments, and prerequisites. *Bus. Strategy Environ., 30*(4), 1803-1822. [http://dx.doi.org/10.1002/bse.2717]

Saarinen, A., Aarikka-Stenroos, L. (2023). Financing-related drivers and barriers for circular economy business: Developing a conceptual model from a field study. *Circular Economy and Sustainability, 3*(3), 1187-1211. [http://dx.doi.org/10.1007/s43615-022-00222-5]

Stefanakis, A.I., Calheiros, C.S.C., Nikolaou, I. (2021). Nature-based solutions as a tool in the new circular economic model for climate change adaptation. *Circular Economy and Sustainability, 1*(1), 303-318. [http://dx.doi.org/10.1007/s43615-021-00022-3]

Sánchez-García, E., Martínez-Falcó, J., Marco-Lajara, B., Manresa-Marhuenda, E. (2024). Revolutionizing the circular economy through new technologies: A new era of sustainable progress. *Environmental Technology & Innovation, 33*, 103509. [http://dx.doi.org/10.1016/j.eti.2023.103509]

Sisaye, S. (2021). The influence of non-governmental organizations on the development of voluntary sustainability accounting reporting rules. *Journal of Business Socio-Economic Development, 1*(1), 5-23. [http://dx.doi.org/10.1108/JBSED-02-2021-0017]

Shojaei, A., Ketabi, R., Razkenari, M., Hakim, H., Wang, J. (2021). Enabling a circular economy in the built environment sector through blockchain technology. *J. Clean. Prod., 294*, 126352. [http://dx.doi.org/10.1016/j.jclepro.2021.126352]

Salvador, R., Barros, M.V., Freire, F., Halog, A., Piekarski, C.M., De Francisco, A.C. (2021). Circular economy strategies on business modelling: Identifying the greatest influences. *J. Clean. Prod., 299*, 126918. [http://dx.doi.org/10.1016/j.jclepro.2021.126918]

Scarpellini, S., Gimeno, J.Á., Portillo-Tarragona, P., Llera-Sastresa, E. (2021). Financial resources for investments in renewable self-consumption within a circular economy framework. *Sustainability, 13*(12),

6838.
[http://dx.doi.org/10.3390/su13126838]

Sgroi, F. (2022). The circular economy for resilience of the agricultural landscape and promotion of sustainable agriculture and food systems. *Journal of Agriculture and Food Research, 8*, 100307.
[http://dx.doi.org/10.1016/j.jafr.2022.100307]

Torgautov, B., Zhanabayev, A., Tleuken, A., Turkyilmaz, A., Borucki, C., Karaca, F. (2022). Performance assessment of construction companies for the circular economy: A balanced scorecard approach. *Sustainable Production and Consumption, 33*, 991-1004.
[http://dx.doi.org/10.1016/j.spc.2022.08.021]

Takacs, F., Brunner, D., Frankenberger, K. (2022). Barriers to a circular economy in small- and medium-sized enterprises and their integration into a sustainable strategic management framework. *J. Clean. Prod., 362*, 132227.
[http://dx.doi.org/10.1016/j.jclepro.2022.132227]

Velasco-Muñoz, J.F., Mendoza, J.M.F., Aznar-Sánchez, J.A., Gallego-Schmid, A. (2021). Circular economy implementation in the agricultural sector: Definition, strategies and indicators. *Resour. Conserv. Recycling, 170*, 105618.
[http://dx.doi.org/10.1016/j.resconrec.2021.105618]

Vernimmen, P., Le Fur, Y., Dallochio, M., Salvi, A., Quiry, P. (2017). *Corporate finance.* Wiley.
[http://dx.doi.org/10.1002/9781119424444]

von Kolpinski, C., Yazan, D.M., Fraccascia, L. (2023). The impact of internal company dynamics on sustainable circular business development: Insights from circular startups. *Bus. Strategy Environ., 32*(4), 1931-1950.
[http://dx.doi.org/10.1002/bse.3228]

Yang, Y., Ma, G. (2023). How can high-speed rail promote inter-city collaborative innovation across regional borders? *Cities, 138*, 104367.
[http://dx.doi.org/10.1016/j.cities.2023.104367]

Zhao, W., Yang, T., Hughes, K.D., Li, Y. (2021). Entrepreneurial alertness and business model innovation: The role of entrepreneurial learning and risk perception. *Int. Entrep. Manage. J., 17*(2), 839-864.
[http://dx.doi.org/10.1007/s11365-020-00637-2]

SUBJECT INDEX

A

B

C

D

E

N

O

P

R

S

T

U

V

W

www.ingramcontent.com/pod-product-compliance
Lightning Source LLC
LaVergne TN
LVHW070949210926
848482LV00002B/146